DEFENDING CRETE FROM THE
FALLSCHIRMJAGERS

DEFENDING CRETE FROM THE FALLSCHIRMJAGERS
MEMOIRS OF A ROYAL ENGINEER & POW

JACK SEED

Pen & Sword
MILITARY
AN IMPRINT OF PEN & SWORD BOOKS LTD.
YORKSHIRE - PHILADELPHIA

First published in Great Britain in 2023 by
PEN AND SWORD MILITARY
An imprint of
Pen & Sword Books Ltd
Yorkshire – Philadelphia

Copyright © Jack Seed, 2023

ISBN 978 1 39904 925 2

The right of Jack Seed to be identified as Author of this work has been asserted by him in accordance with the Copyright, Designs and Patents Act 1988.

A CIP catalogue record for this book is available from the British Library

All rights reserved. No part of this book may be reproduced or transmitted in any form or by any means, electronic or mechanical including photocopying, recording or by any information storage and retrieval system, without permission from the Publisher in writing.

Typeset in Times New Roman 12/16 by SJmagic DESIGN SERVICES, India.
Printed and bound in the UK by CPI Group (UK) Ltd.

Pen & Sword Books Ltd incorporates the imprints of Pen & Sword Archaeology, Atlas, Aviation, Battleground, Discovery, Family History, History, Maritime, Military, Naval, Politics, Social History, Transport, True Crime, Claymore Press, Frontline Books, Praetorian Press, Seaforth Publishing and White Owl

For a complete list of Pen & Sword titles please contact

PEN & SWORD BOOKS LIMITED
47 Church Street, Barnsley, South Yorkshire, S70 2AS, England
E-mail: enquiries@pen-and-sword.co.uk
Website: www.pen-and-sword.co.uk

Or

PEN AND SWORD BOOKS
1950 Lawrence Rd, Havertown, PA 19083, USA
E-mail: Uspen-and-sword@casematepublishers.com
Website: www.penandswordbooks.com

Contents

List of Illustrations vi

Foreword viii

Chapter 1   Capture on Crete 1

Chapter 2   The Road to Galatos 20

Chapter 3   Salonika 39

Chapter 4   To Germany 52

Chapter 5   Lager 413 Dabendorf 1941 75

Chapter 6   Lager 520 Grossbeeren 1942 99

Chapter 7   Mühlburg-Saxony 1943 134

Chapter 8   Zwickau-Saxony, 1944 148

Chapter 9   The Days of Reckoning 178

List of Illustrations

1. The Author 1945.
2. Maria Sahm – Zwickau 1945.
3. Trooper T.B. Caselli, 1945.
4. Sergeant Ali Riza Tewfik, 1945.
5. Marine L.N. Walker, 1943.
6. The Author, 1945.
7. The Author, 1945.
8. German Parachutists before take-off for Crete, May 1941.
9. German Parachutists dropping over Canea-Suda area, May 1941.
10. German Parachutists dropping over Canea-Suda area, May 1941.
11. One of the railway working parties taken with 'Mad Harry', the German ganger, near Grossbeeren, Berlin, in the spring of 1943.
12. POW Identity Tag of Author.
13. Record Card taken from German officer after liberation.
14. A piece of an allied night bomber found at Hoppegarten, east of Berlin, 23 August 1943
15. Prisoner of War Camp Money, equal to 1 Reichsmark.
16. A One Mark note exchanged for POW camp money, 1944.
17. Para boys Camp, Zwickau I Working Party, 1945.
18. Para boys Camp, Zwickau II Working Party, 1945.
19. Para boys Camp, Neumark Working Party, 1945.
20. Para boys Camp, Werdau Working Party, 1945.
21. Para boys Camp, Mosel Working Party, 1945.
22. Para boys Camp, Staff, 1945.
23. Frontispiece of a POW lettercard.
24. Contents of a Next of Kin Parcel.

25. Photographs of entries from author's notebook.
26. Some German Second World War Medals.
27. German Party Badges.
28. Other Nazi Party Badges.
29. Copy of the report of the Red Cross Parcel Affair.
30. General layout of Crossen C58 POW Camp Zwickau.
31. Plan of routes taken on night of 17 June 1944.

Foreword

I am honoured to write a short foreword to Jack Seed's self-written account of his time in uniform between 1941 to 1945, both fighting the Germans in Crete and then in long captivity in numerous hutted Prisoner of War (POW) camps in Nazi Germany, employed as cheap labour. Written with a deft, engaging, and often matter-of-fact hand, *Defending Crete from the Fallschirmjagers* is a fascinating and brutally honest account of everyday challenges in imprisonment that, despite the passage of time, deserves to be heard. Perhaps consciously, the author focuses almost exclusively on his personal journey from initial capture during Operation Mercury, through four years in detention (and several camps), to ultimate liberation and repatriation. Sadly, we know very little about Jack's background, career, or his key achievements. His own day-to-day experiences, reactions, and observations, at a critical time in world history, provide the thread running through the book. What we do know about the author is that he was a Sapper (a Royal Engineer) and at the start of his account he belonged to a field company of engineers. We also know that he 'joined up' in 1936–7, initially in the Queen's Own Yorkshire Dragoons, then part of the Territorial Army, and that he departed 'Blighty' in 1939. Little else is known about the author, perhaps less his postal address in Dunbar, East Lothian and that, post captivity, winemaking and beer brewing became one of his hobbies.

Therefore, this is not a book that sheds fresh light on the machines, strategies, politics, events, and warfare that shaped, arguably, the world's greatest conflict – the Second World War. Instead, it is a deeply personal account of camp life, burnt indelibly into Jack's mind, and seemingly unaffected by the passage of time but grounded firmly in the realities of harsh captivity. Therefore, the likes of hunger, body lice and bugs, German brutality, appalling living conditions, severe winters, psychological effects, and petty thieving, all receive a fair and understandable airing. And, throughout, a deeply compelling element of the book is Jack's honesty. On one occasion he asks simply: 'Does anyone think the Politicians and Generals thought twice about us after we were made prisoners?' And responds: 'Not on your life they didn't. We had served our usefulness, we had gone through hell for them, we had seen so many men of both sides killed and wounded, maimed for life, shell shocked (or is not the modern term, Battle fatigue) and now we were, to use a good old army term, written off.' But there is also warmth and insights throughout the narrative. The value of Red Cross parcels, letters from home, kindness from the local German population and others, the black-market trade, Maria and Frau and Herr Sahm, and the importance of discipline, to highlight but a few examples, also pepper the narrative, each combining to provide a sense of balance, shade, and, importantly, hope.

Even so, this was a dangerous and uncertain existence for Jack and his colleagues. Aerial bombardment – both German and Allied – was a relentless hazard at various stages of his captivity. During one raid, the Royal Air Force, whilst bombing the Teltow area of Germany, inadvertently hit the camp that Jack was resident in, killing one man. Others simply found the monotony of captivity and the lack of hope too much to cope with. Most were mentally prepared to sustain serious injury or death in battle, but few contemplated the reality of being captured by the enemy and a long period of incarceration. Jack notes that on one Sunday morning, a fellow prisoner had been found hanging from the rafters and, despite attempts at resuscitation, was pronounced dead by the Medical Officer, Captain Neale. He recalls: 'I know our very existence was tough at that time and must have proved too tough for this one poor soul, who had decided to make an end of his tormented life.' But, on a more positive note, he goes on to say: 'The incident had a long-lasting effect on us all, making us more determined to survive.' But, despite these realities, the business of attempting to escape often ended up in a heated dispute. It was not just a question of getting out of the camp, the main problem was getting out of Germany. And, as Jack records: 'There is always two sides to everything, and as it was with our thoughts and arguments on the subject of escaping. Why should we escape? Why should we risk our lives again and again, and for what? A grateful country eager to have us back so that we could be used as gun fodder again?'

Defending Crete from the Fallschirmjagers describes vividly the highs and lows of captivity at the hands of the Germans. In so doing, it enables the reader to acquire an authentic picture of life as a military POW in Nazi Germany which, for those in captivity, was a tough and often lonely row to hoe. He describes events at the time, through vivid memories, and distinguishes clearly the occasional afterthought reached with the benefit of hindsight. It also exposes human failings on both sides, but also human strengths of determination and resolve, even when the odds seemed stacked against an Allied victory. The year 1941 was particularly disquieting for those in captivity. Just about the whole of Europe, from the Baltic to the Balkans, the shores of the Mediterranean and in North Africa, nearly to Alexandria, was held by the Germans. In such an account, it would be quite understandable if a certain measure of overlap and repetition occurred; but there is little, if any, of this. Instead, through many interesting twists and turns, and an engaging and often fast-paced narrative, we uncover the tireless resolve of Jack and what makes him tick – and through his experiences and feelings, we find out about many aspects of his character. In so many ways, this is a remarkable account of fortitude, patience, persistence, kindness, and hope.

It has often been alleged that the POWs from the Second World War are a forgotten generation. Few spoke of their treatment and cruelty at the hands of the enemy. Even fewer articulated lucidly their experiences on paper. Most were keen to move on with their lives post-repatriation. Therefore, it would be remiss of me not to thank Dave Irving – himself, a former serving Sapper and budding military historian. He recognised instantly the importance and richness of Jack's account and pursued a recognised publisher – Pen & Sword. We all owe him a significant debt of gratitude.

There was a very real danger that this important memoir and window into life as a POW could have been lost forever; fortuitously, it was not.

Jack, like many of his colleagues in captivity, was a remarkable man, undeterred by the challenges, dangers, cruelty, and uncertainty he faced, and the account that he tells reflects his qualities. I am convinced that *Defending Crete from the Fallschirmjagers* will enrich the small number of memoirs which cover the exploits of POWs in Nazi Germany.

Major General, Dr Andrew Roe CB

Chapter 1

Capture on Crete

I don't profess to be able to write about the 'Battle of Crete' nor do I intend to try. I can only try to give an account of the events leading up to our captivity, of what I saw, entirely from my own point of view and from bitter memories at that.

The first of June 1941 was a dark day in the annals of the British and Commonwealth military history. Another battle had yet been lost and at 11 a.m. on that beautiful summer's day, our forces on Crete had to officially capitulate to the Germans.

Before this, there had been Dunkirk and Norway, then we had chased up and down the Western Desert, again been chased out of Greece and now Crete.

'Capitulate'! What a horrible word it was to us on that day; it was a Sunday (without a church parade). We, the ordinary common or garden soldier, couldn't understand why we had to capitulate.

There was no doubt we were extremely tired, weary and dirty and also very hungry, yet right up to the last we still had faith that something would turn up to relieve us. We were the British army; our navy was out there somewhere and if we only held out they would come back for us and take us off to safety. But it wasn't to be, they weren't coming back anymore; in other words, 'We had had it, we had missed the boat! We had our backs to the sea.'

It had all started so many days ago, we had almost lost track of time.

After the fall of Greece, things began to hot up on Crete; we were getting air raids several times a day delivered by the Germans. They were beginning to pick out their targets carefully and methodically. Malamie airfield; stores dumps around Canea; the shipping and guns around Suda Bay, Reteimo and Heraklion – all were being 'softened up'.

HMS *York* lying on the mud in Suda Bay was a sitting duck. The Italians had previously fixed that with a suicide raid from the sea. They had brought a ship close in to Suda Bay one night and in the early morning had dispatched three small motor boats filled with high explosives, with a man controlling each one, on a suicide mission to blow up the largest target in the bay. They had skilfully manoeuvred through the protective boom barrier and in turn set their course for the *York*.

One boat had missed the stern to explode on the rocks, one had passed the bows and came to a halt on the mud flats without exploding, and the other one had hit the ship midships and broken its back. It was just about first light when it happened and we, living in our 'dug in' tents near Suda, had nearly been blown out of bed by the two loud explosions.

So, HMS *York* was a daily practice target for the Germans, and all through April and into May the raids intensified.

I belonged to a Field Company of Royal Engineers. We had landed on the island about 5 November 1940 and had been met with a very warm reception from the Italian high-level bombers as we were disembarking.

We were the only Field Company on the island and by the numerous tasks we had carried out, we were beginning to think we were more like a construction unit.

We had built roads, storage huts and depots, a small gauge railway, bridges, shelters of all descriptions, 'ack-ack' gun positions and we had even built a jetty – and a host of other things.

It had been a great, welcome change after the Western Desert. The climate was good and the people very friendly; there was plenty of good fruit and the wine was very cheap.

We were camped at the base of the foothills, a few miles from Suda near a village with a name I never knew the spelling of, but it sounded like 'Chick La Rear', and Canea would be a further 6 miles away to the west.

We had been warned some weeks past that the Germans might try and land; consequently, as May approached, we were doing a twice daily stand to, morning and evening, and were confined to our camp area after the evening stand down. During the daytime, we still went off to work at our various tasks, split up in small groups covering an area from Malamie airfield about 20 miles to our west and to Suda Point about 12 miles to our east.

Our unit consisted of a small headquarter section and three field sections of about sixty men each; one of our field sections being recently despatched to Heraklion. We were never to see it again.

On about 12 May, the members of my section had just got back into camp after a trying day, and whilst we were getting cleaned up and having our evening meal, the Germans delivered a concentrated bombing attack on the ships in Suda Bay. It was a furious battle whilst it lasted, with everything possible being fired at the Germans; aircraft were hit and brought down and ships were hit and damaged by the bombs.

Shortly after the raid, we were all mustered, our pumping equipment was loaded into our lorries, and we sped off to Suda docks where we were told we were going to fight a fire on one of the ships.

As we arrived, the only ship which we could see to be on fire was an ammunition ship well out from the shore with its ammunition banging off in all directions; there wasn't a hope of putting that one out. We were actually standing against the ship we were to work on; it was moored to the jetty and had been hit several times.

I seem to remember it was called *Lowgesian*. It was berthed on the east side of the jetty and a much smaller boat, the *Volvo*, was berthed on the west side of the jetty.

The ship was coal fired (I never knew its tonnage), and had been discharging much-wanted aero engines at the time of the air attack. Bombs had landed 'aft', midships, one having gone straight down the funnel, another through the deck of the bridge, through a cable room which had set on fire and finally out of the starboard side of the ship just above the water line. Another bomb had exploded in the coal bunkers, setting them on fire. The worst place to be hit had been the forward hold where men had been unloading the aero engines, and many of them had been killed or wounded. The *Volvo* was untouched. It was already coming dark when we arrived and we soon got our pumps working and climbed on board to put out the fires. The cable room and other smaller fires were soon put out, but the coal bunkers were a much more difficult job as the fires were emitting deadly coal gas. After many hours of hard work, we got the bunkers under control and it was decided we would leave a small party aboard all night just in case the fires started again, and I was one of the party who stayed behind. We were all volunteers and our orders were to leave the ship at dawn the next morning and get back to camp. The only other person aboard was the first officer of the ship.

Our party consisted of a lance sergeant, myself, a lance corporal and six sappers. I was 21 years old. We arranged to do a 'tour of duty' in pairs throughout the night, keeping watch for any fires which may restart. I well remember the next morning when I awoke, for I had been sleeping next to someone's blown off forearm which had a clutching hand and it didn't half give me a nasty turn. We were all glad when we finally left the ship and went back to our own camp and breakfast.

This sort of thing was now a daily occurrence. Our work was being interrupted and so were our meal times, and although air raids at night were not frequent – and then only delivered by the Italians from a high altitude – we were often working into the night clearing bomb damage.

On the morning of 20 May we were up as usual at first light to 'stand to', then after 'stand down' we prepared ourselves for work, had breakfast, boarded our vehicles and the various parties went off to work.

Five sappers and I were to go to a spot near Suda to build air an airraid shelter and headquarters for the naval personnel of HMS *York*, but we never got that far.

Two of my men were late, so I and three others carried our stores to our waiting truck a few hundred yards away, and whilst it was being loaded, I went back to chase up my two men. I found them dashing along to the cookhouse to grab a bacon sandwich each and I urged them on with some good old army language. The three of us then doubled off to the waiting truck, with our haversacks bouncing up and down on our backs, carrying our rifles and ammunition, sweating and cursing under our steel helmets, and the two of them trying to eat bacon sandwiches.

We arrived at the truck quite breathless, climbed on board and set off along the very narrow road we called 42nd Street (named after our Field

Company) which would be about ¾ of a mile long, joining up with the major Suda-Canea road. It was a sunken road with dense olive groves along each side and had been nothing more than a cart track when we had arrived on the island. We had widened it, put in passing places, metalled it and rolled it into a good surface, making it fit for military traffic.

All our other working parties had gone on their way to their various jobs and we were trying to hurry to get out of our camp area as quickly as we could, so that we wouldn't be spotted by any of our officers as being late.

We hadn't gone very far when the most unearthly noise of bombardment started around us. We stopped the truck quickly; even the ground was shaking.

Looking up into the clear blue morning sky, we saw wave upon wave of German heavy bombers coming in over Suda Bay from the east and northeast, dropping their bomb loads from Suda to Canea and further west to Malamie airfield.

We had a very limited view, owing to the trees around us, so to get a better view we climbed upon our vehicle's superstructure. The sight we saw wasn't a very good one; Suda was under a complete pall of black smoke and dust. There were black crosses everywhere in the sky. We were deafened by the noise of bursting bombs, anti-aircraft guns firing and aircraft engines.

This must have continued for at least half an hour, and after a short lull it started again. This time we could hear the unmistakable screaming dive of the Stuka dive bombers, and we got down from our perch very quickly as German fighter aircraft roared in at tree-top level, strafing the main road and the countryside.

I quickly decided it was time to get our truck turned around and head back to camp, so shouting at the driver above all the din we took the truck to the next passing place and started to turn it round. It was a difficult manoeuvre in such a confined space and while some of us were trying to help the driver, others were keeping a lookout around us and popping off their rifles at the aircraft above.

Just as we had managed to get the truck turned and I was telling the boys to get on the back, one of them shouted, 'parachutists!' We couldn't believe our eyes, there they were, long, dark-coloured heavy transport aircraft with men jumping out of them and parachute canopies opening up.

Forty-Second Street was no place for us to tarry; we were soon roaring down the road back the way we had come and still trying to fire our rifles at the targets in the air. This was 'it'; the Germans were arriving.

We parked our truck beneath the olive trees in its usual place several hundred yards from our lines, and ran the rest of the way. There were only two sappers left in camp; one was the cook and the other the storeman. By now, they had seen the first parachutists (*der Fallschirmjäger*) landing and had prepared themselves for action in a slit trench.

I told the storeman to get out the Bren light machine guns and open up some ammunition boxes. The Brens were soon produced, but the ammunition was locked in a steel box concreted into the ground. We told the storeman to open the padlock and he said our section sergeant was away with the key, so there was nothing else we could do but to break it off whilst the storeman was bitterly complaining that he would surely get into trouble for it. We would all be in trouble mighty quick if we didn't soon get some ammunition!

We split up and positioned ourselves between the Bren gun pit for aircraft defence and two slit trenches for ground defence. There must have been some indiscriminating shooting from us at first, picking out targets at random due to the initial excitement, but after being spotted by two German fighters who gave us a nasty few minutes with their guns, we became more cautious. We would then pick out the nearest transport aircraft with its human cargo and all concentrate on the one target, raking it from stem to stern with our fire, hoping we would do the maximum damage.

We kept a sharp lookout for the fighters and parachutists who had already landed. We were reasonably safe from our rear because the towering mountains behind us were not the type of terrain to land parachutists on. Aircraft flying from this direction had to fly high and could therefore not get down close to us before they were away over Suda Bay – well out of our range.

The battle with parachutist troops and aircraft continued furiously all day. We had never seen so many aircraft together in the sky at one time.

They were bursting into flames after being hit by ack-ack and exploding, again with a terrific bang as they plummeted down to hit the earth.

By late afternoon, our section officer, with a few NCOs and men, struggled back into camp having had a busy time trying to get back. We were jolly pleased to see them and they were equally pleased to see we were in control of our own camp area. Later, more men arrived, usually in threes and fours, all having had hair-raising experiences.

Our young officer had congratulated us on being back in camp and keeping control and I thought it best not to mention the fact that we had never even got as far as our job that morning. We were now able to form a better defensive position; we were issued with more ammunition and emergency rations of corned beef and biscuits, and our bomb-happy cook had managed to knock up some hot stew and a brew of tea which we were ready for and thoroughly enjoyed. It was to be our last hot meal for a long time.

Towards darkness, the battle quietened down; we posted sentries and gave out a password and our officer and senior NCOs were able to get in touch with our HQ and the other Field Section, or what was left of them, and our commanding officer was able to reassess what he had left out of his unit; we never did get all our men back.

So the first day of battle was over, it had been a great shock to us. The Germans didn't appear to have dropped their forces in one particular place, but well spread out between Suda and Malamie airfield.

This had created havoc amongst the various units in this area, especially the smaller units like ours, and some had been so badly hit that they never were able to recover again as complete and organised units.

The second day of battle was very much like the first, with the bombers playing havoc with their ground targets, the heavy transporters bringing in more parachutists. The stukas played hell with our ack-ack defences and with the ships still in Suda Bay. The fighters were like hornets, forever blasting up and down, trying to make us keep our heads down.

Pockets of parachutists were being mopped up in different places and one of our unit officers came along with the story of the Australians and New Zealanders who, having captured a German Swastika flag, had been laying it out in a clearing, and the Germans had continued to drop more troops on to it, only to be cut to ribbons by their devastating fire and bayonet charges, and as our officer put it, 'They were having fun and games!'

The Germans also landed glider-borne troops on a plateau east of Canea, only to be met by the 2-pounder anti-tank guns of the Northumberland Hussars.

As the days passed, the bulk of the fighting centred around Malamie airfield, the nearby flat ground of Galatos where the 7th General Hospital was, and towards Canea.

Germans had also landed at two other towns on the northern seaboard, one being Reteimo about 40 miles away, and at Heraklion about 80 miles away, and we were led to believe that all three places were well under our control.

One night there was much shelling out at sea and later we heard it had been our navy preventing the landing of German troops. There was no doubt, however, that the Germans were determined to get a foothold at our end of the island. They crash-landed hundreds of aircraft transporters at Malamie with troops and supplies. They took over the 7th General Hospital and placed the British sick patients exposed in front of them as a shield against the weapons of the Welsh Regiment; consequently, many of our own men were killed by our own bullets. Some of our sappers were sent off to Suda Point where there were some large naval guns positioned, pointing out to sea. They were to assist in turning them round to enable them to be fired in the direction of Malamie.

When this had been done and the guns started firing, we could hear the whine of the shells as they sped on their path of destruction; it was a frightening sound.

Our ack-ack defences around Suda Bay were gradually being thinned out by the stukas, but there were still a few mobile Bofor guns left in action. The naval ships able to sail had left the bay and those (or what was left of them) left behind were lying at all angles.

Of our air force we saw absolutely nothing. There were supposed to have been three old Gladiator fighters and three Hurricanes at Malamie but they must have been put out of action 'early doors'. There is no doubt that they were used to the utmost advantage against an enemy vastly superior in numbers. We always said that Crete would have been a different story had we been able to put fighters into the air.

This was a new type of warfare; our methods were antiquated. The Germans had the air power from the start, their stukas were 'dead eyes' once they began their dive on a target; they seldom missed. Ground defences were no match for all the hundreds of aircraft, though they knocked a lot out of the sky. Our navy, likewise, was no match for the stukas and no matter what they tried, we still lost a lot of good ships and brave men for the want of air protection.

My unit's next move was to be reorganised and reallocated to fresh positions east of 42nd Street in the olive groves, where we dug in and faced in the general direction of Canea. The Germans had now got a foothold in the Malamie area and were bitterly fighting towards Canea.

Then late one day we sorted out our stores and loaded some of our vehicles, mostly with explosives, and that night we pulled out of our positions and drove along 42nd Street to the main road.

We expected to turn left and go towards Canea but to our amazement we turned right towards Suda. The whole road from Canea to Suda was chock-a-block with all types of vehicles; they were made to pull in well to the left whilst we were to try to get past. We soon found out why.

The road passing through Suda was blocked by the debris from bombed buildings and we had to set to and get it cleared. There were no such things as bulldozers in those days and it took many hours of hard toil by hand to get the road cleared. The first vehicles allowed through were the ambulances and lorries carrying the wounded, then came all sorts of other vehicles full to capacity with men.

I saw lorries filled with both British and Anzac (Australian and New Zealand) troops which had been stopped by officers who were pleading with the men to get down and reform their units and to go back and make a fight of it, but they wouldn't and the drivers drove on.

Our section moved out of Suda just before first light to a position along the coast road where we could hide our vehicles and get some rest after the gruelling night's work.

From here we were told an evacuation of the island had begun and we would be given various targets to demolish along the road of retreat, and we would be part of the rearguard action as long as we could last out.

Food and medical supplies were now very scarce but again we were told of dumps along the road, there for our benefit. Needless to say, we never saw any.

We had plenty of ammunition and explosives; we even made our own hand grenades from empty detonator tins. These detonator tins were about 2½ inches in diameter and about 5 inches long with a screw-on lid at each end. They normally held twenty-five detonators and a wooden rectifier. Now we stuffed them with gelignite, made a hole for the detonator and fuse to sit in and led the fuse through a hole in the lid. The fuse was about 3 inches long and, burning at the rate of 2 feet per minute, would give us about seven-and-a-half seconds to light and get rid of it. They were better than a hand grenade and more powerful.

We were now allotted to small demolition parties, mine consisting of a lance sergeant, myself, a couple of drivers and six sappers. We had two vehicles, one a 15cwt open truck with the explosives and demolition stores, and a 30cwt truck with other stores such as picks and shovels, sledgehammers and crowbars, also more explosives and ammunition.

The lance sergeant with his driver and the sappers took the 30cwt truck in front and I and a driver followed with the 15cwt truck.

As per our training, we carried red flags displayed on our vehicles to denote explosives being carried, but we soon dispensed with them after nearly being shot up by German fighter planes. It was obvious they also knew what red flags on vehicles meant and there was no point in us advertising the fact any more.

The demolition parties were given their locations and targets on the road of retreat and we set off in our vehicles at various intervals.

Our turn came and off we went. I couldn't help feeling most uncomfortably exposed as I sat opposite the driver on the Mottley mounting seat, much higher than the normal seat and specially made to swivel around from side to side with a Bren gun mounted on the special fitting in front of me. We also had our rifles stuck in the racks at our side and a German sub-machine gun some of our boys had 'won' when returning to our lines during the first couple of days of the battle.

I also remember as we were going along the road, we came across some infantrymen marching towards us in single file on the sides of the road. We exchanged greetings and they told us they were Marine Infantry who had landed during the previous night from a destroyer and that men from the Middle East Commandos had also landed.

This gave us much heart and we saw no reason why more troops couldn't be landed and we could still put a stop to the Germans, and the great 'IF': if we only had some fighter aircraft.

We were now travelling south, across the island, through torturous roads badly potholed, the terrain becoming more and more mountainous.

Eventually, we arrived at our location for demolition; it was a huge culvert round a bend in the road. We unloaded some explosives and equipment and took the trucks a little further up the road into a cutting with rocky cliffs on each side, and also on the next bend. This would protect them from the air. At the demolition site, the cliffs rose straight and high up one side of the road, with a drop of hundreds of feet on the other side of the road.

There were vehicles crammed with men travelling through our new position to the point of evacuation at Sparkia on the southern coast. They all looked as fit as us and, were armed and we still wondered why these men were not being organised to fight. It looked to us as though everyone was running away.

There was one hell of a scatter when the German fighter planes came whizzing overhead; they couldn't come down too low owing to the high mountainous cliffs around, but the mere sound of their guns put the fear of Christ up everybody.

During a quiet spell on the road, a German observation plane, the 'Storch', started patrolling and nosing about up and down the canyons. We kept dead still until he was almost opposite us, then we let him have it with every weapon we possessed. He was a sitting duck and hadn't seen us and I could see the shots from my Bren gun cutting into him from his nose to his tail.

Of course, he was soon out of range, disappearing round a bend, but we could hear others further along the road shooting away at him, then we heard an almighty crash and saw a plume of black smoke rising; at least one more German had bit the dust.

We had a mobile Bofors ack-ack gun parked very close to us for some time. He had probably been sent to give us protection from air attack, but he only made things worse. We had been getting on well with our demolition job before he came on the scene, and now the German fighters were buzzing around us like bees round a honey pot.

Very soon three stukas paid us a visit. They circled round whilst each made a separate diving attempt to bomb the Bofors gun, but again they couldn't dive as low as they normally did, owing to the cliffs. They came far too close for our liking; I was still on the Bren gun popping away as fast as I could. We could clearly see the bombs leave the aircraft, narrowly missing the road to explode down in the chasm below us. They certainly gave us a nasty turn.

When they had gone, our sergeant went along to the Bofors gun crew and told them in plain English to get to hell out of it – and that's putting it mildly. There were some heated words on both sides, but the gun packed up and pulled out, not towards the rear, we were pleased to see, but towards the 'sharp end'. Consequently, we were left alone after that and we got on with our job.

Within a few hours we had our culvert all nice and ready for blowing and all we now had to do was wait for the order to 'blow'. This was the worst time of any.

We could tell when the 'sharp end' was moving to us. Our forward demolition teams would come through and give us the latest news whilst on their way to leapfrog us on to their next job. Again, we would hear the sounds of battle coming closer; one or two Bofors guns would come through accompanied by their crews and ammunition, 2-pounder anti-tank guns, etc.; the rearguard infantry would come and take up positions and lastly two ancient 'I' tanks (infantry tanks) would trundle up the road, covering each other with their fire at each bend in the road, and the last of the infantry with the tanks.

When everyone had passed by us we were usually told to 'blow' by our own OC, a dynamic little man who seemed to be tireless, and by which time, however, the Germans were sending over their 3-inch mortars at us.

Usually, the sergeant and I lit the fuses and after making sure they were properly burning we would leave the demolition as per the 'book' and walk steadily away to our awaiting trucks with their engines running.

It was a nerve-racking few minutes, thinking with every step we were going to walk into a bursting mortar or get shot in the back.

It was more dangerous to run away from a demolition because one might easily fall, twist an ankle or break a leg and again it is always a point of honour for a sapper to walk away, not run.

This then was the general pattern of things now, rearguard action after rearguard action all the way to Sparkia. We lost track of time, we had no food, we tried to live off the land, but many hundreds had been there before us and there wasn't much left for us.

The last demolition job we went on was on the seaward side of Sparkia village, not far from the coast. It was a large culvert about 8 feet wide and 8 feet high and about 18 feet in length. There were now only four of us left; it was late afternoon and we were very weary.

We had just lugged our boxes of high explosive on to the site and were preparing to fix them into position, when along came a corps of Military Police (MPs), sergeant and corporal, who said we couldn't carry on with this job as the general and his party were going to sleep there that night.

I told them to 'get stuffed'; I knew nothing of any general and said they had better find our OC who was the only one we would take any orders from; he had given us the job himself and he was the only one who could take it off us.

They went away and soon returned with some high-ranking, red-tabbed officer who looked as if he had just walked out of Sandhurst. He told us the same story; he was extremely nice about it, but I still wasn't satisfied and told him he would still have to find our OC and bring him back before we would leave the job. I did, however, agree to stop the job until our OC arrived.

The officer went off with one of the MPs whilst the other one, chatting to us, told us who the general was; he was only the famous General Freyberg who had swum the Dardanelles Strait in the First World War and earned a VC.

We still, however, viewed all this with suspicion without saying so, until eventually our OC arrived with the staff officer and the MP. It was right enough, we had to pack up, there was a general and he was going to stay in the culvert that night. The staff officer congratulated us on our doggedness in sticking to our orders and on the good job we had done on the rearguard action. He shook hands with the four of us, thanked us and wished us luck and strode off.

Whilst the four of us carried our boxes of explosives back to our truck, the CMPs with a few more men were carrying in filled sand bags to make a blast wall at each end of the culvert.

That was our last job and it was now Saturday evening, 31 May 1941.

We took our truck back into Sparkia village, which was by this time quite congested with vehicles of all descriptions and other mobile equipment. Groups of men from various units were being marched off to the evacuation beach. Other troops making up part of the rearguard were digging new positions, getting ready for the last stand.

A couple of our men were on the roadside waiting to tell other members of our unit where to assemble. We soon pulled our truck off the road, over some bumpy ground by the side of a building and met the remnants of our unit. Our ranks were now somewhat sadly depleted.

From what I remember of Sparkia village, approaching from our route from the north, the mountains suddenly gave way to a wide steep-sided valley, with the village nestling in the bottom, its houses and other buildings on each side of the one and only road.

From the houses, the land was cultivated in terraces as far up the steep slopes as it was possible to go. The village was several hundred feet above sea level and just beyond it the ground dipped down to the sea in a series of craggy chasms and escarpments with sides of sparsely growing bushes and trees. There was a donkey track leading down a tortuous route to the beach. It started wide enough for the average vehicle to drive along, then became narrower and narrower until it was impossible to turn the vehicle round. Our sappers had tried to widen it and to take out some of the bigger bumps, but they didn't get very far.

This was the evacuation route, thousands of our soldiers had come this way and there were still thousands down there, near and on the beaches.

Our work, however, still wasn't finished. A party of us was gathered, we boarded one of our trucks and went off up the road toward the 'sharp end' again, whilst those left behind were detailed to destroy the remaining vehicles.

Apparently, one of the demolition jobs had gone off prematurely and the 'I' tanks and others of the rearguard were on the wrong side of it and we were going to fill it in again. We drove the truck as quickly as possible some miles until we came to the large gap in the road. The only thing to do was to blast some rock off the cliff side to help to fill it.

There was the merry hell of a battle going on further along the road, which was slowly but surely getting nearer. We worked like the devil to fill that damned gap until we saw the first of the 'I' tanks approaching and with it several infantry men. They stopped a few hundred yards away, took up new positions and started firing somewhere down the road.

Then the second tank came into view with more infantry men with it. Mortar-shell bursts were following them, all sorts of weapons were now beginning to fire in both directions. The tanks were edging closer to us every minute, but they were reasonably safe now as we had got the gap filled in enough for them to get over.

Behind us was another group of infantry in positions waiting for this rearguard to pass through. We were told to get to hell out of it and didn't need a second telling. We kept to the cliff side and made off at the double to our waiting truck.

It was at this time when something burst quite close; the sapper ahead of me stumbled, having been hit in the knees. I reached him and helped him the rest of the way to the truck; we climbed on board and it wasn't until then that I realised I was tasting blood in my mouth, I had been hit on my upper lip. Whether all our party got on board or not, I will never know, but we went off back down that road as fast as we could go. I broke open a half of my first aid dressing and bound it around my face, I could now feel some of my teeth were loose, but the wound didn't hurt.

'Mac' who had been hit in the knees was also attending to himself. He wasn't badly injured; luckily, splinters which had struck him had been very small.

We arrived back in Sparkia village just before dusk. The place being almost deserted now, everyone must have moved off to the beaches. All the air activity had ceased, but it would be back in the morning.

Ditching our truck, we then moved off through the village on to the track which led down to the beaches. We didn't go very far when we turned off the track on to a high ridge where we met up once again with the remnants of our unit.

We took up positions with our backs to the sea; I still selected my favourite, the faithful Bren gun, settling down to what we thought would be a few hours wait until the navy came in to pick us up, as we had been told this would be the last night of evacuation.

I, for one, was very tired and weary, and when darkness came I soon fell asleep still holding on to my Bren gun. I awoke like all the others at about first light the next morning to the sound of a very heavy and large aircraft flying nearby. We then spotted the aircraft; it was a Sunderland Flying boat low over the water coming in to land. Soon a couple of small boats went out to it and several persons climbed on board. The Sunderland then roared away into the now early dawn, skimming over the sea, which was as calm as a mill pond, gradually making a perfect take off. It was a wonderful sight.

Looking out at the length and breadth of the sea, there was not a ship to be seen; nobody spoke, all was quiet now the Sunderland had gone. We now knew we 'had had it'; in other words, there wasn't going to be any evacuation for us.

Then someone's voice piped up in protest at the Sunderland coming in to pick up 'Privileged Persons'. Another voice said that was 'Tommy rot', it had come in to pick up the wounded, and yet another voice making some crack about another aircraft coming in to pick us up. There were lots of voices in protest now, some about why the navy hadn't done their job, others wanted to know where our 'Blankety Blank' air force was.

Some were asking why we had been put out on this 'sticky ridge' to fight to the last man; another protest went up that our OC was entirely to blame as he was probably wanting a 'bar' to his OBE at our expense.

What we didn't know at that time was that the navy had carried out an immeasurable task of maintaining command of the seas around us with no air support to speak of, had destroyed the bulk of a German seaborne invasion force bound for Crete (in the north), brought in reinforcements and whilst attempting to evacuate many thousands of men, had been bombed unmercifully, resulting in an appalling loss of ships, sailors and troops.

We had always bitterly complained about our air force, not of the personnel, it wasn't their fault they hadn't enough aircraft, it was at the controlling powers back home for their lack of foresight and understanding of the type of warfare we now found ourselves in. The complaint against our OC was definitely unjustified, no officer had ever had his troops more at heart than he.

Now, as the sun rose in the east over to our right, the German air force made their grand entry upon the scene once again. There were as many as ever, coming in out of the sun, keeping very low. With guns blazing, they skimmed over the top of us and up the mountain sides, before turning as quickly as possible, diving low along the beaches, blazing away with their guns again on the defenceless men down there.

Further up the ridge, towards the village, the battle had started once again with the crack of rifle fire, machine-gun fire and mortars. The German mortars were flying right over us, screaming as they went, exploding in the chasms down below.

My mouth was now well congealed with blood. I was trying to make a hole through one side with my finger whilst assisting with my tongue from inside, so that I could have a drink of water from my water bottle. I managed alright but I couldn't speak very well. Someone gave me a cigarette which I lit and inhaled deeply. I didn't smoke very much in those days and that first drag made my head spin round, all the trees looked upside down and I felt I was floating on air. This feeling must have lasted something like a minute, I didn't put the cigarette out but continued to puff away. Mentally, it did me the world of good, serving as a tranquiliser and nerve steadier.

Our OC made an appearance, apologising for not being able to give us any food. But now, more important at the moment was his news. He told us the Sunderland flying boat had been to take off General Freyberg and his staff, and his latest orders were that we were to negotiate a capitulation of the island to the Germans that morning without delay to save any further unnecessary bloodshed, as there was nothing to gain by continuing the struggle. He said the senior officer was a Medical Corps colonel, then there was a Royal Artillery major and himself, a Royal Engineer major. They were now going off to confer and make arrangements to meet the Germans.

Soon the shooting and mortaring from both sides ceased; the aircraft though kept circling round; all went quiet.

Shortly afterwards, our OC returned to say that contact had been made, the terms had been agreed, we had to lay down our arms and stand up as the Germans would be arriving any time now.

We had a few young junior officers with us by this time; a couple of them were ours but I don't know where the others came from, as the only officers I remember seeing on the rearguard were our OC and our section officer; the others were strangers to me, but with them being Royal Engineers our OC must have collected them en route.

He now told us that it was a case of every man for himself; he would give anyone the option of trying to make a break for it or staying with him to become prisoners of war.

All the young officers decided to try to make a break for it and off they went. I never saw any of them again. The remainder of us, and there weren't many left (as a few had sneaked away during the night hoping they would get away), decided to stick it out with our OC.

We smashed up our rifles, threw away the mechanisms of our automatic weapons and made a dump of our ammunition.

So this was 'IT', the end of the road, I can't express the feeling I had at that time, I was simply sad.

I took stock of what personal possessions I had left: my haversack with mess tins, eating irons, washing kit, shaving kit, 'housewife', holdall (with its spare pair of laces neatly rolled up), my small kit of socks and a change of underwear, a water bottle which I filled up at the stream below us, a greatcoat and one blanket. My water bottle was to become worth its weight in gold.

The Germans eventually arrived; there was no trouble, they looked just like us: tired and fed up. They came round and shook hands with us wishing us well and saying in very bad English, 'Vor du der Var is over.' Cigarettes were exchanged and smoked and we all started to climb on our way back up the ridge and track towards Sparkia village.

We were now prisoners of war and little did we realise our troubles were just beginning.

Chapter 2

The Road to Galatos

It would be about midday when we climbed the steep track to Sparkia village. The sun was high and blazing hot; there was hardly a breath of air, even so near the sea, and clouds of arid dust rose from the ground, caused by the dryness and many hundreds of tramping boots.

The Germans were now conspicuous by their absence; there were so few of them and so many of us, it was hard to understand how we had lost. We were now told to just keep on marching, there being only one road, back the way we had come, rough and rugged at that.

As we were passing through Sparkia village, now a long column of prisoners, ever increasing, I spotted a building with a huge Red Cross painted on the roof. As I passed by the building, I broke ranks to see if I could get any first aid for my face.

The building was deserted apart from some dead bodies belonging to both sides lying around outside. The place was shot to bits. Others had been there before me, but I managed to find a field dressing and, most important of all, a pound tin of marmalade, about a pound of tea and some lump sugar. I scooped the tea into my mess tin and stuffed the sugar as quickly as I could into my pockets. I then went out by another door, passing some more corpses, and rejoined the marching column, passing as quickly as I could along the ranks to join up with the men from my own unit. All the officers had been separated from the other ranks and kept on their own with a strong German guard in charge of them.

The battlefield around Sparkia wasn't a very pleasant sight. There were vehicles by their hundreds, of every description, parked in every place possible; there were all sorts of guns and their equipment lying at all angles, odd-looking armoured cars, and one of the battered old 'I' tanks which had done so much on the rearguard action.

There were many dead from both sides, but we were now hardened to this and the sight of death no longer meant anything to us. The past two weeks of action had shocked us beyond our normal understanding, numbing our finer senses. We had been living under unnatural conditions for too long, and doing unnatural things. Those who say war is adventure are crazy, it may be exciting for some, but for the majority, if the truth is known, it is a terrifying experience.

Hundreds of men were now breaking ranks and searching through the vehicles, mainly for food, but some who had ditched their kit en route to the evacuation point, were now looking for anything of any use, such as blankets, mess tins, water bottles and greatcoats, etc.

The column continued to move on its way out of Sparkia into the foothills of the mountains. It was a steady climb for mile upon mile on a poorly surfaced road through a huge valley with its steep sides. We had previously only travelled over this road in a truck, not realising how bad its surface was and how much of a gradient it had. We weren't used to marching, we had ridden in trucks almost everywhere. Now we were finding how tough it was underfoot.

But I was young, fit and had a good pair of feet and a good pair of army boots on. I had tied my greatcoat and blanket together to enable me to carry it bandolier fashion. Many times during the heat of the day I was tempted to throw them away as they were becoming such a burden to carry.

My lip was now giving me more trouble; my teeth were aching and I tried to soothe my gums and the inside of my lips with my tongue, and to stop my lips from sticking together I cleaned a small twig from an olive tree, about 1½ inches long, with my jack-knife and then held the twig between my lips. It was a great help and I was able to keep an air passage through my mouth.

There were many others with wounds, mostly superficial, but nevertheless painful and aggravated by the present conditions. Mac, who had been hit in the knees, was marching painfully on with us. Water soon became at a premium. I was thankful I had filled up my water bottle from the stream; it would have to last out as long as possible. I was able to suck a sugar lump every now and then and take with it the least drop of water.

We marched on, mile after mile, climbing all the way, until we really got into the mountains. We had no idea how far we were marching for there were no milestones along these roads; we would have to guess it over a period of time. We were, by some calculations, doing a fantastic mileage at a fantastic speed, but it would be fair to say that on leaving Sparkia at approximately 12 noon and continuously marching until about 7 o'clock in the evening at 3 miles per hour, we must have done at least 20 miles.

The first night halt was on a small plateau in the mountains. Ahead of us we could see campfires and the rumour went around that they were field kitchens: they were, but not for us.

We left the road and lay down in the fields on either side anywhere we could. There was no food to issue out anyway, so the only thing to do was to settle down and get some much-wanted sleep. I did, however, dig out the tin of marmalade and share it with the few of us who had stuck together.

Then it was 'heads down'; we were thankful for the cool mountain air after the hot gruelling day. I put on my greatcoat and wrapped my blanket around me, using my haversack as a pillow and holding on to its strap (so that it wouldn't get stolen), and soon went off to sleep.

We awoke next morning at first light, just before sun up. It was cold and many men who had days ago dispensed with their kit had had nothing to keep them warm and had spent a very uncomfortable night. They were on their feet, already moving about to keep warm, and as the sun came up, they needed no telling to start off on the road for another day's march.

The day started out like most other days at that time of the year, the fresh mountain air and beautiful sunrise creating a kaleidoscope of colour. Oh, for a good hot mug of tea and some egg and bacon, but it was to be a long, long time before we saw that again.

We made for the road and started off once more, our small gang keeping together. There was no method of marching by units or anything like that, we were all mixed up, there were no longer any units. There was no marching in step, one made one's own step.

For the first couple of hours there was plenty of talking, usually about food, or why we lost, or how we could have won. There was no doubt we felt we had been terribly let down by our country.

What were the people in charge doing to let a catastrophe such as this happen? Where was our modern equipment and why hadn't we moved with the times? We had definitely been trained in the 1914–18 methods of trench warfare and always in the defence. Our vehicles and equipment were outdated and obsolete and we had to be good at improvisation. (I remember seeing vehicles of the Madras Sappers and Miners in Egypt which were so ancient they had solid tyres and headlamps of highly polished solid brass, and the vehicles were chain driven.) All sorts of rumours spread back and forth along the column. Sometimes it would be about food being issued just around the next bend, and a classic one was that our troops from Egypt were going to make a landing and relieve us. But, as the sun rose higher and higher and the day became hotter, there was less talking except for the odd curse.

The road back was almost indescribable. There was abandoned equipment lying everywhere on the sides of the road. There were many graves of both German and British where rearguard actions had been fought. We went past where we had carried out demolitions on the road, now mostly filled in again, and always a few graves dotted about the area. The Germans had brought their own black crosses for their graves with them. The British graves were denoted usually by a rifle at their heads with a steel helmet on top.

It was now becoming a grim trudge along the road as the day got hotter. Men were falling out on the roadside, utterly exhausted, compelled to rest for a while before moving on. Even some of the Germans marching with us were feeling the pinch and were having to rest.

My feet were now beginning to give me hell, I hadn't taken my boots off for days, I could feel my heels getting sore, there must by now be huge holes in my socks, and blisters on my heels. I had another pair of good clean socks in my haversack which I decided I must change at the first opportunity, but not now because my feet would be swollen and I might not be able to get my boots back on again. Water was scarce and roadside wells were very few and far between. These wells were usually quite deep and about 10 feet in diameter; many water bottles were lost down them whilst trying to fill them with water, leaving their owners desperate.

In the early afternoon, we arrived at the one and only river in our area. It is probably wrong to call it a river, a huge mountain stream would be a better name, but it was water, clear sparkling water, with hundreds and hundreds of thirsty men getting their fill. I made sure my water bottle was properly filled again. I took the field dressing off my face after giving it a good soaking, cleaned my wound up as best I could and put on the other half of the dressing. It felt a lot better. Then I started on my feet, it was wonderful get my boots off and lower them into the ice-cold water. My socks were terrible, with large holes worn in the heels and toes, but I rubbed them vigorously in the water and wrung them out. They would soon dry again in this heat. My heels were blistered but not broken and the tops of my toes were very sore, but with a fresh pair of socks on and clean feet and managing to put my boots on again, I felt I could continue the march with much better heart.

Again, we were more than heartened when the Germans announced there was going to be some food issued. It was our own 'bully' and biscuits; one tin of corned beef between two men and a couple of packets of biscuits each.

I paired off with a pal of mine, Alex (Jock) Morrison, a dour, tough Scot who had been a recruit with me back at Chatham. We drew our rations and sat down to eat them. I found eating very difficult, I had to mash the corned beef up and push a little at a time into my mouth, and the only way I could manage the hard biscuits was to soak them in water in my mess tin. But I managed, it was essential that I should because by now we were terribly hungry. I shall never forget that feed, the bully and biscuits tasted wonderful and the water like wine.

Soon we began to move on again, much refreshed, so that others behind us could move in and enjoy the water and draw their rations. The heat of the day was passing its zenith, the road now more downhill, leading out of the mountainous terrain towards a wide valley which we knew was taking us ever nearer to Suda Bay. My feet felt much better, but towards evening time I was definitely feeling the strain again and was only too grateful when the second day's march was over and we settled down off the road for the night. It was estimated we would reach Suda by midday the next day.

Early next morning we started once again. The night hadn't been as cold as the previous one high in the mountains, but the day started with its usual freshness. The mountains, ever dominated by the snow-capped Mount Ida, were slowly but surely receding behind us.

Many men were now complaining they had lost some of their personal possessions during the night, such as water bottles, haversacks and packs, and even boots had been stolen. There were a few ugly scenes as men started to argue amongst themselves. From now on one had to make doubly sure that one's kit was not left lying unattended, not even for a second. We steadily tramped on, mile after mile, the sun again gradually becoming hotter until it became almost unbearable. Most of us still wore our steel helmets as protection against the sun, but they were heavy and made one sweat a lot.

Later, several vehicles came along in our direction, edging their way slowly past the column; they were loaded with officers and wounded men. The vehicles were some of our own that had been repaired back at Sparkia by cannibalising other vehicles. The occupants were given many cheers and ribald remarks as they passed.

There were four distinct places on this road which I should never forget. One we had already passed by up in the mountains where we had left an old Cretan peasant at his one-roomed stone house at the side of the road near one of our demolition sites during our retreat. He had set himself up with an old single-barrelled shotgun in defiance of the oncoming Germans, and no matter how much we had pleaded with him, he was adamant he would stay there to fight. He had stayed there alright and had still been there when we had marched past again, but this time he was dead, stone dead. I wondered how the brave old man had fought his last battle.

The second place was a stone-built arched bridge which had been prepared for demolition, but had never gone 'off'. By the signs in the area of the bridge, there must have been quite some battle. Our sappers and infantry had tried and succeeded many times to get back to the bridge during the battle, but for some unknown reason it just wouldn't go off. The third place was where we were now marching. It was a large copse on each side of the road, and the scene of more than one battle. My unit had been caught there by German aircraft whilst we had made it an overnight stay. We had been bombed and machine-gunned unmercifully for hours on end. What our losses had been I don't know but we were pleased to leave as quickly as we could with what vehicles we had left. Other units had also been caught by the aircraft there, both before and after us.

The rearguard must also have had a big battle there. The whole area was littered with burnt-out vehicles. There were numerous graves and bodies still lying around and some even wedged in the forks of trees; there was an awful stench of decaying bodies.

The fourth place was still to come for it was on the Suda road, which we were now approaching. The sun was high in the sky, it was midday, and the heat was terrific as we joined the coast road and turned left for Suda. We could now see the whole of Suda Bay, it was a scene of utter chaos. It was the first time we had seen it in daylight since before the Germans had landed.

The submarine boom defences were still there, but every ship in the bay, no matter how large or small, was sunk. They were lying at every conceivable angle, some with bows sticking up, some with sterns sticking up, some on their sides, some with just the tops of funnels showing, and so on. In the far distance, HMS *York* still sat on the mud near Suda; it looked as if there was nothing the matter with her, but we knew differently.

Every ack-ack gun position we passed had been destroyed by bombs from the German stukas; they were just a mass of scrap iron and bent barrels now. Everywhere, on either side of the road, was utter desolation.

This was the hottest part of the march and the bright glare off the sea was agony to our eyes. We reached Suda and rested in the shade of some of the buildings that still stood. It was here we were given another packet of biscuits each, but there wasn't enough 'bully' to go round.

It was here that we also saw some Italian prisoners of war who had been captured previously in Greece on the Albanian front and brought over to Crete. When we saw them, they didn't seem much better off now they were supposed to be free, because they were having to work for their ally, the Germans, who didn't appear to be treating them very kindly. It was only a short halt; we were soon on the move again. We were told we were going to the area of Galatos, but that was still some miles away, having first to go through Canea.

Every step was now becoming agony to me. I could feel my feet were like two lumps of raw meat, my blisters broken and bleeding – but so were everybody else's.

We just had to keep going, knowing that our ordeal would be over once we reached Galatos. It was a case of the survival of the fittest. Anyone without broken and bleeding feet was most fortunate. Passing the end of 42nd Street brought back happier memories, I wondered what our old camp looked like now and whether or not my khaki drill tunic was still in my tent, with a couple of uncashed postal orders in one of the pockets, and whether or not the large metal key our blacksmith had made for my twenty-first birthday was still hanging on a tree by the side of my tent. When Canea came into view, the inhabitants lined the pavements to watch us straggling through. Some of them walked alongside us to give us things to eat and to pass us bottles of water, which was wanted more than anything else. We had always got on well with these very poor hard-working Cretans, and the kindness they showed to us when we were down on our luck will never be forgotten. The column was by now thinning out somewhat. We were amongst the first 500 at its head and away behind us the column must have stretched as far as Suda, as there were thousands of men in it. It was evening time and we had arrived at our destination, a large flat expanse of sandy ground which reached down to the beaches between Galatos and Malamie. This was the area where the bulk of the first four or five days of fighting had taken place. There were some prisoners already there who had been taken during the early days of the battle. Those last few miles from Canea had been sheer hell. I, like many more, had prayed openly and aloud to God to be given strength to carry on.

In the years to come, I was to do a lot of praying to God, harder than I had ever thought possible, sometimes that I might live and survive, and sometimes in desperation that I might die, quickly, not to suffer any more.

Surely if there was a God Almighty, he wouldn't let such suffering happen to us. But it did, and if ever there was a hell, then this was it, we might as well be dead, there couldn't be anywhere in the afterlife worse than this. It was becoming last light when we finally found a place on the sand to flop down. Jock and I cleared a patch of ground and decided that was where we were going to make our 'home' for the night. Aching in every limb we lay down gratefully on our backs next to each other, looking up into the fast-darkening sky, watching the stars appearing, until we dropped asleep. I had never felt so weary and despondent. All through the night more and more men kept arriving, utterly exhausted. They found themselves a patch of ground, sank down on it and went straight to sleep. By next morning, there were men lying around as far as the eye could see in all directions, and still they kept arriving, stragglers who had fallen by the wayside and couldn't keep the pace. In fact, they were coming in for days. The first thing Jock and I did on that morning was to collect our kit together and get to the beach where we spent some considerable time in the water trying to get ourselves clean. My feet were cut, blistered and bruised, and they didn't half smart as I went into the seawater. We also took turns to look after each other's kit whilst the other was in the water, thus safeguarding against getting our kit stolen. The sea was refreshing, it was good to feel clean, all we wanted now was feeding, but that was asking too much.

The next few days were full of activity with the Germans organising and supervising the erection of barbed wire compounds on all sides of the T road junction we had settled upon, this being the main road from Canea to Malamie with the road junction leading off to what had been the 7th General Hospital. Tents and marquees were produced and erected, one of each to each compound. A water pipeline had to be laid with branches and standpipes to each compound, and latrine trenches had to be dug. Senior NCOs tried hard to compile nominal rolls of the men in each compound, but this just wasn't possible to do by units any more. There had to be some form of order and reckoning of the men to enable food to be issued. It was entirely up to us to do this quickly as the Germans were in no hurry to issue anything before they knew our numbers. In the end, the men in our compound paraded and the nominal roll was soon sorted out. It was a couple of days before bread and thin lentil soup began to be issued to us. The water pipeline didn't produce very much water, and one had to wait in the queue for hours on end before being able to get any. The best time to get water was after most other men had gone to sleep. The latrines, being open trenches, were soon swarming with flies and mosquitos, there being no disinfectant available to kill them off. During the day, the sun was unmercifully hot, the coolest place being in the sea but one couldn't stay there all day, so we erected crude sun shelters using our blankets and salvaged pieces of timber.

There was also a punishment compound erected which wasn't far from our own compound. It was quite a small area, being ringed with barbed Dannert wire and had one 180-pounder tent which was for the use of the German guards. This was what the Germans called *Der Straf Lager*. Anyone causing the displeasure of the Germans was quickly forced along the road and thrown into this punishment compound. Then for all to see, the punishment began. This took the form of a beating-up by several guards, then the unfortunate soul was stripped to the waist, made barefooted and made to lift an empty 3-inch ack-ack shell case from the ground level to above his head until he dropped flat on his face through sheer exhaustion and suffering from the heat of day. He would then be revived and the punishment would start all over again until finally the man would be a physically battered, gibbering wreck, to be thrown out of the compound into the road for his pals to come along to carry him back to his own compound and nurse him back to life again.

I've always remembered seeing one man in there who had a mass of red hair. I believe he was a Liverpudlian and many months later I got to know his name as 'Ginger' Connelly. He was a tough man, hard as nails. He would take on four Germans at once and would inflict much damage on them before he was battered senseless to the ground. More will be heard of Ginger later. The Germans seemed to delight in picking on the Australians and New Zealanders for the *Straf Lager*.

Some leaflets had been dropped from the air by the Germans during the battle, stating that their parachutists had been found mutilated after being killed on the battlefield, this being attributed to the Australians and the New Zealanders, and if it didn't stop the Germans would refuse to take any of them prisoners. Needless to say, many hundreds of Australians and New Zealanders had been taken prisoner on the capitulation, the Germans doing their best to keep them separate from we British, and now they were treating them roughly. Whether there was any truth in the German allegations of the atrocities or not, we never found out, but there were no mass executions. During the first few days, we were paraded and visited by several German officers. We paraded in lines of five deep in open order so that the Germans could walk round the ranks and see each man. They were all dressed in excellent fitted uniforms, wore highly polished riding boots and displayed medals and decorations on their left-side tunic pockets. Then with the air of arrogant authority they started their quick inspection. They all stopped in front of me, jabbered away in guttural German, until one of them asked me in perfect English what was the matter with my face, and without waiting for a reply lifted up the edge of the bandage and had a look for himself. Then with a distasteful look on his face, turned to the others, speaking in German again, and the one word I caught was 'gangrene'. Without further to do he told me to go straight off the parade and report to the hospital down the road and he would be along later.

So, with a nod to Jock and with what bit of kit I possessed, I made my way out of the compound, pausing to ask at the marquee if I could have my ration of bread – which was given to me very reluctantly – and I then walked out on to the road to the hospital. However, I hadn't gone very far when a German with a motorcycle and sidecar came roaring along the road from behind me. He pulled up and called me over. He was a tough, hard-looking individual and could speak barely any English. I soon understood by his gesticulations that he wanted to know if I had a wristwatch to give him for a small loaf of bread he had. I showed him by bare wrists and also turned out the pockets in my shorts to indicate I hadn't anything. He then asked me where I was going and I told him as best I could, by making the sign of a cross and pointing to my face, that I was going to the hospital down the road. I also put on a look of agony for his benefit. He promptly indicated to me to get into the sidecar and he took me all the way to the hospital reception. He talked, or I should say, shouted to me all the way, conversationally like, and I couldn't understand one damned word he was on about. At the hospital reception he had a good talk to a German medical orderly who appeared to be in charge, then turning to me gave me the loaf of bread, a packet of boiled sweets and ten German cigarettes.

You could have knocked me down with feather, I was absolutely speechless; whilst up the road they could dish out the most atrocious punishment, here was the entire opposite with a great show of kindness. He grabbed my hand and shook it, then with an *aufwiedersehen*, he jumped on his motorcycle and roared off on his business. The German medical orderly spoke quite good English and told me that my German 'friend' had spoken well of me and wanted him to make sure I was well looked after, and he would be back to see me in a few days' time. A friend in need was a friend indeed, my fortunes seemed to be changing somewhat for the better. It also appeared that my 'friend' was an Unteroffizier (a corporal). Next the orderly took me into a tent, gave me the necessary hot water and lint to enable me to bathe and clean up my gangrenous-looking face. I was at it for a long time, until finally the German MO arrived. Other British prisoners had also been arriving at the reception centre, suffering from all manner of things, and like me had been picked out from the parades in the compounds. The German MO was quite young, very businesslike and confident; he didn't waste any time and was soon examining and issuing instructions to both German and British orderlies as to what treatment to give to his patients. When it came to my turn, he again looked very disapprovingly at my lip, complaining that I should have been given treatment days ago. He gave me an injection in my right arm, took out three very loose top teeth, gave instructions for the dressing and told me to report back the following morning when he would be able to give me some further treatment.

I was now allocated to one of the many marquees, and was able to take stock of what had once been a very orderly and well-run British Military Hospital. This area had been the scene of some of the most bitter fighting. The Germans had shot up every marquee with their fighter planes; the evidence of this was plain to see by the ripped and ragged tentage. Many patients had been killed and many more wounded. The Germans had then dropped their parachutists who had quickly taken over the hospital, again killing and wounding more of the patients and forcing them as hostages and as a shield in front of them when other British troops had tried to retake the area. The whole place was a complete shambles. The marquee I was allotted to held about ten badly wounded men. They were still clothed or partly clothed, lying on bare mattresses on the beds, and some covered over with a blanket. There were no vacant beds so I was given a blood-stained stretcher to sleep on, and settled down at one end of the marquee. I felt pretty miserable and lonely being away from Jock and the others in the compound. There was no one here I knew; I found it difficult to try to speak but if there had been anyone there I had known, I could at least have tried. The men on the beds in front of me were too ill to talk. My lip gave me no pain, it felt much better now it had been properly cleaned up and the loose teeth taken out, but how was I going to eat?

I was ravenously hungry and all I could manage to do was drink water from my bottle. Two things I decided must be done: one, I must find some way to eat; a rubber tube was what I needed so that I could suck the food into my mouth; and two, I had to get out of this marquee which, with all due respect to its inmates, was more like a morgue and I wasn't going to stay watching these very unfortunate men. I had to get with those who could move about like I could. So I went in search of an orderly. The first one I met was the German again. The rubber tube took a bit of explaining so I wrote it down and the German cottoned on, and it wasn't long before he produced a piece of rubber garden hose. After giving it a good clean I soaked some bread and water in my mess tin, mixing it up into & soggy mess and tried out my new invention. It worked splendidly, but it also gave me wind, and later diarrhoea. But I didn't care, I was pleased to know I could at least eat after a fashion, providing my food was a soggy mess. I stayed in the marquee that first night, and next morning found that three men had died. Later that morning two other men who were due for major surgery were flown with others to Athens in Greece. That was half the tent gone, so I was now able to have a bed and two more 'walking wounded' arrived. To my delight one of them was Mac, the pal and fellow sapper of mine who had been injured in the knees. The other man was a gunner who had been injured in one arm.

On my next meeting with the German doctor, he patiently cleaned my wound, then he inserted a metal strip on the inside of my lip, which had a thin piece of cord fastened to it that led out of the corner of my mouth and was tied to the dressing, so that I wouldn't accidently swallow it. This was all very well, but it made it more awkward to get the rubber tube into my mouth. The doctor would not put in any stitches but used some very small clips to hold the bits of flesh together. In the days that followed, the treatment I was getting began to show dividends. If I thought I was badly off, there were those around me who were much worse off. I could at least move about and use my arms, making myself useful in the marquee helping the other wounded. I was also getting on well with my bit of rubber tube. I often wondered how Jock and the others were getting on in the compound; we had no means of communicating with each other at present. One day, the German medical orderly came to me and said my 'German friend' had come to see me. This could only be the soldier on the motorcycle. He greeted me like a long-lost friend. Using the orderly as an interpreter, he wanted to know all about me and how I was getting on. Most of the conversation was, however, between the two Germans. Of course, he was naturally full of German propaganda. He said they had now overrun most of Europe and were steaming ahead into Russia, also pushing our forces back in the desert campaign. London was 'kaput' and so was Malta. All in all, the war should be over in a few months and the Master Race of the Third Reich would make the world a much better place to live in when they had sorted out all the capitalists. There is no doubt, however, that he was well meaning towards me, and when he was ready for leaving, he again gave me bread, boiled sweets and cigarettes. He would come every three or four days to see me, always bringing me something. His name was Rudi something or other, which I have long since forgotten, but he was a good soul and a Godsend to me, German or no German.

After about three weeks, Rudi told me that the prisoners in the compounds had started to be moved off to Germany. This disturbed me, as I did not want to find myself completely parted from those I knew in the compound. I was getting on well, or so I thought, and decided to ask if I could be discharged and get back to my pals. I also tried to get a message through to Jock by the way of the men being discharged, but, having had no reply, didn't know if my message had got through or if Jock had been moved or not. However, by the end of June I was finally discharged. Rudi came to collect me on his motorcycle and dropped me off at the compound, giving me the usual bread and things. We shook hands and said cheerio to each other; I went into the compound and he went roaring off up the road with a great flourish. That was the last I ever saw of him. I reported to the marquee which acted as 'Office Stores' and held about a dozen British warrant officers and senior NCOs. They were well and truly established, controlling the comings and goings of the compound. My name was checked and put on the ration strength, but I didn't get any bread from them that day. They said I should have received rations from the hospital before I left and should have been carrying my 'unexpired portion' with me. Luckily, and thanks to Rudi, I had enough food to last a few days so I wasn't unduly worried. On the other hand, they were quite prepared to 'flog' me some bread in exchange for some of the cigarettes I had. I told them to 'get stuffed', I would see them in hell first; it was obvious they were 'fiddling'. One of them threatened to hand me over to the German Straf compound and I wouldn't have put it past him either. I went off to find Jock and the rest.

By this time, after one month of captivity, the compound had become a real shanty town. Shelters of every description had been created out of old tentage, blankets, timber and tin sheets. Men were living closer to Mother Nature than ever, and no doubt getting more like animals every day.

I found Jock sitting in a queue; there were queues for everything, taking so long to get anything that one had to sit down on the ground and move along accordingly. He was queuing for water to fill up his bottle, so he told me to give him my bottle as well, which he would fill, whilst I went to join another queue forming up for drawing the day's ration of very watery lentil soup.

The foraging parties which the Germans had allowed during the first few days had been stopped after many of the men had failed to return to the compounds. Many had escaped into the mountains to join the Cretans and many had been recaptured and shot dead in the process.

There was now stricter security on the compounds. The Germans would allow small working parties out who received payment by way of being given extra food, but not everybody could go on these. The only thing we had plenty of was sun and seawater.

Soon the day came when we were officially told we were going to move to Germany. We had to be ready the next morning to march to Suda where we were to board ship and sail for Salonika in the north of Greece. We were issued with a double ration of bread that day to save issuing the next day because we would have to be up bright and early and on the march.

There were many rumours and much speculation and wishful thinking that when we got to sea our submarines would suddenly appear, capture our ship and we would be free. Such was our simple faith in our beloved country. Through all the trials and tribulations of nearly four years of captivity we never gave up hope that one day our own side would liberate us.

Rudi had even tried to tell me what a wonderful place Germany was, that we would be well treated, well housed, well fed, providing we worked for the *Vaterland*.

Jock and I took stock of what few possessions we had. I had managed to get another pair of K.D. shorts and a shirt whilst at the hospital, these having once belonged to someone who had since died. I also had appropriated a 1lb bar of army carbolic soap, giving Jock one half. It was rough on the skin but better than nothing, and was to last us for months. We made sure of filling our water bottles that night.

The next morning, we packed up and cleared out of the compound. There was no parading, we were just told to get moving along the road via Canea to Suda, the German guards moving along with us at intervals. We had no regrets at leaving. By the time we had marched the first few miles to Canea, the sun was well up in the sky, the heat was becoming unbearable and the ever arid dust rising from the road, sticking to our sweating bodies and stuffing up our noses so that we could hardly breathe.

We had a roadside rest when we had passed through Canea, for about fifteen minutes, then we set off again for Suda. Once again, the march developed into a mere trudge as the day got hotter; it was heads down and keep moving forward. I was very thankful my feet were in good condition again and I wasn't feeling any signs of blisters forming.

Once again, the Cretans came out into the streets to see us as we passed through Canea and again many of them handed food and water to us. They were friendly to us right to the bitter end and I shall always remember those poor, hard-working people with my greatest affection and gratitude.

Suda Bay was very much the same as we had last seen it, except that the jetty had been made usable and some of the wrecks had been moved out of the way. HMS *York* still stood proudly upright in the mud; it looked magnificent from a distance, and someone made a crack that it was going to take us home.

The ship we were to sail in was tied up alongside the jetty. It was a small dirty looking coastal tramp cargo vessel; I never did know its name. There was a long wait whilst men were being herded aboard so Jock and I took the opportunity to fill our water bottles again.

Eventually it came our turn to embark and slowly we merged into a single file, climbed up and over the side of the ship and climbed down an iron rung ladder into the holds, a German at the top of the hold counting each man down.

Jock and I, with some others, found ourselves being pushed down into the bottom hold in the stern of the ship. We passed two other holds on the way down cramped full of men. Naturally, the first ones had taken the top holds.

It was like descending into hell itself, coupled with the Black Hole of Calcutta. The hold was very dirty, stinking putrid, and quite dark except directly underneath the hatchway. The decks were sloping and being well below the water line, very cold. There was still one hold below us, this having a slatted hatch cover over it which was barred and padlocked. Someone said it was the bilge, this being where the awful smell was coming from.

Again rumours were going the rounds, it would take us two or three days to sail to Salonika; rations were to be issued when we sailed; the navy, bless them, were sure to intercept us, and what would happen if one of our submarines put a torpedo into us?

As to the last rumour, if one of our submarines torpedoed us, we, in the bottom holds, wouldn't stand much of a chance to get up two flights of ladders with all those men above us. It was a terrifying thought that it could happen.

After a while, our eyes began to get accustomed to the gloom and looking around the hold we realised there were not as many men as we had first thought; it had seemed overcrowded because everyone had tried to get a position near the shaft of light coming down the hold.

So men began to move back and spreadeagle out, putting on greatcoats and wrapping up in blankets, some talking and some going to sleep.

The Germans above were still shouting orders out to everyone; no one was allowed on deck and the upper hatch covers, which were slatted, were slid over the top of the holds.

This, I thought, lying back with my head on my pack, was where I came in. It was now a matter of waiting for the engines to start up to sail out of Suda Bay, having been on the island for about nine months. Even now I can see a vivid mind's eye picture of my first sight of Crete from the deck of HMS *Perth*. It was about the fourth or fifth of November 1940; we had sailed from Port Said in Egypt bound for an unknown destination.

The advance troops were aboard HMS *Perth* and HMS *Ajax*. We hadn't been allowed on deck until the morning we approached Suda Bay. What a beautiful sight it was after having spent months in the Western Desert.

Such beautiful mountain grandeur with Mount Ida, snow-capped, dominating the whole scene; the wooded, rugged and rocky cliffs down to the steep foothills which were terraced and under cultivation; and down to the more gentle slopes and miles of olive groves, tangerine groves, orange trees and grape vines. The colour stood out vividly, every colour imaginable.

Suda Bay was 'bottle-necked' with a small island near its entrance, giving way to a large anchorage; the water on that day was as calm as a millpond.

We had tied up on each side of the jetty, where we now sat in this stinking prisoner ship, and as we began to disembark, the Italian heavy bombers had flown over and bombed us.

I and one or two more had been halfway down the gangway, not knowing which way was best to go, there being no cover on the jetty and all hell had been let loose on the decks of the cruisers by anti-aircraft guns blazing away.

The air raid had continued for quite a while, we having an uncomfortable grandstand view. Suda village was hit and smoking, bombs exploded on both sides of the jetty, but the cruisers were not hit and I don't think any of the disembarking troops were hurt.

It had been a great reception with no bands playing, but the Cretans came and shook us by the hand and gave us a great welcome. Now we were waiting for our departure with still no bands playing, going into a future we knew not where, or how it was all going to end.

Chapter 3

Salonika

The ship's engines started up during the late afternoon, causing a steady throbbing vibration from stem to stern. It would not be long now before we were on the move, but we seemed to wait hours and hours. Eventually, we felt the throbbing increase, the ship's bell rang and a shudder ran through the ship as it moved away from the quayside. The ship developed a steady rhythmical throb; we were on our way.

Our eyes had by this time become accustomed to the gloom of our stinking hold way below the waterline. There were fewer men in our hold than we had first thought, but the upper holds were jammed solid. We called out to those above to tell the German 'so-and-so's' to open the hatch top to let in some light and some fresh air. The stench from the hold below us was now becoming nauseating; it wouldn't cost the swines anything to give us a bit of fresh air.

Nevertheless, they would not open the hatch covers, so we hurled up all the abuse we could lay our tongues to, which brought no response until we laid tongue to their beloved Führer, Hitler, and a few of his cronies, including the club-footed cripple, Goebbels. Then a small hatch above the iron-runged ladder opened and in climbed a screaming German, but he did not come very far down. Wrapping his arm around the ladder he fumbled to withdraw his pistol from its holster, nearly falling off the ladder in the process, amidst loud cheers from us.

He started waving his pistol around indiscriminately, then pointing it down into the bottom hold where we were, began firing until he had emptied it. We soon ducked out of his line of fire, the shots thudding into and ricocheting off the top of our hatch cover. Luckily no one was hit.

The German then let out a bellow; someone in the upper hold had taken off a boot and thrown it at him, hitting him fair and square in the middle of his back. He quickly pocketed his pistol and scrambled back up the ladder to safety, howling with rage.

No more Germans appeared, the small hatch cover was closed with a bang, the large hatch stayed closed, and we had to settle down as best we could amongst the filth and stench of the ship.

Another scourge which had invaded us was body lice; we were getting covered with the horrible little things. They bit deep into our pores to suck their fill of blood, then they hid in the seams of our clothing to lay their eggs. They made us itch something awful, but it was fatal to scratch as dirty fingernails would soon cause a mass of pus-running sores, for which we could not get any medical treatment. It had become a daily routine searching through our clothing to pick them out and kill them by squashing them between our thumbnails until our fingers were covered in blood. Another way of killing them was to light a thin piece of rope and burn them out, being careful in the process not to burn any holes in our clothing.

Everyone spent a very miserable first night huddled together to try to keep warm. Next morning when it was light the large hatch cover on top was withdrawn, letting in a shaft of brilliant light and much-wanted fresh air.

We, in the bottom holds, were ordered up on deck first, thinking that now we were for it. But as we climbed up the long iron-runged ladder and over the top on to the deck, nothing happened. We were just told to form an orderly queue around the deck of the ship to attend the toilets.

The toilets were very crude wooden structures erected over the sides of the deck; it was a tricky feat to climb on to them, but they served their useful purpose.

The brilliant sunlight hurt our eyes, taking some time to get used to it.

The ship was well guarded with machine guns and crews stationed at strategic points. We were passing through a series of small islands which looked ever so near us, but there was little chance of escape.

Now for the first time I noticed someone standing on the bridge of the ship in a different uniform. Black from top to toe, a young-looking 6-footer in an immaculate fitting uniform. His cap badge and collar dogs were shining silver-coloured skull and crossbones; the chin strap of his silver-braided black peaked cap was a double braided thick silver cord, and above his cap badge was the German winged eagle with the swastika below it.

His rank was shown by the type of braid on the shoulder epaulettes of his well-fitting black tunic, and he wore a black swastika on a round white background high on his left arm. His riding breeches and highly polished riding boots and waist belt were also black. On his belt he sported a Luger pistol on one side and a thick black dog whip on the other. He displayed a complete air of Aryan arrogance. We didn't know it then, but he was a member of the dreaded SS (Schutz-Staffel) *Totenkopfverbände*, or Death's Heads regiments, in charge of concentration camps.

The SS force was divided into three categories: the selected Germans first served a compulsory period in the Reichsarbeitsdienst (the Labour Corps) before entering the SS. Then they were posted to the Allgemeine SS (General SS) in which service was not permanent; the SS-Verfügungstruppen or regiments quartered in barracks and the SS-Totenkopfverbände.

We were allowed about half an hour on deck, then we were chased down into the holds again and the next lot took their turn on deck. I had spent every minute of that precious time deep breathing the fresh morning air. There was no water to be had for drinking or washing and no rations issued, but we had managed to persuade the Germans to fix an awning up over the hold to catch the air and direct it down the shaft of the hold, which made it far more tolerable for us down below.

While the morning's activities went on, some of us were lying near the hatch cover of our hold when someone whispered to look down through the slats into the hold below. I looked through and could see three motorcycles and sidecars. Lo and behold in the sidecars were stacked British army ration boxes. This must have been someone's private loot, being taken to Salonika. The question was, 'How were we going to get at it?' The hatch cover was barred and padlocked, there was no chance of getting through that way.

Then someone said 'Let's move the railway sleepers in the corner of the hold, there might be a trap door under them.' We worked quickly, and there it was, a trap door, unlocked. It took a lot of work getting it open and now we had to find a way down below as there was no ladder, but a drop of about 15 or more feet.

Everyone was told to carry on as normal as possible, while some of us tried to make a rope out of blankets. It is the devil's own job to tie army blankets together.

At last, in sheer desperation the 'rope' was made; we fastened one end to a railway sleeper and lowered a man down below, quickly followed by another. Soon up came the food: bully beef and biscuits, Maconochie's stew, steak and kidney pudding and fruit. Distribution was made, the tins being stuffed into haversacks and packs, and we all had a damned good feed.

In fact, most of us ate far too much, but we couldn't help it as we were ravenously hungry.

There was no chance of the Germans coming down and finding out, we kept it quiet to our own particular hold. All the empty tins and broken boxes were taken down below to get rid of them.

We then lay back and slept, it being nice to feel one had a full stomach again. Later, men were wanting to go to the toilet, as one could not eat without wanting to relieve oneself. We decided we mustn't give the game away by going up on deck so each man had to climb down into the hold below to do the best he could in the bilge water, making it more foul and stinking than ever.

Drinking water was always a most precious commodity, there being none whatsoever to be had on this ship to replenish one's stock. It had to be made to last as long as possible and it was just too bad for those who had none, they had to stay thirsty. Thus, we got through yet another day and night.

Early next morning, our third day at sea, we were called up on deck for our half-hour ration of fresh air. Again, we asked about being given food and water, but the Germans just laughed at us telling us that only those who worked were entitled to food and non-workers did not need any food,

In the late afternoon of the third day, we docked at Salonika. The ship had been sheer hell and we were not sorry to be getting off it. We climbed up on to the deck, down a gangplank to form up on the quayside, hoping we would soon march away before the Germans had time to find out we had stolen their ill-gotten gains. Someone was going to be unhappy over it. We soon split up and mixed amongst the other prisoners so no one could tell which hold one had come from.

German guards were there to meet us carrying out their customary shouting of orders, pushing and shoving us into line till eventually we marched off.

We were by now a dirty, unkempt, unshaven, bedraggled lot of ruffians, looking like anything but proud British soldiers. We also soon found out that the German guards were a different breed to those we had previously met.

The streets were full with Greeks watching us marching through on our way to the prison camp, and when any of them tried to get close to us to give us anything, the guards set about them with rifles and bayonets, also dragging some of the menfolk into our ranks to make them march with us. There were hundreds of German guards marching alongside our ranks on each side of the road at every 3 or 4 yards. They were vicious and bullying, being urged on by their officers and senior NCOs, making sure none of us got a chance to escape by breaking through the ranks into the crowded pavements.

The camp we marched to was a large Greek barracks, several miles outside Salonika, the Germans forcing us to keep up a fast pace to get there quickly.

The barracks were built on sloping ground, with large single-storey barrack blocks built of stone down each side of a massive open square or parade ground. Around the whole of the camp was a formidable-looking, double barbed wire fence about 10 feet high, with a mass of entangled barbed wire in between. At each change of direction of the fence was a high machine-gun tower fully manned, and at the bottom side of the parade ground and in the centre of the fence was another high machine-gun tower which commandeered the whole of the barracks. We could see that every tower was equipped with searchlights, telephones and binoculars.

Running round the inside perimeter of the fence was another single-stranded thick plain wire at approximately 18 inches from the ground and 6 or 8 feet from the fence. We were soon to find out what this wire was for.

Guards also patrolled along a 'bunny-run' on the outside of the fence. As we reached the barracks, we were counted through in batches of 200. Then a number of guards marched us away to one of the barrack blocks where we had to crowd in and stay in until the other barrack blocks had been similarly filled.

The barrack blocks were split in half, having the entrance, toilet and ablution facilities in the centre. They were absolutely bare of all furniture.

We sorted ourselves out, 100 to each room, making four rows of twenty-five to each room. There was no doubt about being overcrowded as we tried to squat down on the dirty wooden floor to wait to see what was going to happen next.

We were dirty from top to toe; brown smelly dirt from the hold of the stinking ship we had just left. Our clothing was dirty, our hair dirty and terribly overgrown; we had not shaved for weeks and to cap it all, we were very lousy. We squatted down like a lot of caged monkeys, picking off lice.

The Germans next move was to organise someone to be in charge of each block; a Feldwebel or Unteroffizier who in turn selected one of our numbers to be in charge, to produce a nominal roll. Usually, it was our WOs or senior NCOs. The barrack-block seniors were then taken off to the camp commandant where a German interpreter read out camp standing orders, and orders for daily routine.

On their return to the blocks, the information was passed on to us. We were told we could move out and about the barrack blocks but were not allowed to pass over the parade ground to the other side, nor should we trespass over the low wire fence running on the inside of the perimeter fence. Some food would be issued that day.

The toilets and ablutions were in a disgusting state. The drinking water was a mere trickle, while the toilets were overloaded, refusing to function. The water taps were obviously all turned on at once; the toilets could not get water, there not being enough pressure in the main water supply, or else, as we later thought, the Germans had deliberately turned the pressure down. On the other hand, the whole camp was terribly overcrowded.

Luckily, between two of the blocks there was a well with a hand pump which produced water non-stop all day. This water wasn't supposed to be for drinking unless it was chemically treated or boiled, but as we could not produce either of these facilities the water was drunk nevertheless, causing a lot of 'gippy tummies' and dysentery.

Some men must not have been told or heard correctly or bothered about the order forbidding anyone to cross the parade ground, but the first time someone tried, the machine guns opened up to show that the Germans meant business. The shots went dangerously close to the trespassers, making them scurry back to the safety of the barrack blocks.

The daily routine as far as I remember was something like the following:

0600 hours reveille;

0700 hours, line up, draw a small cup of ersatz coffee (no milk, no sugar);

0800 hours, parade outside the barrack blocks and march on to the main parade ground for check parade (which lasted for hours);

1300 hours, a very thin lentil-cum-bean watery soup was dished up;

1700 hours, bread and dry rations issue;

1930 hours, another check parade outside the barrack blocks;

For the first week we had to stay in the barrack blocks immediately after the evening parade until reveille the next morning. To set foot outside or even show a face out of a window meant being shot at by the trigger-happy sentries.

Check parades were always a complete farce, the Germans being hopeless at counting. We would parade in rows of five, one German counting along the front rank and one counting along the rear rank. They only had to count forty rows of fives to give them 200, but it would take them hours to agree. Of course, while this was going on the morning was getting hotter and hotter; we grew more discontented with standing so long, so we would sit down, with the Germans ranting and raving up and down the ranks.

Ersatz coffee was just that, substitute for the real thing, it was a horrible bitter-tasting dirty brown-coloured liquid, but we drank it and queued up for the coffee dregs to eat.

The soup, once per day, was very thin, made from lentils and large white beans. One was considered very fortunate to get five beans in one's ration. Most men having dysentery or diarrhoea meant the soup ran almost straight through one's body, lentils and all.

For our dry rations issue once per day we received 300g of black rye bread (less than three-quarters of a pound of bread per day), a very small pat of ersatz margarine, a spoonful of sugar or jam, and sometimes a small piece of inedible cheese or a small piece of sausage meat. In all, there was not enough to feed a cat.

Those of us who had robbed the ship were lucky to have extra food for a few days, but it did not last long. There is no doubt the Germans worked to a pre-determined plan concerning prisoners: one of starvation, degeneracy and humiliation, to reduce us to the lowest level of human endurance before they took us into Germany. They would not show us off to their populace as fit, fine-looking British soldiers but as horrible specimens of human beings.

Yes! it was good for German propaganda, but there was one important thing they had forgotten; they bred into us a deep smouldering hatred for anything German. This, in turn, kept a spark of life in each and every one of us which they could never put out. We knew that one day they would be made to pay in full.

So each day at Salonika we became more hungry, our stomachs shrank, and we lost a lot of weight, we were living on our previous fitness. The days were hot and the nights were warm, the whole place infested with malaria-carrying mosquitos and millions of flies, which bred in profusion amongst the dirty excreta-covered toilets. Trying to sleep at night was absolute torture; apart from being hungry and being covered with lice, there were masses of fleas to add to the constant itching.

We developed huge sores on each hip bone which constantly ran with vile pus, for which there was no medical attention.

There was not enough floor space to enable one to lay on one's back, there being far too many men in the one room. God help the man who got up during the night to go to the toilets, he would have to fight his way back to his own bit of floor space.

During the day our main occupation was delousing and debugging in general, and sitting on the ground in queues for food or water.

One day I came across a man who was cutting hair, so Jock and I had ours cut (all off) for the price of one cigarette each. The next job was to try and have a shave so we sharpened an old razor blade on a glass window and with a bit of carbolic soap and precious little water we hacked away at our stubbly growth of beards, managing quite well notwithstanding a few cuts and scratches. It was impossible to get enough water to wash oneself.

The brutality of the Germans at Salonika had to be seen to be believed. Several men were beaten up and dragged off to the Straf Compound at each daily check parade on the main parade ground, this being part of their processing machine to have a psychological effect upon us.

One man who hung a towel over the low wire fence was instantly shot dead by one of the guards patrolling on the outside of the wire; the man had not even been given any sort of warning.

Another man stepped over the low wire to pick up something which had been thrown over by one of three passing Greeks; he was instantly shot dead, as also were the three Greeks; and another man who went to give assistance was also shot dead. Five lives in a matter of minutes.

On another occasion, two German guards were searching through some of the blocks on our side of the camp when suddenly they gave chase to one of our men. He ran through several blocks to try and evade the guards and on reaching our block he disappeared into the toilet room, banging the door shut behind him. The two Germans realised he must have gone into the toilet room and not being able to open the door, one of them dashed outside and lobbed a hand grenade through the toilet window. There was a terrific bang, then screaming and shouting in the toilet room, the Germans running off, away to the main gate, while some of our men knocked the door down to help the unfortunate men inside. That little episode cost us five men killed and three men badly wounded. For what? We never found out.

The sound of small-arms fire was heard so often during the day or night that we became used to it. The machine gun on the tower which overlooked the whole parade ground was tested every night when a new crew took over. One night the gun was fired several times, although most of us did not remember there being anything out of the ordinary about it. But next morning, as we assembled and marched on to the parade ground, we saw three dead men lying not far from each other and two more against the barbed wire fence. Nearby was a manhole with its metal top off. These men, who were Cypriots, had been the last of a party of men who had found an escape route down the manhole, about 15 feet deep, into a main sewer which ran out under the camp. The men had been spotted in the searchlights and mown down. Whether the others escaped to ultimate freedom we never knew; we could only hope they had.

The five dead bodies were left on the parade ground the whole day in the blazing heat and not even covered over. Our representations had no effect on the Germans whatsoever and the men were not moved until dusk. This was the sort of daily conduct by well-armed German troops against men who could not defend themselves.

One day I managed to get on a working party while Jock stayed behind to look after both of our kits. I took my empty haversack with me just in case I managed to pick up some food.

Outside the camp, the working party was split up into smaller parties. I was in a party of six men who were handed over to a well-armed guard and taken away to some nearby stables, where we had to clean them out, groom the horses and attend to their water and feed.

We were most interested in the horses' feed: amongst it were buckets full of hard crusts of black bread collected from the German barracks, far too good for the horses to eat, while there were starving men about. So we managed to fill our haversacks and pockets while the guard, I am sure, turned a blind eye. When we marched back into camp, we were given an extra ration of bread as we passed through the gate; our reward for working.

Jock and I had a good scoff that night, the bread was a bit hard and sour but it went down very well. Working parties were few and far between, not that we wanted to work for the Germans, it was a case of being able to get outside the camp for a change of scenery and to try and obtain food, and maybe a chance of escape.

Our days were long and monotonous, with a lot of men cramped together in the inadequate space of the barrack blocks or outside the blocks sitting in the shade. Some men were already feeling the rigours of captivity, lying in the barrack blocks for days on end, not speaking to anyone, losing strength and faith and not even bothering to draw their meagre daily rations. Others would draw their ration and taking it to them, force them to eat.

The whole situation was so sordid and hopeless that it looked like never ending as July gave way to August.

We had, however, managed to get two very important concessions from the Germans. One was being able to construct and erect a deep trench latrine at the end of each barrack block near the edge of the parade ground, owing to all other sewage facilities having failed, but no one chanced to use them at night for fear of being shot at. And two, with the weather being so stifling hot we were granted permission to sleep outside on the pavements around the barrack blocks, giving us much more room to spread out.

This was where the best and the worst came out in each of us, our true colours coming to the forefront. What had we been told just prior to our capture? 'Every man for himself.' Some of our WOs and senior NCOs shone with distinction in their efforts to keep men united together in some form of soldierly order, and also in their dealings with the Germans in charge of the barrack blocks. Other WOs and senior NCOs failed miserably to lead or show any form of soldiery to the junior rank and file, and used their rank purely for personal gain.

The discipline we had once known was slipping. Men now needed every ounce of self-discipline which could be mustered.

New natural leaders came to the fore. It did not matter whether they had any rank or not. These were men who could be trusted both in mind and in deed. When men are starving they will do anything to obtain food, even to the point of fighting and stealing from each other. There is much mistrust and bitter feeling.

They also become most embittered to the cause they have always been led to believe was worth fighting for. It fosters intense hatred of their captors.

But there is that great minority of men who in times of great stress come to the forefront as natural, dependable leaders, nothing seems to get them down, they look upon their tormentors with pity and give moral comfort to their fellow men. Such a man was Les 'Lofty' Rowsell, a mere lance corporal bandsman in the Argyll and Sutherland Highlanders.

He was a Yorkshireman by birth, having gone to live in Canada when quite a small boy and, returning to England just before the war started, had joined the army.

He was 6 foot-odd, big and well made, striking angular features sporting a 'sergeant major-like' moustache which could be 'twiddled' at the ends. His voice was quiet, well spoken with a soft Canadian drawl, creating a calm confidence in people; he had a magnetic personality and he could settle an argument with apparent ease.

There was one thing he always carried, a book, the Holy Bible, which never left him. It was leather bound with a zip fastener. I can picture him now striding along with his Bible held to his chest like the local vicar on a Sunday morning. Although he had done some evangelistic work in Canada, he never tried to ram the Gospel down anyone's throat.

His pal, a wee Jock who also sported a moustache, was a lance corporal regimental medical orderly in the Argylls. They were probably drawn together by the fact that they had seen much action together, but they were as different as chalk and cheese.

I met Lofty purely by coincidence. There was a group of us lying around talking one day and I must have mentioned my home town. Lofty, having overheard, came to me saying his mother lived in the same town, telling me the name of the district and road, which I knew well. This started off a great friendship between us having something in common to talk about. We even met at his mother's house after the war ended.

As the weeks went slowly by, August giving way to September, we became more and more hungry and despondent. Lofty would often read passages out of the Bible to those who wanted to listen, bringing much comfort. I wasn't a very religious man, nor am I one today, but I must admit that in those days of great stress the Bible was a great comfort. I used to try hard to read my small copy of the New Testament, sent to me in Egypt by well-wishers at home. I still have it today. Lofty had great faith in God; I must admit shamefully that I could not reconcile myself with God because of the fact we were in such an awful plight and surely if there was a God, he could not possibly let this happen to us.

Sometimes I prayed so hard and sincerely to live, other times praying that I might die and be spared the awful agony of hunger and want. It was a shocking dilemma to be in, but it is true, I make no bones about it. I certainly was not alone in my views.

At this time there were very strong rumours going around that we were due to move anytime now. There was much speculation whether it was going to be to Austria, Poland, or Germany itself.

In three months of captivity, we had only been able to fill in one postcard to let our families in the United Kingdom know of our capture. It was a small buff-coloured card on which were printed the basic facts: number, rank and name; address of next of kin; I am well, I am not wounded, or vice-versa; I am a POW, and so on.

There were rumours relating to the Geneva Conventions: treatment of prisoners of war; Red Cross parcels; what we were entitled to; letter writing; non-working camps for NCOs; and lots of other things which the Germans obviously did not give a damn about. As far as the Germans were concerned, we were not entitled to anything.

Then came the day when we were told we were to prepare to move the next day. There was not much to prepare. Jock and I attended to our few belongings.

After the journey in the hold of that stinking ship we wondered if our next move could be any worse. We were determined to try and be prepared for any eventuality. We were now in the state of the 'the survival of the fittest'.

Our forthcoming journey was going to be a long one by train, where to, we had not yet been told. We did not care where we went to as long as we got out of Salonika; there simply could not be a worse place than this. But we were kidding ourselves.

Chapter 4

To Germany

It must have been the end of August or the beginning of September when one early morning we assembled for check parade on the huge parade ground at Salonika prior to moving to 'somewhere in the Fatherland'.

Jock Morrison and I, Lofty and wee Jock, stood together on parade and decided to try to stick together en route. It seemed pretty certain we were destined for Germany.

There was a lot of counting and recounting until eventually the first block of 200 men moved off towards the main gate of the barracks. The Germans were bustling about their business shouting orders, counter ordering, cursing and causing a general state of chaos as they moved their blocks of 200 men slowly forward a little way towards the main gate. Each time we moved forward and stopped we would sit down on the ground; then on a bit further, sitting down again. Finally, as we neared the main gate, we saw what was causing the holdup. The Germans were issuing rations for the journey.

I remember them down to the last ounce: to each man was given one-and-a-half loaves of bread about 1.5kg; it was rye bread, hard and stale. Also, five small tins of meat paste spread, one-and-a-half Italian hard tack biscuits, these were white inside and about 4½ inches square and ½ inch thick. Lastly, we were given a packet of boiled sweets. We were told the journey would take about five days by train and these were our rations for five days.

We then marched off through Salonika to a railway marshalling yard where we had visions of a train with decent seats waiting for us. We were not without our usual brand of rumours and wishful thinking.

At the marshalling yard, we found our 'Pullman' was a train made up of box wagons, each wagon having a single-seater sentry box at each end for a guard to sit in, the rest of the train being made up of coaches to accommodate the accompanying German troops.

On the side of each wagon was a small metal plate which our enthusiasts on German, interpreted as reading 'twenty horses or forty-two persons' or something like that. The Germans forced at least fifty men into each wagon, slid the doors shut, dropping over the door catch to lock us in. There were two small barred windows high up on each side of the wagon, and only a person of Lofty's size could see out, so he had to keep up a running commentary of what was going on outside.

We could not all sit down at the same time, it was bad enough some sitting, some standing, we were terribly cramped. My God, this was terrible, the wagon got absolutely unbearably hot and stinking by midday.

Some men were shouting to the Germans to open up, while others were calling them by the foulest language they could put tongue to. I was in the latter group, but it made no difference. Some were desperately wanting to go to the lavatory and were trying to find something to use as containers.

It was mid-afternoon when the guards opened up the wagons allowing us to get down. We could not move quickly enough to get our pants down to squat down on the side of the nearby line, whilst the Germans looked on, treating the whole sordid scene as a huge joke.

Yes! They were going to have a lot to pay for one day.

We were soon hustled back into the wagons, the doors slamming shut and the catches dropped into position.

We decided this time to sort ourselves out into some sort of order to enable us to lie down.

This was where Lofty came to the forefront by sheer size and weight of personality. He got us all to lie down like a lot of sardines in a tin until we were all packed in. Then we rehearsed half sitting, half standing, and it worked; we could do it.

Lofty took out his Bible and read a passage to us; there was dead silence in the wagon. There was only one other thing: he had almost forgotten to arrange himself a space to lie down because he had been standing, directing operations, whilst everyone else had been lying down.

The clanking of buffers and the buffeting of the wagons brought us quickly back to reality. The train was waking to life and we were slowly getting under way. It was now evening time after a very trying day, our first of many trying days to come which we were to endure.

The train gathered momentum, we were off, the wheels making a clackety-clack as they went over each rail joint. There was generally silence, I think all our minds must have been keeping time to the noise of the wheels making their rhythmic music on the rail joints. It was hypnotising because we had not heard this noise for years. I tried putting all sorts of words and sayings to it. It became a game, there was nothing else to do anyway.

We could tell by the setting sun that we were travelling in the general direction of north. Our train chugged slowly on its way, on through the night, never picking up much speed. We all lay down on the dirty, hard, uncomfortable floor of the wagon trying to sleep, and although by now we were used to a hard bed, this was made worse by the vibration and rocking from side to side. We were packed in like sardines so we did not move very much – we couldn't have moved if we'd wanted to. Uncomfortable wasn't the word for it, it soon became sheer hell and that first night seemed never ending.

Eventually, daybreak came, with the train still moving slowly. Somewhere along the line during the night we must have stopped to hitch on another locomotive, because now we had two slowly pulling us through very mountainous country. Those nearest took it in turn to try and peer out of the high, gridded windows of the wagon to give a commentary on what they could see. Apparently, the scenery was splendid, we were travelling through Yugoslavia.

We passed through several small stations whose names were difficult to pronounce, let alone remember. We shouted to anyone we saw, but no one took any notice of us. Many notes explaining who we were, were written and thrown out on to the stations as we passed. What good it was going to do us we did not know, but at least it helped our peace of mind.

During that day, the train stopped once for water and refuelling and to let the Germans carry out their ablutions. We shouted like mad to be let out, but our calls fell on deaf ears, the Germans taking not the slightest bit of notice of us.

Soon the train was rumbling on its way again.

When one man started to dig into his rations for something to eat, he set everyone else going, and being so hungry we did not know when to stop eating. Some men ate everything up in the first two days.

We four decided to try and ration ourselves out for five days, although what we had could be eaten in one day. I still had the tea in my sweaty sock, and although I could not possibly eat it, I did try to smoke it using the very fine soft paper out of my New Testament to roll it into a cigarette. It was awful, it made me so terribly dizzy that I soon gave it up, vowing never to try it again.

After being locked up in the wagons for many hours, there was again the old problem of how to cope with the call of nature. One man in one corner of the wagon had found a small hole in the wooden floor about a couple of feet from the corner. It looked like someone who had been in the wagon before us had tried to cut the hole, probably for the same problem as we were trying to deal with.

One small, not at all sharp, pocket knife was soon produced and further whittling commenced. It was a slow, laborious undertaking, the floor being about 2 inches thick of hard seasoned timber, but time was on our side and there was no shortage of labour. It could have started off by being a knot which had been knocked through somehow, but someone had definitely had a go at it with a knife, later giving it up as a bad job.

We took turns to have a go, it was something to do, we must enlarge it, it was going to be our toilet. Soon the blade of the knife broke, bringing a cry of disappointment from those close at hand. The hole was nowhere near large enough. The smaller blade was next brought into use, making the already arduous work much slower, but there was no shortage of volunteers, with each telling the one using the knife to be more than careful.

There was a lot of sweating and swearing, but this would be countered by Lofty giving one of his daily recitals from the Bible.

When the hole became a bit larger, we were able to attack it with sharpened table knives, until at last the hole was about 4 inches in diameter. It was a draughty hole but it served its purpose well. We made a rule that he who used it cleaned up around it afterwards and stayed on the hole until someone else wanted to use it. The system worked very well indeed.

Our greatest problem now was how to pass the time. We could not sleep all the time although most of our time was spent trying. There was one pack of very well-worn playing cards for ever in use, and there were a few books. I had got hold of a copy of *The Seven Pillars of Wisdom* by Lawrence of Arabia. It was a large heavy book but I read it from cover to cover and then passed it on to someone else.

The chief topics for conversation were food, Crete, the prospects or surmise of our future and what we were going to do when the war ended. It usually ended up with a heated argument about Crete and back to food, of what one had eaten in the past, whether mother's home-made baking or some sort of a 'nosh up' in the NAAFI was a story well worth listening to. One could even make up a good story 'as you go' giving even the NAAFI some worthwhile praise.

Yes! eating was the main topic while women were very seldom mentioned.

The rail wagons were not opened until early on the third morning. It was a pleasure for the train to stop, and music to hear the wagon bolts being drawn and the doors slid back. The doors were only opened on one side of the wagons, the guards having previously been posted along each side of the train, but most of them on the side we were allowed out from. We were in the middle of nowhere, the back of beyond, with uninteresting flat land for miles in every direction.

The sudden extra-brilliant early morning light flooding into the wagons hurt our eyes, making us blink. We were able to move about only in the vicinity of our own wagon to stretch our aching limbs, at the same time taking full advantage of some deep breathing.

There was no chance of escape, the guards being well posted and very alert.

We could not get any information of where we were now or to where we were going.

We still had our two large locomotives and for the first time we noticed we also had with us an ack-ack wagon, which was fully manned. Our brief respite was very short lived; we could not have been out more than ten minutes when we were ordered back into the wagons accompanied by shouts of '*Schnell, schnell, einsteigen*', 'quickly – quickly, get inside', and threatening gestures with rifle butts.

The train then set off again on its slow monotonous journey while we settled down again to sitting, standing, delousing and dozing.

We were descending into a sorry state, getting weaker every day through lack of food and water, this all being part of the methodical German processing methods designed to lower our resistance, forcing us into a complete state of submission. There was no difference between one day and the next, only that we were in a different part of Europe and gradually getting colder.

By the time we got to the fifth day, with our meagre rations finished and still no prospect of being anywhere near our final destination, we were a very miserable, dejected, despondent lot. We blamed everyone from Churchill downward to our general who had deserted us in our most desperate hours; someone had to be blamed. Our route so far as we could determine had taken us north into Yugoslavia passing through Skopie to Belgrade, then further north into Hungary to Budapest, then north-west into Czechoslovakia to Prague, where we were shunted into a siding one miserable rainy evening.

After a few hours in the siding, we heard the Germans bustling about outside the wagons. One of our watchers said wagon doors were being opened then shut again almost immediately. Suddenly it came our turn, the bolt was snapped off and the door slid noisily back. Three huge loaves of bread and a packet of cigarettes were thrust into our midst by two civilian women, then the guards slammed the door shut, dropping the door bolt into position again.

Lofty organised the distribution of the bread, there was only a little bit each, three 2,000g loaves between about fifty men – just over 100g each with a few puffs on a cigarette.

During the mighty feast, Lofty read the bit from the Bible of the three small loaves and five small fishes. It was an apt moment; we fervently blessed the two kind ladies who were from the International Red Cross. This was our first link with any form of Red Cross organisation.

We stayed in the siding all that night, setting off again next morning after parting company with half the train. This was our first inkling we were getting nearer to our destination, but we did not move very far as it was a day of stops and starts as if someone did not know where we were bound. On the seventh day, a signpost to Dresden was spotted and soon we passed through Dresden itself. We now knew we were definitely in Germany. Our journey had now become terribly slow, we were often put into sidings to wait for hours on end, then on a little further with more stops.

When it came light on the morning of the eighth day, the word was passed from wagon to wagon that we were standing at a place called Luckenwalde.

It was a fine sunny morning and soon our German guards were bustling about in great activity up and down the siding. We heard heavy rhythmical steps of many marching boots as a fresh company of German soldiers arrived on the sidings. There was a lot of heel clicking and saluting and orders being given as they got ready to receive us out of the wagons that had been our living hell for so many days.

The wagon bolts were being lifted and the door slid open letting in the fresh morning air and brilliant light which, as usual, hurt our eyes. We were ordered to get down and form up on the siding.

We were by now in a pitiful state, a rough-looking lot. We were very dirty, must have stunk to high heaven (but we didn't notice it, we had got used to it); we were unshaven and had matted lousy hair, though Jock and I were fortunate as we had had our hair cut very short.

We were definitely very lousy, having almost got used to them, it had become a pastime catching and killing them, wishing each one was a German as we squashed them between our thumbnails.

I nearly fell out of the wagon as I tried to climb down, I was so weak in my legs and what little bit of kit I had was becoming an awful burden to carry. There were some men who were too weak to climb down off the wagons. The guards climbed in setting about the unfortunate men with boot and rifle, but most of them were too weak to move.

Our so-called five days' journey had taken eight. I had made the rations I had been given, plus a few crusts I already had, last five days. My water had lasted eight days by just wetting my lips about twice per day and using the least drop to keep my top lip clean as it was not yet quite healed up. I also had a large running sore on each of my hip bones.

The Germans were soon shouting and bawling at us, pushing us into line with rifle and bayonet as we prepared to march off.

We set off in a shambling, limping gait in batches of 200, marching through part of the town where civilians, mostly women and old men, had gathered to watch us. They asked our guards who we were and where we were from. They were amazed to hear we were 'Englanders' from 'Crete'.

As soon as they heard this, they became very angry, jeering and spitting at us and some of them started to throw stones. They knew they had lost the cream of their parachute army over Crete, making them very bitter towards us and now they were able to give vent to their feelings.

The guards did nothing to stop them but kept us moving. Then suddenly something wonderful happened, one solitary voice somewhere in the column had the courage to start singing, *It's a Long Way to Tipperary*, Immediately, the remainder joined in singing as hard as we could, squaring our shoulders whilst trying to get into some sort of step.

It was a great effort to rally, which left the Germans cold. The stone throwing and spitting stopped as if by magic. The guards didn't know what to do about it whilst our civilian audience just stood and gaped. What with the front of the column singing *Tipperary* and the rear singing *Pack Up Your Troubles*, it must have been a sound to shock anyone, but it did the trick.

I don't know how far we marched from the sidings to the camp we were now approaching. It seemed many miles, each step being an effort. We had long since given up singing as we had left the town.

The camp ahead was hutments with a huge entrance gate and wide main cobbled road running straight through the middle of it. There was the usual heavily barbed wire fence with large high watchtowers running right round the whole of the outer perimeter.

Above the main gate hung a huge sign which read 'Stalag IIIA'. On each side of the main road were a number of huts in their own compound enclosed with more barbed wire fences. Nearest the main gate were the German soldiers' quarters, administration buildings and stores.

It was a very large camp obviously built with the intention of housing thousands of prisoners. It was a French Stalag.

As we trudged along the road past the huts, the inmates of the compounds came over as close as their barbed wire would allow, to see who we were; we all exchanged greetings. They were mostly Frenchmen, but there were also some Serbians. We went along to the last compound on the left of the road where, before entering, the Germans insisted on carrying out a search of each man's few possessions.

Passing into the compound we were allotted, in our batches of 200, to a large barrack hut, told to stay inside whilst a sentry was placed at the doors at either end.

The whole area was very flat with pine forests almost surrounding us. The soil was sandy, this was Germany; we were not sorry our journeying was over and we had finally reached our destination. The inside of the hut was reasonably clean. There were treble tier bunks arranged in groups of four down each side of the room. Down the centre were several 6-foot long tables, with two benches to each.

There were two slow combustion stoves positioned an equal distance from each end of the hut. There were plenty of windows, but the daylight could not penetrate into the room on account of the bunks being so high and so many packed in. There were, however, several low wattage electric light bulbs distributed throughout, which gave off a very poor light.

Placed on each bunk was a rough, coarse palliasse filled with paper cuttings, with bolster to match; three blankets, a metal 1-litre soup bowl and one soup spoon.

We four occupied two bottom bunks, one centre and one top bunk. The hut seemed like a palace whilst the bunks were absolute luxury after the months we had spent on the floor.

Soon the sentries on the doors passed the word around that we all had to be ready with our bowls and spoons to go to the cookhouse for soup.

We needed no second telling; we could not get there quickly enough. The cookhouse was situated a little further along the road and on the same side as we were.

It was a huge place with many large steam pressure cookers standing in rows with French cooks in attendance. They were supervised by Germans and worked in shifts around the clock, serving the whole camp.

I, like many more, will never forget that first bowl of soup. It was made of potatoes, the inevitable lentils, and some sort of fish (fins, bones, heads, the lot put in) plus some sort of seasoning.

There was no pushing and shoving as we formed up at the hatchway to receive our ration. There was many a spoonful being eaten on the way back to the huts and it tasted wonderful. We all declared it was the best soup we had ever tasted. We ate the lot, bones and all. The bones had been boiled so much that they were quite soft and not a morsel was wasted.

After eating, we all lay on our bunks, dozing off, feeling much better now there was something in our stomachs.

There was a German Feldwebel or Unteroffizier in charge of each barrack hut, and they now proceeded to make themselves known and sort us out into some sort of 'organised state'.

They first wanted to know who could speak and understand German, but there were very few. Next was to sort out someone to be *Stube Dienstälteste* – barrack-room senior – this being where our old friends, the warrant officers, came to the fore again. They were commonly called the 'Forty Thieves' because given the chance, they were experts at fiddling, especially the rations, for themselves.

The WOs in turn picked their pals to give them a hand. They were responsible to the Feldwebel for our general discipline, getting us on check parades, trotting off to the cookhouse for our bowls of soup, seeing to the general tidiness of the huts and the drawing and distribution of the daily dry rations.

Our hut was divided up into four sections, each of the four sections having a leader who made out a nominal roll and the four rolls then tallying with the grand total in the hut.

Rosters were drawn up for hut fatigues (which most of us tried to dodge doing) and for collecting the rations (which everyone wanted to be doing).

Thus, we gradually got organised, which pleased the Jerries no end. We then received our first day's dry rations, and as far as I remember, these were something like the following: Bread (black rye bread), 300g each, a small pat of margarine, a soup spoonful of sugar, a soup spoonful of jam, and a small piece of sausage meat (or some days a small portion of cheese or cheese spread). As at Salonika, 'breakfast' was a cup of unsweetened ersatz coffee. We were so hungry we could never save our dry rations until the next morning.

Luckenwalde Lazarett (Military Hospital) was full of our men who had been carried in from the train and also those who had fallen by the wayside during our march to the camp.

Men who had refused to get out of the wagons due to their weakness had been ill-treated by the guards. Many of them had been pushed out of the wagons only to fall on the ground and lay helpless and injured. Any of us who had tried to help them were bashed with a rifle and made to move on.

The way in which we had been presented to the German civilian population of Luckenwalde in our dilapidated and dirty state didn't show us off as being part of a proud and efficient British army. It was good propaganda for them, carefully worked out by their Nazi masters – but our day would come.

Our second day at Luckenwalde was spent in getting through documentation, delousing and a general clean up all round. We lined up by huts for check parade, then marched off to the documentation area, where, after a long wait, we gave our army number, rank and name, our next of kin, and home address.

We then sat on a stool to have a photograph taken from the front and side, each man also holding a card with his POW number on; mine was IIID 11131. Each of us was given a metal identification tag with our POW number stamped on and a length of cord so that the tag could be worn around the neck like our own army tags.

Next, a gang of French POWs were waiting with hair clippers to remove all the hair on our bodies. Then we went into the next building to strip off, putting our belongings on a coat hanger together with our boots and socks. The coat hangers were then hooked on to a metal mobile rack and wheeled away to be put through a delousing oven. At this point we fastened on our new identity tags.

We, left standing in our birthday suits, were given a dab of soft soap and went through into another room which was the communal showers.

The water was hot for about three or four minutes, in which time we made the most of it, rubbing vigorously and then rubbing each other's backs. It was glorious as we had not had a bath for months. Then suddenly the cold water came on, which made us gasp for breath. There was joyous screaming and laughing with a lot of backside slapping to get out of the cold water.

There were no towels with which to dry ourselves. Instead we passed on through a series of hot air compartments in the form of a tunnel and as we came out at the other end, dry, we found ourselves in a waiting room where we received our deloused clothing, etc.

Before dressing again, we turned each garment inside out to shake out the dead and cooked lice. After dressing, we all felt on top of the world again; it was wonderful to feel clean. One of the first words of German I learned was *Sauberkeit*, meaning cleanliness. It was screamed at us on every possible occasion at Luckenwalde.

So now we were officially prisoners of war and our next of kin were being notified. After the war I learnt from my brother that the War Office had informed him that I had been officially posted 'missing, believed killed', until they had received confirmation of me being a POW in Germany – so the little buff army forms we had filled in whilst on Crete could not have gone anywhere. During the first night after being cleaned up and deloused, I, for one, was able for the first time in months to get a good and peaceful sleep.

During the day, we would stand near the barbed wire of our compounds facing the road and the Frenchmen, hoping they would throw biscuits and other food over to us, but whenever they did there was one hell of a mad scramble for it, causing many a man to get hurt. The Germans decided this had to stop so they waded into the Frenchmen and made them stay at the opposite end of their huts and compounds.

It was then decided we would have to have something to do to occupy our minds. So each hut was paraded on the compound and the Germans in charge commenced to try and give us some foot drill – IN GERMAN.

In our case our Feldwebel paraded us in FIVES. He stood out in front and commenced a demonstration of various movements to the German words of command. They 'Stand at Ease' rather differently from us, with the feet apart but with the left foot slightly forward and with the hands together in front of the body – his command for this was *ruhrt-euch* sounding something like 'rear-doyeh' then his command for 'Atten-shun' was *Achtung* with no precautionary word of command.

He demonstrated these two movements several times, he was quite smart at it, but we thought it was very funny, and after the last one we gave him a hearty round of applause, which pleased him no end. He did not realise we were taking the 'Micky' out of him.

Then we tried it several times and deliberately not always doing it correctly, we were not interested, but he seemed satisfied.

He next went on to show us his 'Left and Right' turns at the halt.

He painstakingly explained the words of command, *Links Ump* for Left Turn and *Rechts Ump* for Right Turn, also going through the complete demonstration several times and again we gave him a round of applause.

Again, it was our turn. He shouted, *Achtung* and we came sloppily to attention, then after a pause gave *Links Ump*. Some of us turned right, which caused a roar of laughter. Even the Feldwebel had to laugh, it was so funny. Then we practised it several times, not without humour.

Eventually, we got browned off and the Feldwebel, realising this, conveniently brought the session to a close, dismissing us saying there would be another session the next day, but he would now be visiting our hut for inspection so we were all required to 'stand by our bunks'.

It was obvious what we were to expect on our next drill session, so we decided to play along with him. He was not a bad old so-and-so, up to now he had been reasonable with us, he was not the Nazi bullying type although he was firm. He was definitely an old soldier and later we learnt he would have retired on long service had it not been for the war starting. Thus, he had been put on prisoner of war camp duties for the duration.

Whilst we waited for his barrack-room inspection, the chief topic to talk about was 'drill' – how these bloody German so-and-sos had the audacity to drill us like a lot of bloody recruits and in German at that. The next session would be 'marching', so we decided to have more fun and games. We were now inquisitive to know what the German words of command were, so we got our interpreter to write them out for us, we would be ready for the next day.

After the barrack-room inspection, we were chased outside and the huts were locked up. This was to make sure we were not lounging in our bunks. We walked up and down the compound like a lot of caged animals, for that was all we were.

We talked about everything under the sun. Sometimes we sat in groups listening to one man 'telling the tale'. There was nothing to do to pass the time but talk and wait for meal times.

There would be numerous visits to the D.T.L. (deep trench latrine), otherwise known as 'the Bog' or the 'Information Centre' and other names. One would ask, when sat on the throne next to others, 'What's the Griff' (news) and believe me, some hellish news came out at times – and smells.

We had one very good British interpreter who came around each day with news which had been translated from German newspapers, *Volkischer Beobachter* and the *Fumf Uhr Blatt*, by kind permission of the camp commandant. But the camp commandant did not know that our man also brought us the yesterday's BBC news which the French prisoners supplied from their hidden secret radio receivers.

The news at this time was not at all in the British favour. We had lost Western Europe; the Middle East was in a sorry state with Germans and Italians knocking on the door of Alexandria. The German advance into Russia was tremendous and it looked as if they were going to walk right through. They were sinking our ships every day and knocking hell out of London and other cities with their air force.

They often told us we could not win, that we would have to stay and work in Germany for the remainder of our lives and never see England again. They always used the term England and always referred to us as Englanders or Tommies no matter whether we came from England, Ireland,

Scotland or Wales. We were never referred to as British and amongst us we had all sorts including New Zealanders, Australians, Channel Islanders, Spaniards, Cypriots, Palestinians and God knows what else.

Some of the New Zealanders and Australians had preferred to mix and stay with us. The few Spaniards were exiles from the Spanish Civil War who had joined the French Foreign Legion and later came over to the British forces during the time of the Syrian campaign and had eventually become members of our newly formed Middle East Commandos. They were lively, likeable fellows but though a bit sharp tempered, got on quite well with us.

When the barrack huts were opened we would surge in, going straight to our bunks to get our tin bowls and spoons. We knew it would be getting time 'to feed the animals' so we would form up to wait our turn to be marched to the cookhouse to draw our daily bowl of stew. Once we had drawn our stew and wolfed it down, we would lie back contentedly on our bunks until the call to collect our dry rations of bread and etceteras.

The loaf of bread had to be cut up into five equal pieces by someone. Lofty usually cut ours, using a measuring stick we had made, the length of the loaf and carefully divided into five. The loaves were always a similar size, but the man who cut had to cut straight!

We then numbered the pieces of bread, one to five, having five other numbers on bits of card which were shuffled face down, put in a hat and we would take it in turn daily to put one card on each bunk. We then took the piece of bread corresponding to the number. What could be fairer than that?

Some groups only put the numbers on the bunks and none on the bread, so that the first to pick a piece would take his time inspecting each piece minutely (without handling), moving around the loaf several times before choosing what he considered to be the largest piece. Then the second man would have a go, taking as long to choose, and so on with the third and fourth until it came the turn of the last man who would pick up the last piece, with a shrug of the shoulders.

There were many other ways, such as he who cuts the loaf has the last pick. These five would have permanent numbers, each man taking it in turn to cut up the loaf, the one who cut was the last one to pick, the other four taking it in turn of their numbers.

The Cypriots even got down to making a set of very efficient scales out of bits of wood, tin cans and string, and although all of these methods were aids to giving fair shares, they also helped pass the time, I thought the Cypriots were taking it a bit too far.

The common or garden tin can had now become part of every prisoner's standard equipment as a receptacle to drink from, each tin can being fitted with a piece of wire for a handle and fastened to the waist where it was always handy.

I wanted to make a brew of tea. I must have been the only one at that time with tea. There was no fuel for the stoves, that was out, the official winter months had not yet started, it was just like the British army, waiting for the first of October for the official winter months to start before being issued with fuel.

So, one day when drawing my ration of stew, I asked our interpreter, who used to stand at the food counter with each German in charge, if I could have some boiling water put in my can to brew the tea. He asked the Feldwebel, who in turn looked astounded, he could not believe his ears, TEA! What tea? Where did it come from? How much did I have? I was one of his men, where did I sleep?

Needless to say, I felt like Oliver Twist. Yes! After a bit of explaining, I got my water but not before my tin can with the tea in was passed from one to the other on both sides of the counter for the Germans and French to have a good look at, as they carried on a loud garbled conversation of which I understood not one word.

Back in the barrack hut we talked about the incident, wondering if the Germans would be coming along to confiscate it. So, with the aid of my pals, we found a place to hide it.

The brewed can of tea was dosed with our four rations of sugar (no milk) and passed round in turn to drink. It was not so bad, but it did not taste like the tea we used to know, maybe I had made it too strong or maybe the sweaty sock had not done much for the flavour. Whatever the reason, we were a bit disappointed.

When the Feldwebel came round later for the nightly check parade, we, as usual, paraded down the centre of the room after moving the tables and forms to one side. As he passed down the line making his count, I knew he had spotted me because he made a slight pause when he got opposite, staring me straight in the eye.

When he was satisfied with his count and had dismissed us, he sidled up to my bunk and demanded to have another look at my tea, So, keeping him occupied with language difficulties my pal, Jock, retrieved the tea from its hiding place and then passed it through the bunks to me. The Feldwebel looked distastefully at my grey army sweaty sock, then putting a little tea on the palm of his hand sniffed at it, exclaiming how *wonderbar* it was.

Looking around him to make sure no other Germans were watching him, he fished out a Nescafé tin from his pocket and filled it with tea. Then he brought out a 2,000g loaf from underneath his coat and offered it to me. My God! I could have bit his hand off before he had time to lay the bread on my bunk. We did the deal in double quick time, he putting the Nescafé tin quickly into his pocket and putting his forefinger to his lips indicating to keep quiet about the affair, then he was off like a shot. One did not have to *verstehen Deutsche* to do a deal like that.

I shared the loaf between the four of us, letting Lofty cut it up, so that night we were able to enjoy eating our bread ration knowing we had some more left for the next day, and I hoped I would not wake up in the early hours of the morning with the aching pains of hunger in my stomach.

The tea I had picked up and carried all that way was now proving to be of immense value. There was now no point in making it into a drink when I could get bread to eat for the four of us, and I had quite a few loaves of bread out of the Feldwebel whilst at Luckenwalde.

Another day started at Luckenwalde with the Germans rousting us out of bed at about 6 a.m. It was now towards the back end of September and quite dark and cold in a morning.

Someone (a party of men) had to fetch the jugs of ersatz coffee at about 7 a.m. and dole it out. After that we would make up and tidy our bunks, clean the barrack room in general in readiness for the grand entrance of 'His Highness Herr Feldwebel' to make his morning check parade and inspection.

One particular morning, the Feldwebel gave instructions that seeing we were going to do some marching drill under his tuition, there would not be enough space on the parade ground for everyone to drill at the same time, and therefore only three or four huts would parade at the one time, the others staying indoors to take their turn later. Our hut was going to be amongst the first to drill. The other Feldwebels and Unteroffiziers from the waiting huts were going to give assistance with the drill. It took some time to get us out of the huts on to the parade ground, but eventually we were formed up in some semblance of military order ready for the fray.

As I have said earlier, we had a good idea of what was to come next and we had prepared ourselves to some extent for it. We also noticed on this morning that the doors at each end of the barrack huts had been left open.

Our Feldwebel started off in great style by recapping through the previous instruction, not without humour and our usual applause. Then came the moment when he started to show us how to – march off – left and right wheel – and halt. He went through the German words of command: *tret marsch, links* and *rechts schwenkt* – and *halt*. Halt meant stop in anybody's language.

It then became our turn, we came slovenly to attention, turned in all different directions and slouched off to the four winds, with us laughing and joking about it, whilst the Feldwebel and his helpers were frantic and livid with rage trying to halt us and get us back into line again.

At the same time as we were going through our antics, the men from the other huts on the parade ground were also doing the same. It was general chaos for some time.

Starting off from scratch again, going through each stage very slowly, the Germans managed to get us all turned the same way, then we marched off, but not all in the same step, that would have been too much to ask for.

We marched alongside one of the barrack huts, turned left at the end, continuing along the front of the next hut. As our tail end passed by the open door at the end of the hut, men from the rear files smartly disappeared inside, some more doing the same when passing the next hut, and so on. When we finally arrived back at our starting off point and halted, the Germans realised they had lost half the men.

Again, there was utter confusion with shouting and raving Germans trying to get our men out of the barrack huts, but, as fast as they were getting us out, more were coming in from the other marching parties, through doors and windows.

It was a hopeless situation the Germans had got themselves into. They even tried to enlist the services of our own WOs and senior NCOs who, having no heart for the job, made a poor attempt, and we would not take any notice of them either.

In the end they had to give it up as a bad job and that was the end of the drill sessions. They must have thought we belonged to a right ragged army. Needless to say, we were locked out of the barrack hut for the remainder of the day.

Just as the Germans were leaving the compound, a party of our men formed up in three ranks with a sergeant in charge and gave a splendid drill display for the sole benefit of the Germans, who were by now standing on the main camp road gaping at us. They trooped down the cobbled road in disgust, with us giving them three hearty cheers.

An incident I remember very clearly happened at Lunkenwalde one evening.

We were sitting, as usual, in groups on our bunks talking, when some men who were seated at one of the tables, having been playing cards, started off an argument about spiritualism. Those of us nearest to the table began to listen in as this sounded as though it was going to be interesting. The argument, moving from spiritualism to hypnotism, became centred on two men. One was a small stockily built New Zealander who, by his dark skin, appeared to be part Māori. The other man was a Britisher who had grave doubts on spiritualism and hypnotism.

The New Zealander said he could prove to him that hypnotism was a fact and he himself could prove it by making him 'the Britisher' get down on all fours and bark like a dog.

The Britisher, disbelieving these powers, told him to go ahead.

By now the room was almost silent, a crowd had gathered round the table and nearby bunks. All eyes were on the table and the New Zealander.

He asked the Britisher if he would take the word of those around him and would he sit quite still, putting his hands face down on the table in front.

There was no need to ask for silence in the room, there was a deadly hush already.

The New Zealander looked into the face of the Britisher for a short time. Then speaking very quietly said that when he gave a signal the Britisher would get up from the table, kneel on all fours on the floor and howl like a dog. True to his word, the Britisher slowly got up from the table, knelt down on the floor on all fours, then lifting up his head howled like a dog.

The New Zealander then left the table and going to the man on the floor began once again to talk quietly to him, at the same time helping him to his feet. He told him that when he snapped his fingers, he would awaken but would not remember anything that had just happened.

As soon as the New Zealander snapped his fingers the Britisher came back to his normal self, looking somewhat dazed, not really understanding why he was standing up. Sitting down at the table again he admitted he had no idea what had just happened.

It was uncanny, he had lost a few moments of his life which he would never be able to recall, but he certainly changed his views on the past argument. The incident was talked about for days.

The days at Luckenwalde were now growing into weeks and most of us had recovered from the effect of the terrible train journey from Salonika, but there were still many very sick men in the camp hospital.

We were now in need of much warmer clothing, we were still in tropical kit. The Germans were asked every day 'when were we going to get some?' and the answer was always – 'soon'.

Those of us who had greatcoats were now very fortunate. We had carried them through blazing heat and dust, I had often been tempted to throw mine away when I felt it had been getting too much of a burden to carry. I was glad now I had not and I was wearing it all day and every day. I even slept in it, mostly as a safeguard to prevent it from getting stolen.

It was the same with boots. Boots were at a premium, most were getting thin and if one took them off at night and put them on the floor under the bottom bunk, one could be sure they would disappear by morning and a useless pair substituted. There was a lot of petty thieving, it was fatal to leave anything lying around unattended.

It was about this time we were told we would soon be moving to working camps. Warrant officers, sergeants and corporals could, if they wished, elect to go to a non-working camp. The remainder were to form three working camps of about 450 men to each camp.

We would be working for the German State Railway and housed by them in good clean camps, well clothed and fed and there would be plenty of recreational facilities.

We also heard about Red Cross food parcels for the first time and that we were allowed to receive one Personal Clothing Parcel every three months from our next of kin. We would also be allowed letters from home and we would be allowed to write and send four postcards and two letter cards per month.

The camps we were going to would have canteens, where we would be able to buy goods with the special issue of POW Camp money that we would be earning working on the railway.

It all sounded very rosy, in fact it sounded too good to be true. We had by now seen enough of the Germans to know they could not be trusted and their word meant nothing.

Within the next few days, we were all inoculated, with what and for what for, we were never told; it was just a matter of sixpenny-worth in each arm, and that was that.

Another highlight at Luckenwalde was Ginger Connelly, he simply would not keep out of trouble. A German guard gave him a push whilst he was sparking off trouble on check parade. Ginger took one step forward, belted the German on the chin, laying him flat out. Within seconds he was mixed up with four other German guards. He fought like a tiger, with fists, boots and head, bowling over the Germans like ninepins. Other men dashed in to put a stop to it which nearly made matters worse, the Germans thinking they were being engaged in a mass attack. Then suddenly it was all over, with a German putting Connelly down by hitting him on the head with a rifle butt. As he came to, the Germans grabbed him and dragged him off to the 'Cooler'. That was the last we saw of him for a few months.

One night, very late on, around midnight, when everyone was asleep and all was quiet, we were awakened by the distant noise of ack-ack guns firing and steadily coming closer. Someone tried the electric lights but all had been switched off from a central point. We crowded the windows, the camp perimeter lights were switched off, we could see many searchlights raking the sky with their powerful beams. Now we could hear the steady, powerful rhythmic note of the aircraft's engines.

It was bound to be one of ours, or was there more than one?

Some of us managed to get outside the hut to stare up into the clear night sky to watch. One of the aircraft was now caught in several searchlight beams and ack-ack shells were bursting all around it; it never altered its course, going, we presumed, for Berlin.

It seemed a long time before the slow-moving aircraft moved out of range of the searchlights and guns, which then turned their attention to others, but amidst all the clatter of guns we heard the sound and rumbling of bombs exploding.

We were all jubilant, and as the sound of ack-ack gradually died down and the searchlights were extinguished, we wandered back into the huts hoping the bombs had reached their targets and there would be many more to follow. (That was an understatement of thought.)

Soon the Germans gave us more definite news of moving out of Luckenwalde to permanent working camps. We were going to form three or four working camps in the Berlin area for the German State Railway constructing new permanent ways. We were not looking forward to it.

The Irish were the first to leave. Most of them, whether from the north or south, had been put together in one party, the Germans thinking they would be able, through their propaganda smooth talk, eventually win them over to their side since Southern Ireland was neutral.

They went to a camp at Spandau but no one knew what work they were going to do. We did not see or hear of them again until about August 1943 at Wulheide, east of Berlin, which is another episode I will relate later on.

All that remained now was our movement orders which we expected any day.

We were given the opportunity to sort ourselves out once we knew there were to be three camps, one at Genshagen and two at Dabendorf. These three camps were situated a few miles south of Berlin and a few miles from each other.

Jock Morrison and I, Lofty and wee Jock decided to go to Dabendorf I, although there was nothing to choose between them.

Chapter 5

Lager 413 Dabendorf 1941

We left Luckenwalde one dull dismal morning in early October 1941 in rather a different state than when we had arrived. Still dressed in our tropical kit but feeling much cleaner we marched in better order, with heads high, to the railway sidings in the town. There were not nearly as many guards with us this time and very few of the townspeople bothered to turn out to gape at us.

The train waiting in the sidings with steam up was a normal third-class, workers' passenger train, with real wooden seats. We entrained, so many coaches to which ever camp we were going, and were soon under way, travelling for the best part of three hours with many stops to enable us to be shunted on to other lines. Eventually, the Genshagen part of the train was uncoupled and we went on the few remaining miles to Dabendorf.

Dabendorf was a small wayside village station seeming miles from anywhere. We formed up in our two camps, then marched off through the village towards our new abode.

The road through the village was cobbled, the houses looked cold and dark, even the trees looked lifeless, whilst shedding their leaves. We saw only one person; an old woman with a heavy shawl around her shoulders and pulling a small four-wheeled cart (common in Germany) containing a huge loaf of bread. The old dear trudged along with back bent and head down looking neither right nor left, there were many remarks passed about the size of the loaf of bread which fair made our mouths water.

We passed the village cemetery, looking grim and gaunt with its tall headstones where, someone pointed out, lived all the 'Good Germans'.

At the next road junction, Dabendorf II parted company with us. There was a lot of good-humoured leg pulling and cat calling until both parties were out of sight of each other. Then we settled down with some apprehension of what sort of a camp and reception was waiting ahead of us. The guards so far had been quite friendly towards us, chatting and giving out odd cigarettes now and then. After marching about 3 miles, we suddenly came in sight of our camp.

It was situated just off the main road and surrounded on three sides by thickly populated pine trees with the fourth side looking out over miles of flat farmland.

The camp had originally been constructed for civilian workers so it was a simple job to convert it into a POW camp by adding a few more huts and the usual heavy barbed wire fences. The perimeter fence, without watchtowers, circumvented the whole camp including the German quarters, but separating the British and German quarters was another fence with a huge gate in it. At this gate stood a grim-faced, steel-helmeted, fully armed sentry, whilst others looking equally as grim patrolled the outer perimeter fence, making our first impressions unfavourable.

Our day of arrival had turned cold and bleak during the afternoon as we came to a halt at the camp gate to be met by the 'reception committee', which consisted of a vicious-looking Feldwebel and an Unteroffizier of the Wehrmacht and another German dressed in an immaculately fitted black uniform with highly polished riding boots, a smart looking peak cap and sporting a Swastika arm band.

At first, we thought he was another SS man but he turned out to be no more than a Reichbahn Official, namely *der Lager Fuehrer*, the camp leader. Nevertheless, he appeared to be in command for the moment, strutting about like a turkey cock, shouting orders whilst the two arrogant bullying German NCOs detailed us off to the barrack blocks after we had been counted and pushed roughly through the gate.

The buildings inside our compound consisted of four barrack blocks, constructed of wood to hold about 120 men each; a large dining hall which, to say the least, was never used for that purpose; a laundry building with its own boiler house and drying rooms; and, last but not least, a large D.T.L. (Deep Trench Latrine).

The cookhouse, stores and administration buildings were in the German compound along with the guardroom and their sleeping quarters.

The barrack blocks were quite new and clean, although it was obvious they had been previously occupied. A wide corridor ran down the centre of each block with rooms to house us leading off on each side. About halfway along the corridor was a boiler house, ablutions room complete with hot and cold showers and flush toilets. Windows were all double glazed and fitted with blackout blinds, inner walls and ceilings were panelled hardboard with fibre glass insulation.

Our room had twelve double-tier bunks, two long narrow tables with four seat benches, a large slow combustion stove in the corner on the left just inside the door, and a wooden shelf running almost round the room above the tops of the bunks. All in all, we had to admit these were the best quarters we had been housed in since leaving Blighty in early 1939.

Jock and I grabbed a bunk in the corner near the window, whilst Lofty and wee Jock took the next one to us. I went on top with Jock underneath and wee Jock took a top one with Lofty underneath.

There were twenty-four of us in the room, nearly all strangers but with plenty of time to get to know each other. We soon settled down. I found that the British sergeant in charge of our room was a Military Policeman who a few months earlier had chased me over the roof tops in Canea on Crete on discovering me and two others being 'out of bounds' in a civilian house (not a brothel) without the necessary permanent passes. I had evaded capture by dashing up the stairs of the house, out on to the flat roof and had jumped from house to house and street to street, whilst the red-faced sergeant, being quite fat in those days, with a big fine moustache, was left panting and cursing on the roof of the first house and was 'chicken' to follow me.

Needless to say, my two pals were caught and charged. I did not get away with it because the MPs caught up with me the next day, so we took the rap together, an offence for which we were lucky enough to be simply dismissed with a rollicking from our OC.

The sergeant and I were in the same boat together now, we had a little light-hearted banter about the episode, much to the amusement of others listening in, and bygones were bygones so we became reasonably good friends.

In charge of the block was one of the Forty Thieves, he having six more WOs to help him. The senior WO in the camp was an RAF warrant officer who also lived in our block. None of the WOs or NCOs had, as yet elected to go to non-working camps, they wanted to see what working camps were like first, so we were to endure them for another few months.

During the next few days, some new clothing arrived to be issued in place of our sadly worn-out and inadequate tropical clothing. British battledress blouses with French army pantaloons; British and French greatcoats; German underwear of vests with long sleeves and John L type underpants; wooden-soled clog type boots or Dutch clogs; *fuss lappens*, 'foot cloths' instead of socks; a pair of cloth mitts; and lastly, one of those horrible British forage caps which were neither use nor ornament.

I kept my own socks, hosetops and puttees because the French pantaloons only reached to just below the calf muscle, leaving bare legs to the tops of the boots, and I also managed to keep my own boots while still getting a pair of wooden-soled ones when the German storeman's back was half turned; one had to take every possible chance to get something out of them.

We looked quite a comical sight in our new garb, but we did not care about that as long as we were warmer.

After a few days, we were marched into a field near Dabendorf village one fine Sunday morning where there was an official photographer waiting to take our photographs in groups. We were able to purchase a copy later but I am afraid the one I had has been lost over the years, which is a great pity.

We were soon put to work, when early one Monday morning at 4 a.m. the guards came hustling us out of bed. By 5 a.m. we had drawn and drunk our ersatz coffee, scrubbed out the rooms, tables, benches, and the corridor, paraded outside under powerful arc lights where we were counted, detailed into working parties or *Arbeit Kommandos* as they were known from then on, and marched off to work under armed guard whilst it was still dark, to reach the place of work to make a 6 a.m. start.

I shall never forget my first day's work. Lofty and I were singled out with four others and placed on one side with one armed guard. We waited and watched the others march out of camp, then came our turn.

We were taken outside the camp to a Reichbahn lorry and trailer which was being made ready for the road. The driver was stoking a boiler-type appliance with wood chips which when burning gave the vehicle its source of power.

Climbing on board, we were soon chugging along the road in the direction of Berlin. We noticed road signs pointing to Zossen and later signs pointing to Potsdam, so we reckoned we were camped about 20 miles south of the capital.

The lorry stopped in the Berlin suburbs at a railway stores yard surrounded by some tall flats. We were to collect a load of bagged cement, but there being no one at the yard to issue it, the driver went off in search of the storeman whilst we sat with our guard against one of the buildings to wait.

Our guard was a short, stocky man with a round, fleshy face and possibly in his early thirties. He told us his name was Emil, and tried to memorise our names, but conversation was limited owing to the fact that none of us spoke German and he did not speak any English.

At about 10 a.m., Emil pulled out his sandwiches to have his breakfast, whilst we all looked on, watching him like hawks. Our stomachs were empty and we, being very hungry, watched covetously every morsel of food he put to his mouth.

By midday our driver had still not returned. We were getting terribly browned off, but the sun was shining making it reasonably warm whilst we sat around and waited.

However, all this time we had been well observed, without us knowing, by a German woman in one of the top flats. She managed to draw the attention of Emil, who by now was wandering aimlessly about the yard, rifle on shoulder.

Emil looked cautiously around several times whilst at the same time edging nearer to the back door of the flats. Stepping inside the doorway and still able to observe us, he had a hurried conversation with the woman. He appeared again within seconds to continue his slow walk up and down the yard.

After a few minutes more, a window in the top flat opened, out popped the head and shoulders of the woman who began to lower a shopping basket down on a long length of cord. Emil was waiting at the bottom as the basket reached the ground and reaching inside lifted out two handfuls of sandwiches which he shared amongst us. They were made of the usual dark rye bread, spread with some sort of pork fat.

What a Godsend, what a kindness. We dare not shout out our profound thanks for fear of attracting the attention of others. Emil had motioned to us to keep quiet, which we did, but as we all glanced up to see the basket disappearing inside the window again, our silent thoughts of a million thanks went to the woman in the top flat.

We really enjoyed those sandwiches which filled a terribly empty hole for a few hours. It was an act never to be forgotten.

After a while, our lorry driver returned with another man who opened up the store for us to start loading bags of cement on to our vehicle. We made a start, but found we were so weak it took two of us to lift one bag of cement on to the back of the lorry – and that at a supreme effort.

We were going to be hours loading, so Emil realising this put his rifle against the wall and taking off his leather belt and equipment, decided to reorganise the whole thing, by ordering the driver to get upon the vehicle to do the stacking and he and the other German would help us with the carrying. This went well and needless to say the Germans did most of the work.

After several tons were loaded and the driver had restoked his boiler, we climbed aboard and drove off in the direction whence we came, finally reaching our destination on the new railroad at about five o'clock in the evening.

What a sight met our eyes as we alighted the lorry. There were the makings of a sand embankment for as far as the eye could see in both directions. Gangs of our men were emptying tip wagons on a three-quarter gauge rail track of sand whilst others were shovelling and spreading and jacking and filling under the rail sleepers to heighten the line in readiness for more tipping. Guards and civilian railway gangers were bullying and cursing at each gang, urging more work out of men so weak they could hardly lift a shovel.

A ganger soon dashed up to us screaming at our guard and driver to get us unloading the cement quickly into a hut. We got no peace until it was unloaded and by which time it was six o'clock in the evening and the rest of the men were putting away their shovels and other tools and being marched back to camp.

Our first day at work had been easy compared to the poor sods working here.

Emil kept us separate, marching us back to camp on our own where we were counted in and told to parade again in the same order the next morning. He gave us a big wink as he left us at the gate.

That evening the rooms buzzed with conversation about the first day's work.

We drew our ration of thin, dirty looking, watery stew made of potatoes, carrots and lentils, with the dirty gritty potato peel floating on top, but we ate the lot and looked for more. Later, we collected our dry rations going through the usual rigmarole of selection to dish it out to each man.

At about 9.30 p.m. a check parade was held in the corridor which took at least one hour for the square heads to agree we were all present and correct. Then the doors were locked, wooden shutters fastened on the outside of the windows, and lights out. There was nothing else for it but bed. It had been a long day and we were tired and we did not take any rocking to get to sleep.

It did not seem as though we had been in bed five minutes before the guards were rushing about from room to room rousting us out of bed again at 4 a.m. in the morning for work.

I have already said that the first word of German I remember learning was *sauberkeit*, cleanliness, well the second word I learned was *arbeit* meaning work. So *sauberkeit* and *arbeit* was screamed at us many times in the early morning before we left the camp.

Our guard, who was waiting for us on the parade ground, quickly checked us out and took us to our new place of work, which for the next few weeks was helping in the construction of concrete bankseats of a railway bridge which could be seen from the camp. So, we did not have far to go to work and we were usually first back into camp.

This work, although arduous, was much more interesting than the railway embankment. We worked with about eight Germans and some Polish forced labour who detested the sight of the Germans. We helped to prepare the steelwork, shuttering and did the general fetching and carrying of concrete and other building materials. It was a six-day week. They were long hungry days with each day getting colder and shorter as the winter arrived.

Each day one of us would be singled out to be the 'bude boy', 'hut boy', whose duties were numerous but not unpleasant. There were huts to be kept clean where the various workers ate their meals. Some of the Germans lived on the job so their rooms were to be kept clean.

We worked under the supervision of the site cook who kept us busy all day. There were several buckets of potatoes to peel for the Germans' evening meal and a host of other small jobs to do. I enjoyed peeling the potatoes as it meant I could eat a few raw when the cook was not looking. Alas there was no food on the job for us.

When it came my turn for 'bude boy' I soon found out there were about ten rabbits kept behind the Germans' quarters. The German cook whose job it was to feed them would each day take a bucket full of hard crusts of bread and divide them out into the hutches. I had to follow with a bucket full of 'greens', putting a handful into each hutch, whilst at the same time when the cook was not looking, I would quickly pinch a couple of crusts and stuff them into my pocket or inside my battledress blouse.

Whether or not the others did the same when they were on, I do not know. It was not policy to divulge such things for fear of a good thing being spoilt by too many hands dipping in.

It did, however, help to keep the wolf from the door once a week. I was most grateful to the rabbits and hoped one day they would, in turn, with the grace of God, make someone a good meal, but at the time I felt my need was greater than theirs. I also learnt that every rabbit had a serial number stamped in each ear, according to the German law at that time, so it was not policy to pinch one.

After our first week of work, there were rumblings of discontent in the camp concerning our WOs and sergeants. Most of them had to work on the railway the same as anyone else. The only ones left in camp were the camp senior and those in charge of each block.

Those going out to work soon found the shovelling below their dignity and looked for less-manual jobs by exploiting their ranks. They were stupid enough to aid the gangers to get much more work done so that they themselves could get cushy jobs or semi-supervisory jobs. Their action did not go down well at all with us.

We, in turn, had many debates as to what we were going to do about it. We insisted that every man in the working camp be treated alike. The seniors had been given their chance to go to non-working camps and had not taken it, so therefore as long as they were with us there was no rank valid, we were all 'workers'.

The first action of the loading gangs in the sand quarries was to go on strike until the seniors were back on the shovel. *Mein Gott in Himmel* (My God in Heaven). Strikes were unthinkable in Germany, the gangers went stark raving mad whilst the guards clicked their rifle bolts threatening to shoot, but the boys won the day and the seniors were put back to work.

There were many ugly scenes at night in the blocks. Most men were willing to respect the rank of those who were in charge of the barrack blocks. It was obvious someone had to be in charge and that someone had to be able to liaise with the Germans, but as far as the remainder were concerned, we were all in the same boat, and we insisted on equality all round.

The men in the sand quarries had the most arduous job of anyone. They hand loaded tip trucks on a three-quarter gauge track. There were twenty trucks to a train load, hauled by a small steam engine to the place of disposal some miles away on the new embankment.

Each truck held about 4 tons and was filled by two men. On the first day, I believe two trains were loaded, but, by the end of the second week, the gangs were loading at least twelve trains a day. So, a few simple mathematics show that the two men were loading 48 tons per day, and besides that the track had to be maintained and kept close to the sand-face.

Consequently, the men at the other end of the line on the receiving end had more to unload, which did not go down at all well.

Out on the work site we toiled from 6 a.m. until 6 p.m. with two half-hour breaks, one from 10 a.m. to 10.30 a.m. and the second from 2 p.m. to

2.30 p.m. without a morsel of food to eat the whole day and only the water we carried in our water bottles, if we were lucky enough to have one. By the end of the day, we were ravenously hungry, and this for six days a week.

Sunday, the day of rest was anything but. We were rousted out at 5 a.m., one hour later than the normal working day. The usual hut conservancy began at once before the horrible black ersatz coffee came round. A squarehead guard was put in charge of each block to supervise the cleaning; he continually charged from room to room in frantic haste, swearing and bullying until the place was spick and span ready for inspection. During this time, we also had to get ourselves cleaned up, shaving of course was a joke but somehow or other we managed to make ourselves presentable.

At 8 a.m. it was 'Stand by your bunks' for inspection by the camp commandant, otherwise named the Camp Comedian. He and his entourage would stamp into the block, dressed in their Sunday best complete with polished Jack boots and to the shouts of '*Achtung*' as he entered each room in turn, would inspect all the room and us, and there would always be some fault to find just as in our own army. But, to be fair about the whole thing, he had already been round the German soldiers' quarters who didn't get away with anything, they were up and about at the same time as us, the only difference being, they got more food than we did, and able to go home on leave.

When the 'comedian' had been round the camp we all paraded outside for check parade and fatigues. Our Forty Thieves, the warrant officers and sergeants, and one or two of their cronies would parade separately to ensure they went on the spud-bashing detail. This was one of the most distasteful jobs in the British army which no one wanted to do, and usually it was given to the poor old Fire Picquet and the defaulters. But here, now that everyone was bloody hungry there was a rush to get on it, especially by the Forty Thieves.

Of course, it wasn't without its humorous side. They always paraded, now the weather was cold, with their greatcoats on, to be let through the gate to the potato store, a cold and draughty, unheated hut in the German compound. After a few hours peeling the necessary quota of spuds they would return to our own side looking like a lot of pregnant women because of the potatoes they had stuffed inside their battledress blouses, down their trouser legs and into their greatcoat pockets.

All went well until a sentry on the gate smelt a rat and ordered the bashing detail to form a single line (still on the German side of the wire) then pressing the electric button in his sentry box, enlisted the aid of some of the off-duty guards to search the prisoners. There was soon a small heap of potatoes in front of each man, which were collected and put back in the store. The camp commandant was storming up and down raving and swearing and threatening dire punishment but finally let them all back through the gate.

Last man through was tall, with his forage cap perched right on the top of his head. The sentry for no apparent reason stopped him, snatched off his cap and out fell two measly potatoes. He could not help seeing the funny side of this, so he bent down quickly, picked the two potatoes up and without any other Germans seeing, who were by now returning to their own quarters, thrust them into the prisoner's hands and pushed him roughly through the gate wishing him well for his ingenuity. But this was not quite the end of the story, some of the other men had craftily secreted a potato underneath each armpit and in the crutch of their long underpants.

The Forty Thieves, however, were in disfavour and from then on the spud-bashing detail was selected from each barrack hut in turn. Potato stealing still continued and not only became a fine art but a game to see who could get the most past the sentry each week.

The food we were getting was absolute rubbish, totally inadequate, doing nothing to rebuild our strength. This was just how the Germans wanted it, they must keep us underfed, under-nourished, overworked and weak so that we would give them very little or no resistance.

So, life at the moment was arduous enough without having to contend with the stupidity of our senior NCOs. They became intensely disliked, mistrusted and ignored. We had our own code of discipline and comradeship which grew into a great *esprit de corps* through the years, and still prevails today when two or more ex-POWs get together.

It was a great day when the first lettercards and postcards were issued to us to write home. Two lettercards and four postcards to write, the first real contact we were going to establish with our folks at home, and hardly a pen or pencil to write them with. Typical of the German mentality to give us the paper to write on and nothing to write with.

We had to wait a few days until pencils were forthcoming, which were then put into a 'canteen' for us to purchase but with nothing to purchase them with, so the next step was to pay us for working. A pay day was arranged to pay us for our first month's work and if I remember rightly, we were paid about 12 DM in special POW camp money, the remainder of our pay, about 36 DM, being kept back for our 'board and lodgings'.

So, pencils were bought and we set to the task of writing home.

There was plenty to write about but we were not allowed to write it. We had to content ourselves with purely personal things about the family and the 101 things we would like sending in our quarterly personal parcels. I remember asking for dog biscuits to be sent because I was so hungry and thought they were tough enough not to go rotten during transit. But alas, the only food allowed to be sent was ½lb of chocolate with each parcel.

We were given plenty of time to write, which led to lots of discussions within our room, thus bringing us all closer together. There were even those who could not write so very well, but illiteracy, though embarrassing, was nothing to be ashamed of, there being many willing hands to write for them.

Twenty-four men in one small room had to make the most of each other's company. We had all been thrown into the same boat, but that did not mean to say we had to like each other as brothers. There were many arguments and falling out and a few fights, usually over the distribution of food. Men swapped rooms with each other in an effort to try to fit into the community until eventually the problem sorted itself out.

There are a few characters in that first room worth mentioning, men, who for one reason or another are well remembered.

Winn and Riley were two Liverpool lads who worked in the sand quarry loading skips. They were light ack-ack gunners who could tell many a good tale of shooting down Germans, or tales of devilment they used to get up to in Liverpool before the war started. But one never knew where the truth stopped and the romancing began as they could both keep a very straight face when yarning. Their quick wit and good humour never failed to create a laugh, which was very badly needed in those days. They never shirked a chore and were good men to be with.

Sid Tomlinson from Blackpool and his pal Davie Fairbairn, a Scot, were two tall, thin, infantry men. Sid had been a cypher sergeant with Divisional HQ and before the war had been an insurance agent; he was more an intellectual than a manual worker and a good man to get into conversation with. His pal, Davie, I believe was a regular soldier and definitely wore the largest cap badge in the British army (The Argyll and Sutherland Highlanders) of which he was very proud. They were an inseparable pair, sitting for hours on end whispering to each other. If one went for a wash the other one followed suit, in fact, they went everywhere together.

There was my old friend, the now not-so-fat Military Police sergeant, with his reddish hair and large moustache. Being in charge of the room, he did all the fetching and carrying, he was a blusterer and as thick as two short planks and had the 'Micky' taken out of him something shocking. Without a doubt, he took it all in his stride and not without good humour, promising if he ever met us after the war he would delight in 'sticking us on a fizzer'.

Lofty was without doubt one of the most impressive characters of all, who was thought to be an authority on most subjects and whose advice was often sought. He had now developed a peculiarity of slicing his daily ration of bread as thin as he possibly could and making his spread go as far as possible. He would then divide his sandwiches into half, eating one half during the evening and saving the other half for morning. The ones for the next morning would be wrapped in a damp handkerchief and placed at the side of his pillow with his Bible on top. It was a dodgy thing to do in those days, there being so many hungry mouths about, but he had faith that his Bible would protect them, and protect them it did, until one morning Lofty gave a mild cry of alarm which brought most of the room gathering round to hear the worst.

Lofty lifted out his small bundle of sandwiches to show that a small hole had been made through the cloth and in between two slices of bread and into the cheese, which could only have been made by a mouse. His reaction was typical of him, 'God bless the poor little mouse,' he said, 'and if it has made the mouse happy, then so am I.' Nevertheless, he made sure that in future his sandwiches were not so handy for the mouse again.

'Digger' Lowery was an Australian who had found better comradeship with a Britisher than with his own kinsmen. He was a profound talker, probably having been vaccinated with a gramophone needle as a baby, consequently named in soldierly terms as a 'Bull shitter', but a tolerable one at that.

Arthur Weldon – Driver RASC was a happy soul normally. He had experienced great hardships as a child in Birmingham during the 1920s with his belly often more empty than full, until, when he was old enough, he joined the Regular Army to obtain his first square meal. And here he was once again hungry, but as he explained, it was nothing new, he was used to it.

Then there was the quiet, morose 'go it alone' type, who living on a top bunk near the door, placed a photograph of his so-called girlfriend on the shelf near him so that he could sit or lie and gaze at it on every possible occasion. When it came time to undress for bed, he would turn the photo to face the wall so that she would not see him undressing. Funny fellow.

Another 'go it alone' type claimed to be a member of The Magic Circle, that illustrious fellowship of magicians – which no one believed. He was, however, an excellent performer of card tricks and often kept us amused if not a little bewildered. But more about him later.

Then there was George Landa, a small, weak weed of a lad about 19 years old. He lived in deadly fear from day to day that the Germans would find out he was a Jew. Poor George made himself really ill with worry and when one morning someone near him found a repugnant smell coming from him and his bed, we could do nothing else but to take him wrapped up in the smelly blanket across to the camp hospital and the MO.

A few of us used to visit him each evening to cheer him up by telling him the current news and also to kid him on that he would have to be a C. of E. or Baptist or some other than his own religion until the end of the war. He eventually got over it and came back to us and was given a job in the camp for some time.

Such were some of the types it took to make room, from all walks of life, good, not so bad, and indifferent.

The winter was now setting in with a vengeance, with icy cold biting winds sweeping across the flat featureless landscape from the east. We shivered and were half frozen all day on the working sites. Our job was gradually coming to a close because of the freezing conditions putting a stop to the concreting, essential to progress.

The railway work did not stop. Those men had to work through snow, rain and frost come what may. Everyone came back into camp wet through and exhausted. It was difficult to dry off wet clothing because the Germans only allowed us four small coal briquettes per day, hardly enough to light the stove let alone warm the room and dry our clothes.

We would try and scavenge fuel whilst at work, every little helped, providing we could smuggle it back into camp past the guard on the gate. Even then, we had to be careful not to stoke the stove too much because the sentries on their night beat would notice the extra smoke coming from the chimneys, causing an investigation and confiscation of fuel. Any fuel left over for the next night had to be hidden during the day, a simple but effective hidey hole being in the stove itself and also inside the stove pipe with the damper closed. If during the day the stupid square-headed Feldwebel inspecting the rooms checked the stove, he would only look to see if the ashbox had been properly emptied and on finding it spotlessly clean, would not look any further.

Our job at the bridge finally wound up for the winter. So, one morning Emil collected us and marched us off to the railway station at Dabendorf, only to be told we were at the wrong place of work. But the enterprising station master, himself a shrewd old soldier from the 1914 effort, put us to work cleaning the platforms and what have you, whilst he found out just where we should have been. The old devil kept us there until midday, polishing his station, when a middle-aged stockily built German came along to collect us and show us our new job. We did not really mind so much when he rewarded us with some sandwiches, we let him understand we would come back anytime he wanted us and Emil with a wink and a big smile led us away.

We trooped off back towards our camp, then followed the German along a series of cart tracks across the fields, with Emil bringing up the rear, until we finally came across some huts at a site excavation in the middle of a field. At the site were two other Germans, one a blond-haired youngish man who was obviously in charge, and the second an older country yokel type of labourer (another Emil). The blond was Adolf and the one who had fetched us, Carl.

Without wasting much time, we were soon put to work in the hole, digging out heavy wet earth. It was a round hole about 25 feet in diameter being dug down to about 10 feet to start the concrete foundations. We did not get much work done that afternoon for several reasons. We had no adequate footwear to work in the now boggy ground, our feet were already soaking wet through, and Emil was unsure of the way back to the main road to the camp and he insisted we get there before dark

So off we went back to camp where en route we took more notice of what was in the fields. There were still acres of potatoes, sugar beet and carrots to harvest. We eyed all this before us, longingly, wishing Emil would let us pick some which would not be missed amongst all that lot. But our wish was not to be granted that day,

During the next few days travelling the same route, Emil, sensing what was in our minds, would not always walk behind us to keep us in view. We would, therefore, quickly dash off the path, pulling up a few carrots or whatever else there was, and quickly stuff them into our pockets and haversacks. He knew exactly what was going on but knowing we were extremely hungry, turned a blind eye.

Brushing the sandy soil off a carrot or potato and wiping it on the inside corner of our greatcoats, we would continue the remainder of the journey eating them raw. They tasted good; we were sadly in need of them. On nearing the working site, Emil would motion to us to finish chewing and to show no signs of what we had left so that the other three Germans knew nothing about our activities.

There were two huts on the site, one the Germans used which had a stove, the other being a store hut which we and Emil crammed into, but it had no stove and was now getting so cold we were better off walking up and down during our break times.

Adolf, the blond, seeing this, had a few words with Emil and decided to invite us in to share their hut. It was warm inside and we were grateful, we thanked him as we went in and sat down on the benches along one side of the hut.

It was then for the first time after several weeks that we realised Adolf could understand and speak a bit of English. Up to now he had said very little to us whilst on the job, but had given instructions to the others, who in turn had transmitted them to us somehow.

His English was slow, hesitant and very guttural, schoolboy stuff. He would try translating choice bits out of his daily paper, *Der Fumf Uhr Blatt*, which always had its major headlines in red, telling us with delight of all the shipping we were losing, of the tremendous air raids on Britain, and of their massive push into Russia. Usually, he became excited until he lapsed back into Germen without realising it.

Suddenly, one day, he asked us point blank what we thought of the Jewish problem. We told him we did not have a Jewish problem, did he? With that he became very angry, shouting and waving his fist, burst out with such venom, '*Alle Juden missen tote sein.*' 'All Jews must die.'

He had shown his true colours, the other Germans silently gazed at the floor, embarrassed. We now knew he was a proper Nazi bastard, one to be handled very carefully.

One night on the 9 o'clock check parade, the Germans found there were two men missing from our hut. We were counted and re-counted numerous times whilst others searched in every conceivable corner of the camp. Extra guards were put around the camp, the perimeter lights were switched on and Alsatian dogs were brought in.

The news had spread to the other huts very quickly, where delaying tactics were soon employed by making the Germans count too many men. We could not do this in our hut because we were the first to be counted, and none of us had previously known the two men were going to escape.

It took then hours to find out who the missing two were by having to check each man's identity disc against his photograph. The incident, however, created a diversion from the usual drab routine.

On the next day when we returned from work the two would-be escapees had been recaptured and brought back to camp. They were a corporal and an aircraftsman of the RAF who had made a brave attempt to steal away in a German aircraft on an airfield a few miles away. They had watched the aircraft, a heavy bomber, landing, counted out what they thought was the crew and had actually got inside, only to be caught by the rear gunner who had not left at the same time as the other crew members.

Being none the worse for their adventure and treated very well by the air force, they were returned, smiling, through our gates. Nevertheless, both they and the RAF warrant officer who were the only RAF personnel in our camp, were soon removed to a more secure place, and we never saw them again.

Another most sad occasion was one Sunday morning when someone burst into our room to say that a young chap from one of the other huts had been found hanging from the rafters in the D.T.L. He had quickly been cut down and artificial respiration applied. Our medical officer, Captain Neale, of the New Zealand Forces, had done his utmost to save him, but to no avail.

I know our very existence was tough at that time and must have proved too tough for this one poor soul, who had decided to make an end of his tormented life. The incident had a long-lasting effect on us all, making us more determined to survive.

Captain Neale, an astute, diligent and competent MO, though quiet and retiring, had been with us since the start of the camp. We were very fortunate to have him with us and although he insisted in keeping to his own vocation and in the background, he was really a tower of strength to us. I have often thought he must have been a lonely man during those years.

It was about five weeks before Christmas 1941 when on one very cold, snowy late afternoon we trudged wearily into camp, hoping we would not be searched at the gate. The sentry on duty dressed in his big overboots and extra-large thick overcoat shivered and beat his gloved hands together as we passed. We were glad to be getting inside where there would be a little more warmth and somewhere to lie down.

Suddenly, a group of excited voices shouted forth the good news that Red Cross food parcels had arrived that very day. We jumped with joy shaking each other by the hand and even hugging each other. I, like many more, wept with the pleasure of knowing we had not been altogether forgotten and that this was the first breakthrough of our side.

They could not have arrived at a more needy time, not only for our stomachs' sakes, but as a great boost to the morale of the whole camp. But, before we got them there were many arguments with the Feldwebel as to the method of issue.

If there were enough parcels for one each, then we would get one each, but the stupid Germans insisted every tin must be opened at the time of issue, forcing us to eat them as quickly as possible or else they would go bad. We obviously could not agree to this so in the end when tempers were getting frayed, a compromise was reached by issuing one parcel to four men four times per week (with tins opened), Monday, Wednesday, Friday and Sunday, until a proper food parcel store was arranged,

With the parcels were fifty cigarettes per week. The German guards stood goggle-eyed when they saw the parcels opened plus the cigarettes, and there is no doubt in my mind this was the finest piece of propaganda Britain ever put out during the whole war. The food parcels had been so well thought out, not only to get as much in as possible, but to give a man a varied yet nutritious diet coupled with what we got from the Germans.

That first night we had a jolly good feed to say the least. Some men made themselves sick, some were ill the next day, many had diarrhoea later, but no one grumbled. I remember waking up in the early hours of the morning to reach out on the shelf to finish off a small tin of Nestlé condensed milk, it was wonderful, and did me the world of good. I can still taste it now when I think of it.

The advent of the first Red Cross food parcels injected us with new life and hope. It was a great morale booster; we saw life around us in a different light. We could afford to take something with us to work to eat now, and inside no time, instead of trudging miserably along the roads with heads down, with no purpose in mind, there was suddenly an uplift, the chattering of voices and a lighter tread.

Someone sparked off the idea of having a concert party. There was fervent activity in the huts at night before the main doors were locked, to find out who could do what.

We suddenly had a new camp commandant, an old lieutenant bandsmaster who soon made many changes to our advantage. Firstly, he could not agree to the main doors of the huts being locked at night because the windows were also heavily shuttered from the outside, stopping much ventilation and creating a grave fire risk.

So, all shutters and doors were left open, providing the blackout blinds were properly adjusted and the camp perimeter lights blazed all night except when an air raid was imminent.

We were free to pass from one hut to another willy-nilly until lights out, but after that anyone foolish enough to be caught outside in the lights of the compound was likely to get shot.

Being a musician, the commandant managed to produce a piano, which, when installed, he tuned it himself. He was all for having concert parties, doing much to encourage and assist, especially in building the stage, finding materials for 'wings', backdrops and curtains.

Surprisingly enough there was much difficulty in getting artists for the first concert. We produced three out of our room, however: Riley who sang a few of his witty ribald songs, much to the delight of the audience, our Magic Circle friend who, with his card tricks and conjuring, was a great success and lastly, Yours Truly, who when relating a monologue, forgot his lines halfway through, but was gratefully saved by the curtain, lights out and the air-raid siren and whilst groping my way off stage, the audience bolted into the compound as fast as they could to watch the searchlights, Flak and the poor blighters aloft who were being shot at.

After the raid, which was on Berlin, the concert made a brave attempt to continue and, on the whole taking into consideration it was the first, with very little in the way of props, costumes and other aids, it was a great success.

Our conjurer was without doubt the best artist of the night who, when we were talking it over later, made a boast that there was not a lock in Germany he could not open. Somebody shouted, 'bullshit!' and said if he was such a Houdini what the hell was he doing in a POW camp. Ironically, a few weeks later he escaped, or should I say, he left us and went home, because no one knew how he got out of the camp nor when, he just disappeared. A couple of months later the commandant had a letter, postmarked from

England, from him saying he had thought it time to do his disappearing act (at the worst time of the year with snow on the ground). No one else was involved, and he wished him and us all the very best of British luck. He was the only man I know of who 'made it'.

A stroke of luck I had at this time was during one evening when a few of us in the room were showing each other some photo snaps. From a group of soldiers taken somewhere in Egypt, I picked out an old friend of mine, Tom Caselli. Tom and I had 'joined up' at the same time way back in 1936–7, when we had joined the Queen's Own Yorkshire Dragoons TA.

I had been under age, but with the aid of the Permanent Staff Instructor and my brother, I had managed to take the King's Shilling, and later joined the Regular Army when I was 18.

To my delight, I learnt my friend Tom was also a POW in the other Dabendorf Camp, He, having joined the newly formed Middle East Commandos and having landed on Crete during the Blitz, was taken prisoner not so very far away from myself. We must have passed each other many times during the rearguard actions.

The first thing I did was to scribble a short brief note to be passed on to Tom via our MO on his next visit to his camp. It was not long before I had a reply and from then on we kept up a regular correspondence.

One Sunday morning, Tom managed to come to our camp with a fatigue party, it was a happy reunion for we had a lot to say to each other.

In the same fatigue party was none other than our old friend, Ginger Connelly, looking as belligerent as ever. The first question from Ginger was to ask the whereabouts of a certain little fat warrant officer, whom one would have thought he was especially fond of. On being told he lived in the end room on the left, in A block, with five others, Ginger went marching along the corridor shouting, 'Come out you little fat so and so, where are you, come out and fight.' He banged hard on the door with his fist shouting for the lot of them to come out, but the only reply was a chorus of 'F— offs'.

Luckily, the door was locked on the inside, other heads now appeared at each doorway along the corridor to see what all the commotion was about. And as a few men went along to quieten Ginger down and get him out of the block, the guard came running along, rifle at the ready and ordered him outside.

For once in his life Ginger obeyed the guard but not without booting the door and shouting, 'I'll be back, you little bastard, I'll be back,' and then walking out of the block laughing all over his face, There was never a dull moment with him.

Christmas was getting near now; it was definitely going to be a white one, snow was falling, it was very cold and there was no doubt we were in for a bad winter.

Work, however, was still going on to the bitter end, They were blasting in the sand quarries and having one hell of a time unloading the frozen tip skips, the only consolation being we were not working as long because of the very short daylight hours.

Our job also continued through thick and thin. The foundations had been laid in very difficult conditions through mud and rain. And now, in the ice and snow, the brick walls of a circular building were taking shape. But it became so cold and we were so exposed to the elements out in the fields that we split up into two parties in company with the Germans, and whilst one party worked for one hour, the other party thawed out around the stove in the hut.

We had managed to get several brief glimpses at the drawings of the building which looked like some type of electric sub-station. I suppose it was nice to know what was going on, but really we had not much interest in the job nor were we particularly bothered whether it was a sub-station or the Leaning Tower of Pisa.

Preparations for Christmas were coming on well, another concert party was rehearsing, various and numerous 'props' were taking shape, we were even getting some better lighting and different colours of paint, all due to the interest and efforts of the camp commandant.

The camp now boasted of a well-established Red Cross parcel storeroom, properly shelved out to hold about 400 parcels. Each barrack hut had its own portion of shelving to hold its own parcels, with each individual's POW number written on the end of a parcel.

A roster was in force, enabling the members of each barrack hut to draw whatever was required from the parcels on several evenings per week. Each tin had to be opened and inspected by a couple of German guards (just to make sure there were no weapons or escape materials concealed in them).

The door to the Red Cross parcel store had two locks, the keys of one lock being held by the Germans and the other key held by our Red Cross representative, *der Vertrauensman*. This man, no matter who he was or what his rank was, was elected by the whole of the camp for his honesty and integrity in dealing with the Germans and us, hence *Vertrauensman*, man of confidence or better known by us as the confidence man. If he did not do his job right or got into 'fiddles', he was sacked and someone else elected in his place.

For Christmas we were issued with special Christmas parcels, one each, without them even being opened. It was wonderful to hold a parcel in one's own hands, to have to cut the string and delve into the packing to see what was in it.

On Christmas Day we were off work, but were up early doing the usual cleaning chores and making our own preparations for Christmas dinner. We were also getting extra rations in the way of bread and potatoes from the Germans.

I well remember the camp commandant paying us a visit during the morning. He came into A block first, going to each room in turn accompanied by the hut NCO.

There was no accompanying guard to shout '*Achtung*' into each room, as was the rule. Our hut NCO entered first to say, 'camp commandant', whereupon we would stop whatever we were doing and stand up to attention, paying our proper respects to an officer, which was his right.

The commandant would say, of course in German, 'A Merry Xmas, please carry on', whereupon we would return the compliment and offer him a British cigarette or a piece of chocolate, which was always refused.

In fact by the time he got halfway round the hut, he was so overcome by the scene before him that he took out his handkerchief and, mopping his eyes, left the hut in a hurry. Still, I suppose some Germans were sensitive enough to have such feelings and were not ashamed to show them.

The concert party was a great success this time with no air raids to disrupt it. We had a session of carol singing to end the show and, having the Germans present in the audience, the carols had been carefully selected and the Germans had also joined in singing, enjoying it as much as anyone.

It had been a good day as days went in a POW camp. It would have been much worse without the Red Cross parcels.

Christmas came and went and New Year's Eve arrived. We all assembled in the compound in one huge circle just before midnight and on the stroke of midnight we joined hands and sang *Auld Lang Syne*. It was a moving scene all standing out there in the deep snow with the camp perimeter lights on and a pale watery moon showing through. As I got back to bed, I prayed damned hard for the war to end soon and put an end to all this strife.

The year 1941 had been another disastrous one for our side, the news was bad all round. Just about the whole of Europe, from the Baltic to the Balkans, the shores of the Mediterranean and in north Africa, nearly to Alexandria, was held by the Germans. They were also well into Russia; their fronts and lines of communications were thousands of miles long. We had heard that the Japanese had attacked Malaya, Pearl Harbor, the Philippines and Hong Kong in early December. Yes, things looked very black indeed.

Chapter 6

Lager 520 Grossbeeren 1942

Our first winter in Germany was a complete and utter swine. For the past six months the Germans had treated us no better than animals, we lived like animals and acted like animals. It was all part of the Nazi processing machine to lower the resistance of their adversaries and then keep them knuckled under by either making them work hard or confining them in miserable living conditions and always hungry to a point near starvation.

But with the coming of our first Red Cross Food parcels, we found a glimmer of hope. These parcels weighing no more than about nine or ten pounds, so well thought out and so well packed with a stable nutritious diet, were to be the mainstay of our very existence.

During January and February, it was so cold that it was a physical impossibility for us to go out to work on the normal job on the railway, but we were often sent out in gangs snow shovelling and of course our own camp area had to be kept clear of snow.

One day a rumour flew round the camp that we were all going to be moved to another working camp, and a few days later the same news came that our neighbouring camp was also going to move. There was talk about working in factories and it was always amongst food; the wishful thinkers had it that we were going to be put in small groups to work on farms. It was all a lot of gossip which I am sure was often started by the Germans to give us something to talk and think about. Finally, the truth came out, we were soon to move to another railway working camp at Grossbeeren, 12 miles south of Berlin and our friends in the other camp were going to a similar camp at Teltow 2 miles nearer Berlin than us.

In fact, we were not so very far away from Grossbeeren and some of our men had actually helped to build the new camp we were going to, but obviously did not know this at the time.

The day came when we moved by train with all our worldly possessions – which could just about be carried in our greatcoat pockets. We alighted at Grossbeeren and marched off in batches of about 100 to our new camp.

Herr Feldwebel Montag and Herr Reichbahn Lager Feurher Schulze stood near the German guardroom just inside the entrance of the new camp we now approached. The usual steel-helmeted, fully equipped sentries were on duty at the main gate whilst others paraded the 'bunny-run' around the perimeter of the camp.

Once inside the gate and into the German compound we all paraded to hear Herr Montag's speech of 'welcome'.

He stood out in front of us, a tall, middle-aged, thin-faced Wehrmacht sergeant with a serious expression and very cold eyes. He called for silence and then putting his right hand inside of his tunic, Napoleon style, and standing with his jack-booted feet apart said, in German, 'I am Herr Feldwebel Montag the camp commandant, and my orders in this camp will be obeyed, you are prisoners of war and under direct command of the German army, any breaches of discipline will be dealt with by Court Martial!'

The man standing by his side, equally as tall, dressed in an immaculate black uniform with highly polished riding boots and smart peak cap with yards of gold braid and sporting the Nazi swastika on his right arm, was then announced as Herr Reichbahn Lager Feurher Schulze. He immediately sprang to attention, flung up his right arm in the Nazi salute and shouted 'Heil Hitler' whereupon some bright Herbert in the rear of our assembly shouted 'Heil Churchill'. There was one hell of a titter went round the ranks with the Germans shouting, 'No one is allowed to make fun of our beloved Führer,' and someone else shouted 'arseholes'. It was all so damned funny; it had started off as a serious address and the whole business was suddenly through, with Schulze – who was nothing more than a Quartermaster – strutting off back to his barrack hut and Montag giving the orders for us all to go through the usual search procedure before being allowed to pass through to our own compound and our new quarters.

The searching got underway. I was not looking forward to it as I had something, if caught with, I would be for the high jump good and proper. (My feet certainly wouldn't touch the ground.)

During our last few days at Dabendorf, I had been staring at the ceiling above my bed one night when I wondered if the panelling was movable. Even just kneeling on the bunk, I could reach the ceiling easily, so I tried to move the small corner panel, about 18 x 24 inches in size. To my amazement it moved quite easily, letting in a very cold draught of fresh air. The previous occupants must have done this to provide fresh air at night when the windows, shutters and main doors to the huts were locked.

Standing up with my head and shoulders through the hole I felt around inside not knowing what I might find. My fingers searched every inch between the rafters as far as I could reach and my reward was a small tin box about 5 inches long by 1½ inches broad and ¾ inch deep. I searched the remainder of the space then ducked back inside the room replacing the panel after me, making sure there were no finger marks showing on the underside

Back on my bunk I opened the tin box to find half a dozen 4-inch long very fine files; round, square, half round, flat and triangular, oh boy what a find, these would come in most useful.

On leaving Dabendorf, I had wondered whether to leave them back in their original hiding place or to chance taking them with me to the new camp knowing quite well we would be put through the usual stringent search procedure. But at the eleventh hour I decided on the latter; my only problem was where to hide them.

I was filling my water bottle prior to the move when the penny dropped. I bound them with bandage and tied them with thin string and dropped them inside the small neck of the water bottle, one by one. It was ten to one the Germans would not look twice at the water bottle hanging from my waistbelt. But if they did! Oh to hell with it, so what.

When it came my turn, one guard searched my pack, haversack and greatcoat whilst another one searching me just lightly shook my water bottle hanging at my side and detected nothing. I felt a bit hot under the collar and, hoping I did not have a guilty look, passed through undetected on the command, *weiter-machen* (proceed), much to my relief.

Alex Morrison and I went into B block, first room on the right and again a double-tier bunk by the window. This was a smaller room than previously and held only fourteen men. These were brand spanking new huts, they smelled clean and fresh, the paper-filled mattresses and three blankets were new. This was indeed splendid and gave a big boost to our somewhat low morale. There were four barrack huts standing in line and lettered A.B.C.D. A hut held the camp staff, doctor and medical orderly and the small overflow from the other three barrack huts which held over 100 men in each. Each barrack hut had a corridor running full length down the centre with a stout door at each end and, as in our last camp, all windows had shutters which could be fastened from the outside. In the centre of each block was a boilerhouse with ablutions, showers and toilets, but these toilets could only be used at night; during the day the usual deep trench latrine was provided. Surrounding the whole camp area was the usual heavily barbed wire fence, sentries and Alsatian dogs. All in all, the quarters were very good and far better than some I had been in, in the British army.

We were always very hungry and it was a devil trying to keep warm during this freezing winter. The first thing we did on entering our new home was to look for something to burn in the square, upright metal stove which stood in the corner on the left, just inside the door of our room. Our ration of coal briquettes was tiny, there being seven lying at the foot of the stove, just a half each for fourteen men. There was no paper or wood to start the fire with, we wouldn't find anything outside because the whole place was covered in deep snow. So, we turned, as we had done before, to our bed boards. The first two men gave one each and the others would be called upon to do so, in turn, at a later date. Shredded paper was produced from a palliasse and a fire was soon lit and burning merrily, thawing us out and making our lot a bit more cheerful.

During the next few days there was some shuffling around of men between rooms and blocks trying to find the best mates to be with. It was a great difficulty trying to fit oneself into a room to live in harmony and unison with the other occupants. We did not stay within groups of our own units. Our room for instance comprised RE, RASC, Gunners, Argylls, Black Watch and an Australian, and for many months we got on reasonably well together.

The Germans soon had us working, however. It would have been most inefficient of them to have left us alone for more than a day or so. We were now well and truly part of their *Arbeitsamt* labour exchange and *Arbeitsdienstpflicht* compulsory labour service.

Lofty Rowsell and his pal, Jock, being medical orderlies, were transferred to Lager 404 at Teltow where they were put in charge of the sick bay. I was sorry to see them go, but they were not far away and we were able to keep in touch with each other.

We still kept our small working party together but without Emil our guard. We had a new guard now and we went to work at a granary at Litchefelde near the large railway marshalling yard just past Teltow on the way in to Berlin. The new guard, like all new brooms, asserted his authority on the first morning he came to collect us, shouting for the '*Kornboden Kommando*' at the top of his voice, hustling us out of the camp and down the road through the snow to catch the 5.45 a.m. passenger train which would drop us off at Litchefelde. Once there, we trudged across the marshalling yard to the granary to be met by the German in charge.

There were five Germans working here and all pretty old codgers at that. The whole place was under blackout and only dimly lit. We were put to work unloading heavy sacks (whatever they were) from railway vans and wheeling them into the building for stacking.

Stacking was a problem for we were much too weak for two of us to lift them above shoulder height, on to the stack to one of the Germans who completed the stacking. We soon created a hold up and the guard who had been watching the unloading from the vans came in to see why.

He bullied and pushed and showed us how he, one solitary German could easily toss a full sack on to the pile, then he stood back and urged us to get moving again. The next thing he did was to storm off in search of the man in charge, and both of them returned talking quite voluminously and with much gesticulating.

To our immense relief, the man in charge spoke to us in reasonably good English and we were able to explain to him just why we were so weak. He looked in disbelief when we told him we had no food with us and it would be at least 6.30 p.m. before we would get anything on our return to camp. We had only been on the job one hour but the work had to be done and there were many more hours of drudging work to be done. He left us by saying he would try and get us some potatoes for lunchtime, so with a parting word to the guard, stormed off to his office.

Our guard then promptly transformed into a different man altogether, slinging his rifle across his back and helping us with the stacking. We took turns at stacking, emptying the railway vans and wheeling. It was a matter of keeping moving to keep warm for it was just as cold inside the building as it was outside.

As the day became lighter, we took more notice of our surroundings, there being a small rail siding which fed the granary unloading bay where we were now working, and another rail siding into a loading bay to receive the produce after processing. The whole area was ringed by a high chain link fence.

By lunchtime we were well and truly exhausted; it had been a long gruelling morning and we did not have enough strength nor the will for much more. But true to his word the man in charge sent for us, and although he had not been able to produce the potatoes, he had a loaf of bread and some sausage meat already cut up to give us a portion each.

We were ravenously hungry and very thankful for what we received, and told him so. It certainly helped to fill the hole in our stomachs and see us through the afternoon, which, thank goodness was a short one, for after we had loaded a couple of rail vans we were allowed to pack up and go back to camp.

That night back in camp, after we had cleaned ourselves, had our hot, dirty, potato stew and drawn our dry rations for the day, we talked about the different jobs we had all been on. Some had been snow-shovelling, some unloading timber sleepers at a railway siding, some unloading swedes (and many a one stolen and smuggled back into camp), some had been working near the local bakery which had been profitable, and so on.

Inevitably, our WOs and senior NCOs heard all this and quickly reorganised the working parties. One of them came round to tell our gang that we were detailed for snow shovelling the next day and others were told similar tales. The Forty Thieves were going to make sure they were going to have the jobs where there was a good chance of getting some food and working indoors. There were many rows and threats, even a few scuffles and punch ups which ended with promises of charge sheets and court martials after the war. But there was nothing more we could do that night; we would have to wait and see what happened in the morning.

The next morning prompt at 5.30 a.m. our guard of the previous day shouted through the hut door for the *Kornboden Kommando*. Then to his utter amazement out dashed six WOs and sergeants, nearly knocking him over in the process. He soon protested saying volubly this wasn't his gang and he did not want six Feldwebels.

The British interpreter tried to tell him the gangs had been changed but he wasn't having this and came into the hut in search of us, telling us to be quick about it or else we would miss the train. But one of the sergeants tagged on with us insisting he was in charge of the party and again the guard didn't like this as he felt it undermined his authority, but he condescended owing to his haste to get us to the train on time.

There was not one word spoken on the train or across the marshalling yards to our place of work. But once inside the granary, the guard reported straight away to the man in charge who, after we had been detailed to our jobs, sent for two of us and asked us what the upset was all about. We told him, we were quite honest about it, whereupon he said he would deal with the matter.

This man, whose name we never got to know, seemed to have a definite air of authority. The other Germans jumped to it when he spoke, our guard was most respectful to him, and no one said a word when he had produced the bread and sausage meat for us. Maybe he was a Nazi party man or some reserve officer, but whatever he was, he was definitely going to have things the way he wanted them. He phoned the camp and spoke to Herr Montag and seemed to do all the talking. When he had finished, he simply turned to us telling us quietly that we wouldn't have any more to worry about in future, the sergeant wouldn't be with us tomorrow and he would have to do his share of the work today and if he didn't, he wouldn't get any of the 'food' at lunchtime. So that was that.

There was no doubt about it, the whole camp would have to do something about the Forty Thieves. The senior officer in the camp was the medical officer who kept to himself and wouldn't have anything to do with the running of the camp. It must have been obvious even to him what was going on but he just turned a blind eye to it.

Our small gang began to settle down to a regular routine, not only to travelling to and from the granary but also at work, which we were getting used to, and found that with the little extra food we were getting at work and the occasional Red Cross Parcel to supplement our German camp rations, we were gradually becoming stronger. Everyone in the camp now seemed to be getting rid of the lice which had plagued us for months, there was also more British clothing coming through to us of which we were in dire need.

One morning during our train ride to work, some young schoolboys who were also travelling into Berlin asked our guard if they could sit near us to try out their English, which they were learning at school. They tried out their book-learnt phrases, some being more guttural than others; it was a change and diversion for us and they were always most polite and correct in their manners, doffing their caps when bidding us 'Good morning', and a click of the heels and a flung-up right arm with a 'Heil Hitler', for the guard.

After boarding as usual one morning and starting their English lessons, one little boy stood up and blurted out, 'I say, you English are taking a thrashing, aren't you?' 'Yes,' one of our number said, 'It does look that way just now, but did he not know that Great Britain always won her last battle.' He was rather taken aback with this and said he did not know, but would consult his teacher about it. We never heard what happened; it was never mentioned again.

It was still extremely cold with snow on the ground and whilst picking our way carefully over the lines of the marshalling yard we came across an old man who was very poorly clad and with sacking tied round his shoes to keep his feet warm. He was a Jew and wore a yellow star of David on the lapel of his coat and one on his back. His job was to pick away at the ice between the railway points, then oil them and make them function.

Speaking in excellent English, he told us he had been an eminent surgeon until the Nazis had thrown him out, making him work on these sorts of manual jobs, and his wife and children had been taken away to a concentration camp he knew not where. He had no doubts as to his ultimate fate after his usefulness as a manual labourer was ended, he would be sent without option to an extermination camp.

We found this incredibly hard to believe, but then the words of Carl, the blond one, came back to me, 'All Jews must die.' This Jew had no fear of the future, he had resolved himself to his fate in an almost calm, matter of fact attitude brought on by many, many months of suffering and utter despair that there was simply no other way out. There was so little we could do to help him, but we did manage to give him some chocolate, a piece of English soap and a few cigarettes.

Next to our camp at Grossbeeren, about ¾ mile away, was another old hutted camp which had at one time housed German railway workers. Now it was a Political Prisoners Straf Camp, (Punishment Camp). The jailers of this camp were the dreaded SS (Schutz-Staffel). We could see the camp clearly from ours. Inmates for this camp usually arrived in twos and threes accompanied by a fit young SS trooper who would chase them at the 'double', belting them with a dog whip all the way from getting off the railway train at Grossbeeren to the camp. Once at the camp, they would be stripped of all their belongings and clothing and given the horrible coarse ill-fitting yellow- and black-striped prison garb with flat peakless cap to match and footwear of wooden Dutch clogs

They were terribly ill-treated and purposely kept very much underfed. Some of them were made to work in the fields between our camp and theirs, working in long lines to dig the fields over by hand. When one of their working parties passed our camp en route for work (usually before we marched out to work) we could see the look of utter despair and fear of their jailers on their faces. We thought we were badly done to, but our camps must have been luxury compared to theirs. They were often seen arriving but I can never remember any of them departing.

It is all very well for Germans to say, after the war, that they did not know what was going on but they must have done, it was all around them daily. Everything about the Germans appeared grim in these early days, we did not see any smiling people. Maybe this was because of our present grim environment and perhaps we were seeing through malicious eyes towards our captors and of course the bitterly cold winter did not help.

The Germans we worked with at the granary were old and a miserable lot, they very seldom spoke unless it was of work. But one of them, a badly deformed hunchback, used to sidle up to us and looking from side to side to make sure no other person was in ear-shot whispered over and over again to us, '*Hitler scheissen, nicht gut*', in other words: 'Hitler shithouse, no good.' The next time he came along he would repeat the same of the other members of Hitler's hierarchy. Maybe as a cripple he had a grudge against them and their regime for making him work so hard.

Of the others there is only one worth mentioning. He was a tall 6-footer well over 70 years of age, always had a long, grim face, stooped a little and very seldom spoke to us. His occupation was catching mice, attending to the blackout blinds – of which there were many – cleaning out the office and toilets, making the ersatz coffee and boiling our spuds.

He had dozens of the most ingenious mouse traps, which he placed at strategic points, and needed a wheelbarrow to collect up his dead mice each morning, then he took them outside and destroyed them in an incinerator. We thought we would boost his production figures by making sure there was plenty of meal scattered about in places that he could not possibly get at and also in any mouse holes we found.

Also, while we were at the granary it was necessary for us to steal whatever we could in the way of anything edible. Sometimes it was lentils, other times peas, beans, barley or oats; we would take a pocketful, hoping to get back into camp without being searched. Sometimes there would be a snap search when the Kommandos were returning from work, which would reveal all sorts of items from bread to coal and even rabbits.

We devised cleverly made cloth bags to fit under our armpits and on the inside top of our coat sleeves so that when the searchers began, we simply lifted our arms obediently and nothing was found.

The cold harsh winter was now beginning to give way to spring; a thaw set in, the many dirt roads in the area turned to quagmires and our camp being built upon sand became a sea of mud. Our days at the granary were now numbered because as the better weather came every man possible in our camp would be put to work on the new railway embankment construction.

We were also determined to do something about the WOs and sergeants whom we wanted to get rid of. We would be much better off without them and after many meetings and debates we decided unanimously on a vote of non-co-operation and to make life as difficult as we could for them. This was gradually achieved by taking no notice whatsoever of those who went out with the working parties and thought they were just going to stand and watch us work while they toadied to the gangers and guards.

To those on the camp staff we would do everything possible to delay parades for work and the evening muster parade, and on Sundays to make sure that the cleaning and polishing of our rooms and ourselves were late for the camp commandant's weekly inspection. We would do anything to make it difficult for them and to get them in bad books with the Germans. Eventually and inevitably, we won.

One fine day in the summer of 1942, there was a mass exodus of the Forty Thieves from our camp for the sanctuary of a non-working camp, to which they were entitled to go. There were no farewells or goodbyes, for we were glad to see the back of them. They left behind about four or five sergeants whom we considered were honest and worthy of running the camp. From this time on we saw a great change for the better in our camp. On the same day as they left and as we marched back into the camp after our long day's work, though we were tired and weary, it felt as if an awful dark cloud above us had blown away. Similar proceedings had also taken place at Teltow camp and our other camp at Genshagen.

There were not many, if any, Oxford accents with us, nor had we any 'Dons', nor were there any university lecturers, professors or professional men except our medical officer, but there arose from our midst the true leaders, some remarkable talent, wonderful ingenuity and an *esprit de corps* second to none which still prevails today when we meet. There is something about the feelings towards one another of ex-POWs which is so different and genuine from any other walk of life. Maybe it is because we were forced by circumstances beyond our control to start off with nothing and after several years of living as guests of the Nazis and finishing up with nothing, we can still meet each other on equal terms after thirty years and speak the same language as we did then.

Those wonderful Red Cross food parcels were now rolling in, in sufficient quantities to enable us to have one per week and with each, a tin of fifty cigarettes. We were also gradually getting in more British army clothing, footballs and football boots, musical instruments, books and many indoor games, all from the great organisation, the Red Cross.

Herr Feldwebel Montag was typical of the Prussianised German soldier we had always been led to believe existed from our forebears, from the First World War. He was always stiff and starchy. I cannot remember ever seeing him smile or showing any kind thought, word or deed towards us. He was immensely jealous and annoyed with the thought of us getting all these Red Cross parcels and could not believe his eyes when the first batch of personal parcels from our next of kin arrived. His code of conduct of which he was unbendable was, *Dienst ist Dienst und Befehl ist Befehl*, Duty is Duty and Orders are Orders.

Reichbahn Führer Schultz was certainly no better. He definitely had the Nazi doctrine stamped into him with indelible ink; his heart was as black as the uniform he wore. At the least provocation he delighted in joining Montag in imposing petty penalties on us, which was often. His favourite penalty was to cut our rations and to make sure that the potato soup or the carrot soup had all the dirty peelings in it and dished it up no better than pig swill. We had to strain it the best we could before we could eat it.

But we were gradually getting stronger every week, we were not now quite so hungry, we could even afford to take a bit of food out on to the job for our midday meal. We were better clothed and consequently began to take more pride in our turn out.

Sunday morning became a real spit and polish day. The barrack blocks and ourselves were ready for inspection on time. We even held competitions to see who had the best turned-out and tidiest room for the week. The Germans of course were delighted with our *Sauberkeit*, cleanliness, and were stupid enough to think that they were the cause of it. They were most annoyed when we told them we were preparing for our day of liberation.

We soon found that there were certain items in our Red Cross food parcels that the Germans coveted, such as Nescafé, cocoa, chocolate, soap, tea, etc. Their coffee was ersatz, whilst cocoa, chocolate, tea and our Lux toilet soap was simply unheard of; they had not seen any for years. Their cigarettes were so inferior to ours and their soap was a latherless, scentless block of rubbish, with which they somehow managed to keep clean.

So started a huge black-marketing trade between us and the guards and anybody else we came in contact with. We did not want money, we mainly wanted bread, of which we never had enough. Any of the aforementioned items would be exchanged for a 2,000g loaf of bread.

This of course led to another game with the guards and our railway gangers and even that Nazi bastard Schultz, by the way of blackmail. We became very adept in this art as a matter of necessity for our own comforts for they were terrified of being found out as black-marketeers. They knew the penalty for being found out was the 'chopper' or *Straf Kommando*, punishment detachment, on the Russian Front which was probably worse than the chopper.

Of course, there were very few exceptions, guards who would not trade at all, either because of their Nazi principles or because they were scared. These were usually the bullying type of guards, the unbendable ones, but we had other ways and means of dealing with them.

The bread usually found its way in when the guards were on night duty. They would sometimes bring it in just before the nightly check parade, or they would come round later and open a blackout shutter passing the bread through the window which we opened from the inside. (Montag insisted on the hut main doors and all blackout shutters being locked at night, a rule which he never relaxed.)

If the guards were on the 'bunny-run patrol' they would throw the loaf of bread over the wire fence to the man who awaited on the other side. One enterprising baker in the village brought forty to fifty loaves of bread in one go, when a certain guard was on duty, passing them through a specially selected part of the barbed wire fence on a long pole, he was very adept with the pole having long practised reaching and drawing bread out of his bakehouse ovens.

Of course, since most of this sort of carry on was done after dark, it meant we had to get out of the barrack blocks somehow and to the fence and back without being seen by other patrolling guards or seen from the Germans' quarters. The blackout shutters could be fixed so that we were able to open them from the inside after the nightly roll call and the guards had departed back to their own quarters. The perimeter lights were not always switched on at night, making it easier, although even with them on passage back and forth to the wire was not too difficult because there were no towers with wandering searchlights.

In selecting a place along the wire to operate, some favoured the furthest corner out of sight of the German quarters, others were for the nearest corner to their quarters, but still on the blind side; a lot depended on which barrack block one was working from – most important was to cover up our tracks afterwards.

I had started making keys with my valuable set of files. The patterns were the originals obtained by bribing and blackmailing the guards, to be 'borrowed' for a few hours, whilst correct sizes and dimensions were taken, then passed on to me to make. The pieces of metal I had to work with were not always very suitable and were difficult to fashion.

In the first six months I must have made a key for every lock in the camp, the padlock keys being the most difficult with having a hole down the middle. My main worry was hiding the box of files, and I had by now obtained a small hand vice. Searching of the huts was carried out frequently by Herr Montag, Schultz and company while we were at work and my tools found many and varied hiding places: under the floor; in the roof; buried outside the hut; placed in the lavatory cisterns; and even in a hole whittled down the inside of the corner post of a bunk bed, or in the underside recess underneath a stove. Needless to say, they were never found. One had also to be careful of informers as there were some men who would stop at nothing to fulfil their personal gains.

As the spring of 1942 arrived giving way to better and warmer weather after the most severe winter experienced around Berlin for many a year, my pal Jock wanted to move to another room. There was no upset between us or with anyone else in our room, but I did not want to move because it was a small room, when most other rooms were much larger with more men in them, and I got on reasonably well with those in it. So Jock swapped rooms with another, who took his bunk above mine. We were still in the same block and still stayed good friends throughout.

The newcomer, Len Walker, was a Marine infantryman who had also landed on Crete during the battle to help us out. He was tallish, well built, about 27 or 28 years old, one of the early Militia men, married, with a little boy about 3 years old. His home was Whitby, Yorkshire and he was a painter by trade. He and I soon became friends and decided to 'muck in' with each other, which we did for a long time.

Red Cross food parcels began to roll in more frequently, letters from home were arriving and the first personal clothing parcels arrived. More British uniforms, boots and socks were available for issue to replace our French clothing. A Church of England padre came to take up residence with us and later, Catholic padre.

The warrant officers, the majority of sergeants and some of the corporals moved off to a non-working camp. We were pleased to be rid of seniors; we could manage more than well enough without them. All these things helped to make our daily life more bearable. So began the foundations of one of the best-organised Stalags in Germany.

The two padres would visit the rooms to talk to us during the evenings. They held their church services on a Sunday and visited the other camps at Teltow and Genshagen. Their congregations were never very large, the majority of men had simply got out of the habit and had more material things to do, especially on a Sunday, the one day of rest. I have never bothered to remember their names.

Our job at the granary came to an end, as did other inside jobs which we had been assigned to during the winter. Every available man was now wanted on the railway construction. The German railway gangers were efficient at their jobs, there being no labour shortage and there being enough gangers to do the job. We gave most of them nicknames such as 'Mad Harry', a member of the original 'Brown Shirts' toughs who had been knocked about a bit and was as mad as a March hare. 'Cowboy' was another one, a tall, slightly bowlegged man who wore a large Stetson hat, while the 'Sheriff' was a short arse of a man who also wore a large Stetson, a three-quarter coat, trousers and leggings and sported a droopy moustache; we even made him a tin five-point star badge which he wore when at work and if he refused to wear it, we refused to work. Then there was 'Lofty' and 'Fatty' and 'Bomb-head'; others were called by their Christian names. 'Boxer' was a towering brute of a man who boasted he used to be a sparring partner to Max Schmelling. And so it went on.

Life inside the camp was taking better shape. Slowly but surely, we were obtaining recreational aids from the Red Cross, such as playing cards, chess games, draughts and dominoes, footballs and kit, books and musical instruments. We also managed to acquire a piano which cost some few thousand marks, collected around the camp, in POW money, which we had been paid for working. The money had then been legally changed into Reichsmarks and the piano was bought from some old dear in the village.

Herr Schultz, the strutting, arrogant black-suited Nazi that he was, had a thin veneer. Underneath he was bent, he could be bought, he would accept items out of the Red Cross parcels. He would like to have taken many a parcel but he was too well watched, he never got the chance. But nevertheless, we could, on occasions, wheedle things out of him if he thought he was also getting something out of it.

We made a football pitch just outside the main gates on some ground adjacent to the new railway embankment, the goal posts being acquired through bribery of the guards and gangers. It was a good pitch and used every Sunday, weather permitting, for a game in the morning and one in the afternoon, provided that Herr Montag was in a good mood and agreed to supply the necessary guards.

Jock Mackay, a sapper pal of mine, formed our first band out of a few harmonicas and a set of home-made drums. Ken Stow, an excellent pianist, would give recitals on a Sunday evening, for one hour only. He was so good, he always had a huge audience to whom he gave much pleasure.

Much later, in 1943, a Feldwebel, enquiring of Ken's ability to play so well, had a brilliant idea on learning that Ken had played a Wurlitzer organ in Birmingham before the war. He made arrangements to take Ken to a Wurlitzer in Berlin where he played before an audience of Stalag officers, whom he kept so enthralled with his music he was given a certificate to say that he was to be given light work and so protect his hands. Ken was proud of the certificate and was given a job in the camp picking up paper and general light work. He was worth it, but it is hard to believe such things were possible in Nazi Germany.

We were not, however, without our air raids. The RAF still managed to get as far as Berlin and more than once did we pick up used flare boxes in and around the areas where we worked. Listening to them coming over at night was like music in our ears. It was usually very late on when we were in bed. We would hear the distant sirens go, then our camp siren would wail out, whilst we lay quietly in our bunks listening to the sound of distant flak until the engines of the aircraft were audible above the much closer flak. Then we would hear the crunch of bombs, never thinking it was possible that maybe one day some of those bombs might fall on us.

'Oh,' said the wishful thinkers and the knowledgeable ones, 'the maps they have are all clearly marked showing exactly where our camps are and they wouldn't possibly bomb us.'

We really believed this and felt confident that we were safe. It also gave us the little bit of hope we needed and reminded us that although the air raids were infrequent, and that news from the fronts was not very good, we were still in the fight and, it was being delivered into the heart of Germany.

On the 19 August 1942, myself and one or two more POWs were working on a new road which had something to do with the railway system. At about midday, a French POW farm worker pedalled past on his bicycle and shouted that the Tommies had landed at Dieppe that very morning and this must be the second front, the invasion of Europe. Jumping with joy we told the guard and the ganger who simply would not believe it. But later news confirmed it was true, a landing had been made.

There was much merriment in the camp that night and speculation on how much longer the war was going to last. Alas, next day our hopes were dashed to the ground as we learned that the raid on Dieppe had been crushed. A force of about 5,000 Canadians with some Commandos had landed, backed up by the navy; they had very heavy losses, with about 2,000 prisoners. Another defeat, our hearts sank down to our boots. When would our side start to win? Our only consolation in those days was to hear the sound of the few aircraft penetrating the Berlin area and the deep satisfying rumbling of bombs exploding.

One Sunday, I was going through A Block to see one of the men in the staff room about something or other. On arrival, I found one of the cooks, Jimmy Wright, showing off his skill at hand balancing on the end of the table and assisting any would-be trier to have a go. Naturally, I was asked to have a go, and to Jim's amazement and delight I was able to do the balance without any assistance. Gymnastics had been a hobby of mine since starting it at the age of about 12 and I had carried it on in the early days in the army when the facilities were to hand. Jim asked me if I would start doing a bit in the canteen of an evening, but I honestly was not very keen, my excuse being I was not yet strong enough. Pooh-poohing my excuse, he promised there would be nothing too strenuous, we would take things gradually and he would see that I got the odd extra bowl of soup or potatoes or anything going 'baksheesh'.

A friendship was founded there and then, and we discussed the problem of equipment. We would have to make our own, and being a cook, he was able to flannel round Herr Schultz, whom he was sure could be persuaded to help.

We first acquired three palliasses which we filled with straw and fastened together into one long length to make a tumbling mat. Our next task was to build a set of parallel bars. Jim was able to procure the materials and tools through devious means, the construction being carried out in the huge dining hall adjacent to the cookhouse whilst a guard was present, because this part of the camp was outside of our own compound and actually part of the German compound. When we had finished our evening's work on

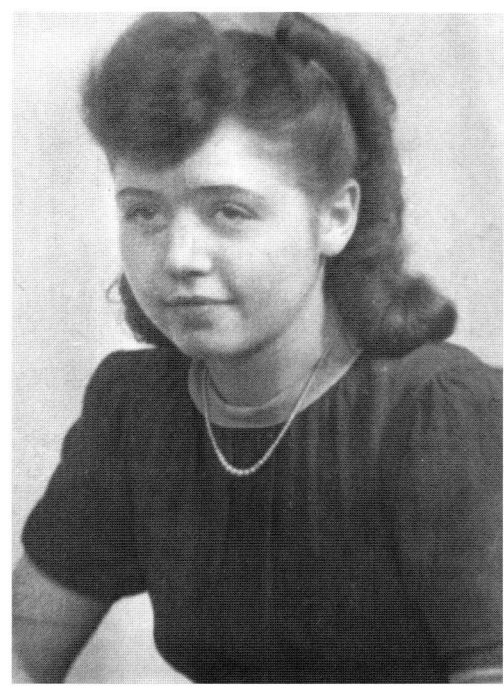

Above left: 1. *The Author 1945.*

Above right: 2. *Maria Sahm – Zwickau 1945.*

Right: 3. *Trooper T.B. Caselli 1945.*

Above: 4. *Sergeant Ali Riza Tewfik 1945.*

Left: 5. *Marine L.N. Walker 1943.*

6. *The author 1945.*

7. *The author 1945.*

8. *German parachutists before take off for Crete, May 1941.*

9. *German parachutists dropping over Canea-Suda area, May 1941.*

10. *German parachutists dropping over Canea-Suda area, May 1941.*

11. *One of the railway working parties taken with 'Mad Harry' the German ganger, near Grossbeeren.*

12. *POW Identity tag of author.*

13. *Record Card taken from German officer after liberation.*

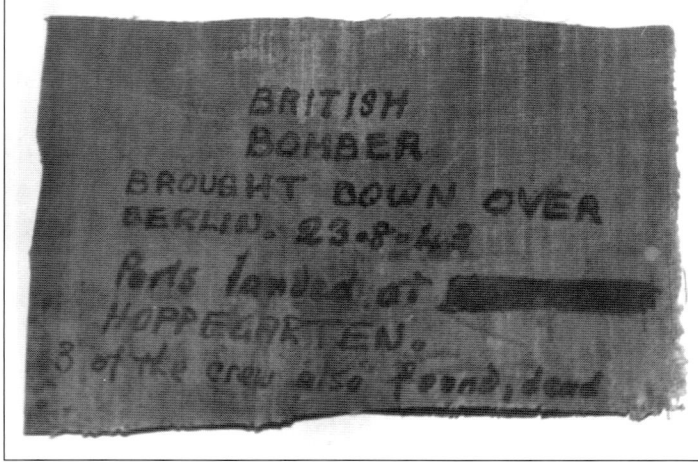

14. *A piece of an allied night bomber found at Hoppegarten, East of Berlin, 23.8.1943.*

Above: 15. *Prisoner of War Camp Money equal to 1 Reichsmark.*

Right: 16. *A one mark note exchanged for POW camp money 1944.*

17. *Paraboys Camp Zwickau I Working Party 1945.*

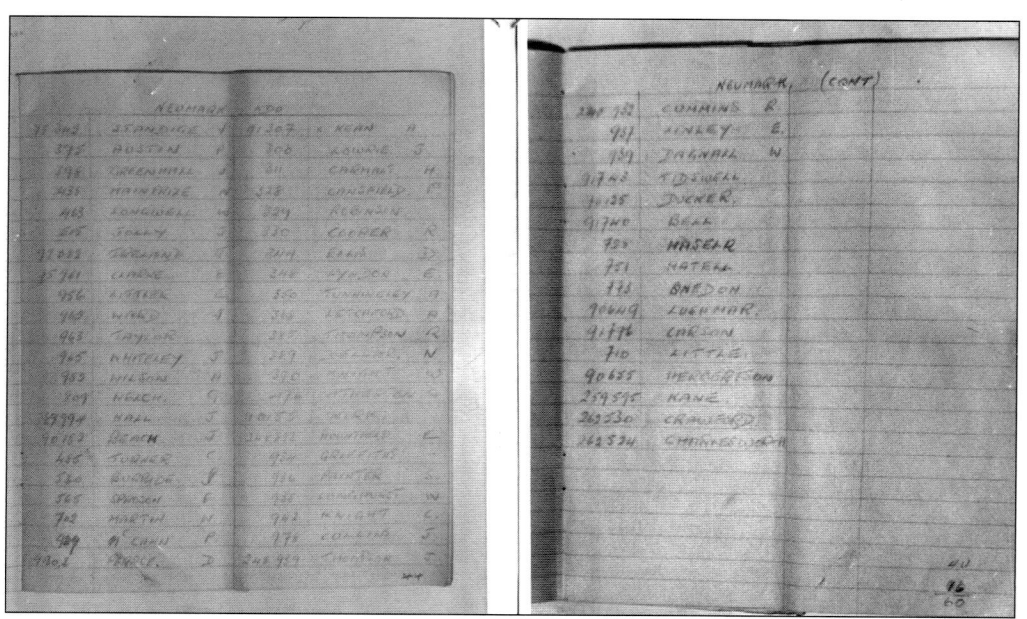

Left: 18. *Paraboys Camp, Zwickau II Working Party 1945.*

Below: 19. *Paraboys Camp Neumark Working Party 1945.*

20. *Paraboys Camp, Werdau Working Party 1945.*

21. *Paraboys Camp, Mosel Working Party 1945.*

```
                STAFF
  1131      SEED    J       CAMP LEADER.
  247467.   ORD.            MAN OF CON;
  12330     CASTELLI.       INTERPRETER
  90624     TRIM.           L. P.
  91436     SIMPSON.        L. P.
  90016     HUNT.           TAILOR.
  68        McGAUGE         SHOEMAKER.
  106       DIROLA.         BARBER.
  8577 H    PETCH.          COOK.
  249073    LANE.           COOK.
  91341.    NICHOLSON.      DINING ROOM.
  91162     FITZPATRICK.    COOK.
  91474     FITZGERALD.     SANITATOR.
  248935    POLLEY.         INTERP.
                                            14
  91876.    McDOUGALL.      SICK.            1

            14 Camp Staff.

                                            15
```

22. *Paraboys Camp Staff 1945.*

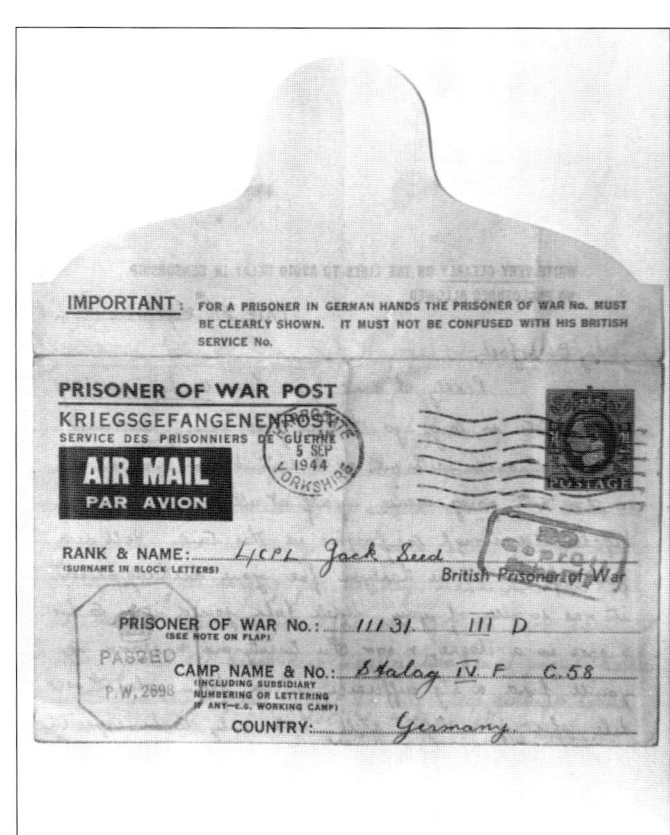

Right: 23. *Frontispiece of a POW lettercard.*

Below: 24. *Contents of a Next of Kin Parcel.*

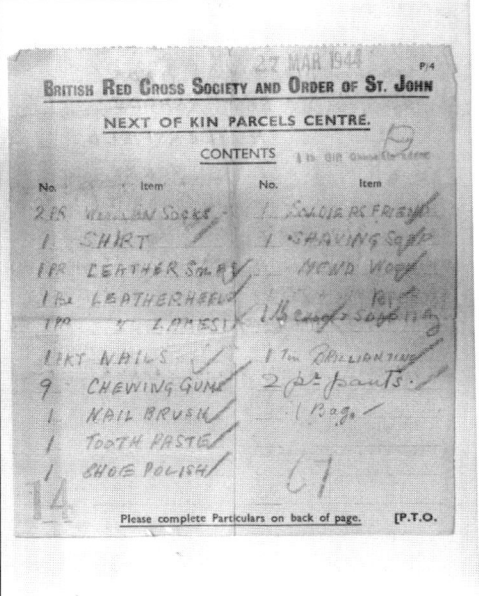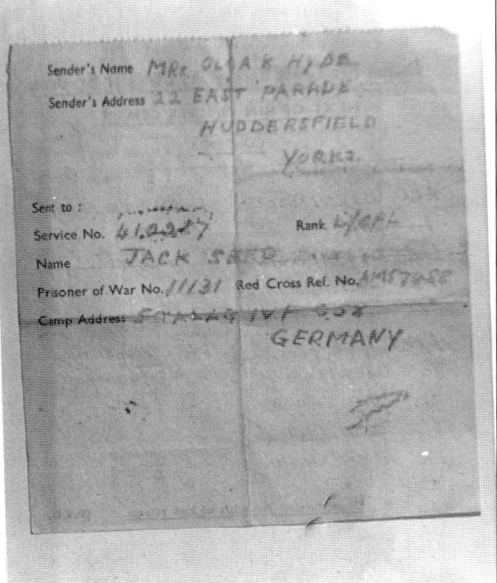

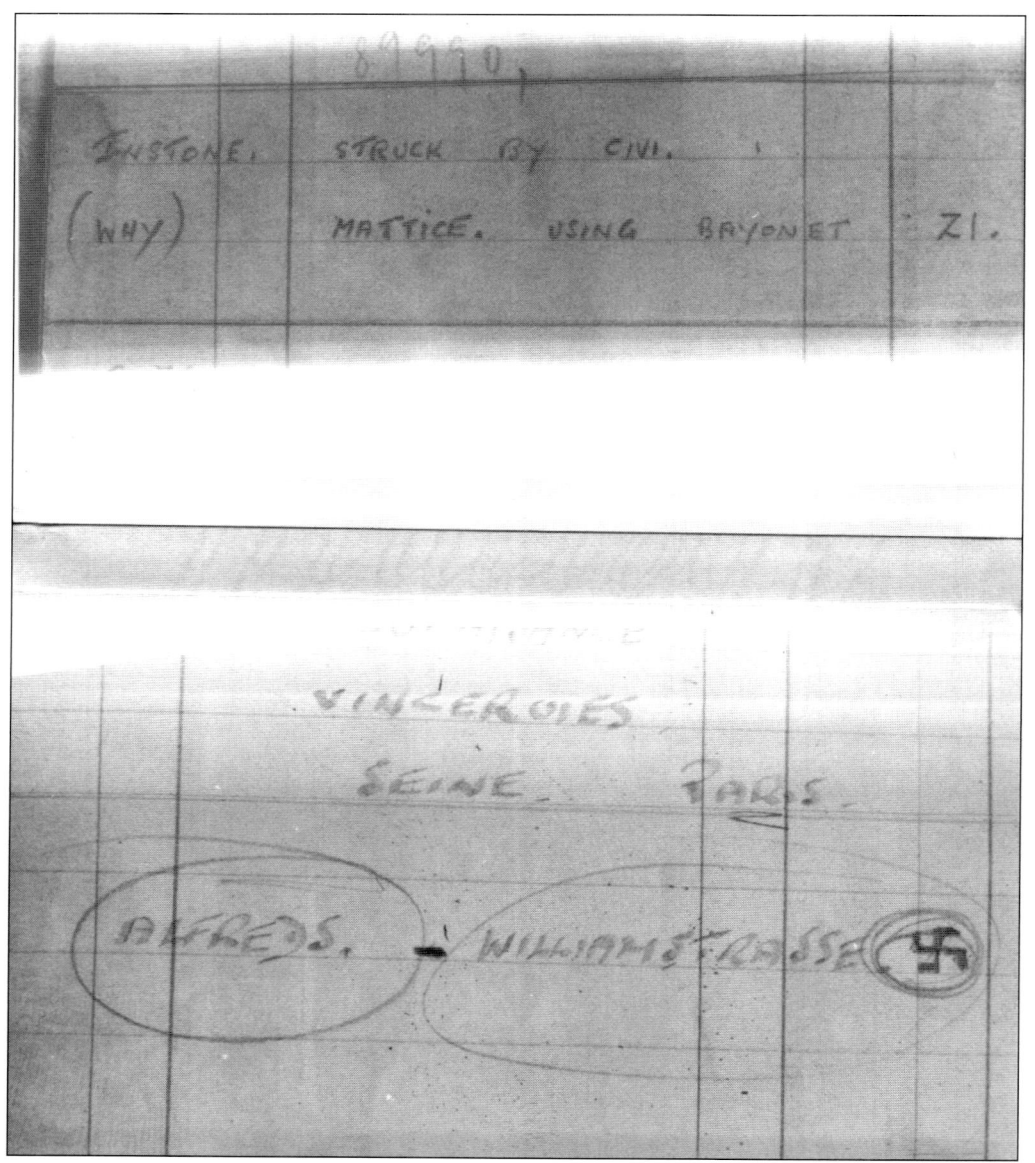

25. *Photographs of entries from author's notebook.*

Right: 26. *Some German Second World War Medals.*

Below: 27. *German Party Badges.*

28. *Other Nazi Party badges.*

G58, IVF. Crossen Horde.
Zwickau. Sax.
18.6.44.

SIR,

I BRITISH P.O.W. NO 11131, L/Cp. JACK SEED RE. HAVE TO REPORT, THAT ON THE NIGHT OF 17.6.44. I WAS ON DUTY IN THE RED CROSS STORE, ACCOMPANIED BY CPL. H. HAMMERTON (LAGER POLICE). WE WERE LOCKED IN, THE PADLOCKS BEING ON THE OUTSIDE. IN THE EARLY HOURS OF SUNDAY MORNING 18.6.44. WE HEARD THE LOCKS AND BARS BEING REMOVED. THE DOOR OPEN AND CLOSE, A LAMP SWITCHED ON TWICE. WE ARRESTED [SENTRY FISHER. POSTEN], IN THE BRIEF STRUGGLE THE BATTERY AND BULB FROM THE POSTEN LAMP FELL TO THE FLOOR. WE THEN INFORMED THE OTHER SENTRY ON NIGHT DUTY 3.35 A.M. WE AWOKE OBERGEFREITER SEIFERT, THE UNTER OFFICER, LANDY WAS CALLED AND THE CAMP INTERPRETER. SGN FRANK HOPE. ON RETURNING, TO THE STORE, 3.45 A.M. WE FOUND POSTENS FISHERS' RIFLE LEANING AGAINST THE WALL OF THE BUILDING 12 TO 15 YDS OPPOSITE THE STORE. THE SMALL LOCK WAS HANGING ON THE DOOR.

WITH KEY. THE KEY OF THE INDOOR TO THE KITCHEN BEING USED. THE LARGER LOCK WITH KEY ON THE GROUND. THE BATTERY AND BULB STILL ON THE FLOOR INSIDE THE STORE.

Jeed. J. No.51 IIID
L/Cpl. Royal Engineers

29. *Copy of the report of the Red Cross parcel affair.*

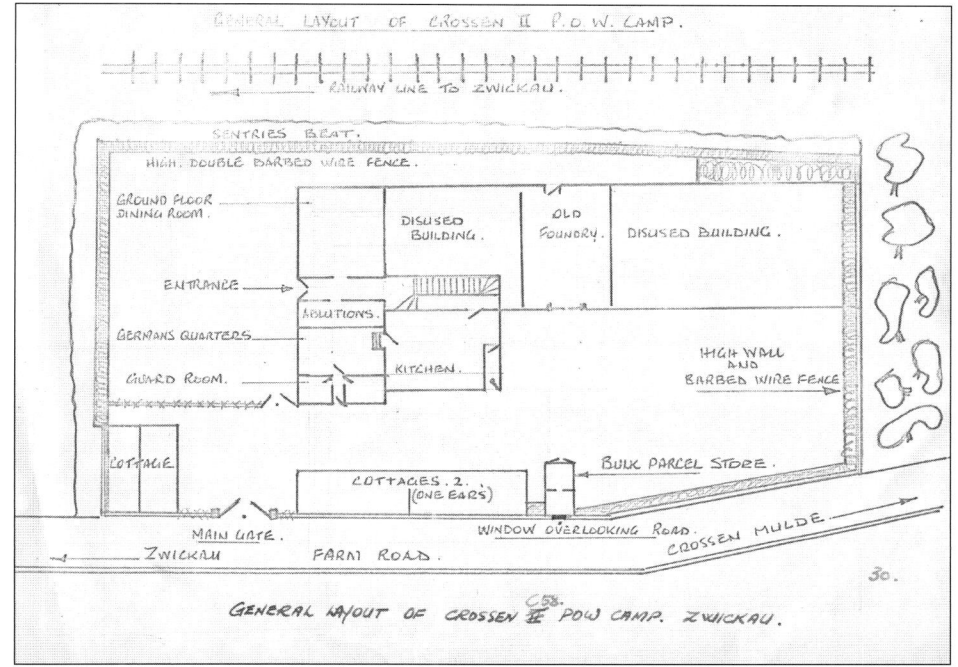

30. *General layout of Crossen C58 POW Camp Zwickau.*

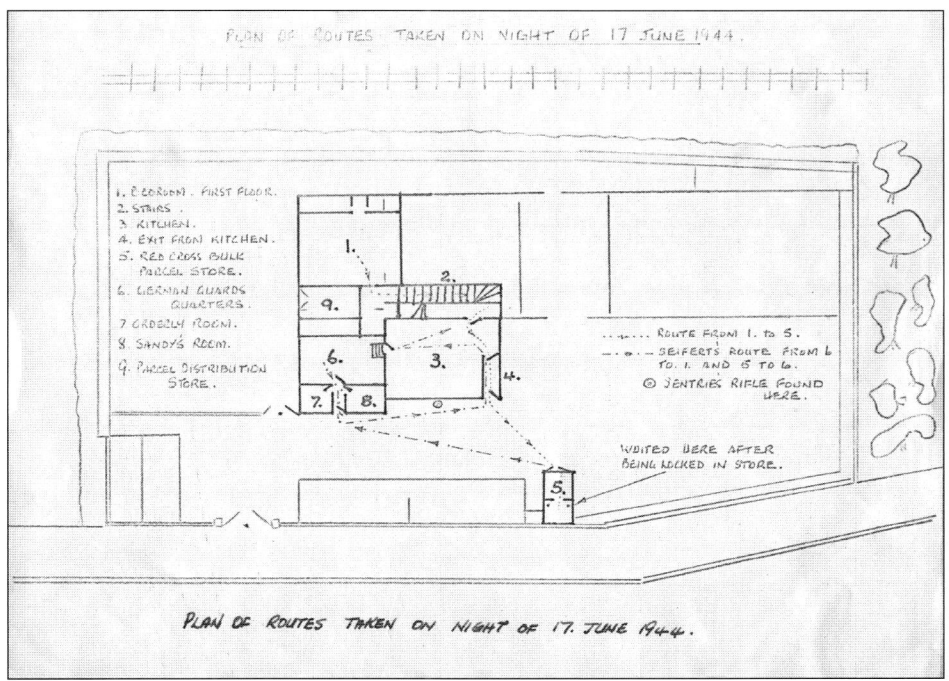

31. *Plan of routes taken on night of 17 June 1944.*

32. *Stalag III D British POW Camp 520 Grossbeeren, near Teltow, Berlin 1943.*

the equipment, the guard would see us back into our own compound (just before check parade), after locking up the dining hall.

Thus, we slowly manufactured our own equipment whilst still finding time to do some preliminary training. It gave us something other to do than the usual moping about the camp in the evenings. We now had something to look forward to of an evening, an aim, something to achieve, and we might be able to get others interested.

We next made a boxhorse, but came to grief falling foul of Schultz when we cut up an old tabletop we found lying against the kitchen wall for a springboard. Schultz played hellfire with us and the guard who was supposed to be looking after us, threatening us with Straf Lager. Straf Lager was a place to be dreaded, it being a punishment camp where harsh treatment was meted out by bullying thugs who had been taught their sadistic trade well. The Straf Lager was at Litchefelde where one started to do everything at the 'double' when arriving half a mile from the camp. Even the accompanying guards were glad to make a quick handover of prisoners and get to hell out of it.

One was sentenced by Order of Court Martial held by the Wehrmacht which one did not attend. A written order, stating that so and so had been found guilty of such and such a thing on such and such a date and was sentenced to so many days Straf under aggravated conditions, signed by order of General Von Eckenvort (I think that was the name), would be posted on the notice board and the offender unceremoniously led away.

The first three days was solitary confinement in a small cell 8ft by 4ft, with very little ventilation through a high grid in the wall, too high to see out of. An electric light shone all the time. The bed was hard wooden boards with pillow to match, one blanket and your greatcoat if you were lucky enough to have brought it with you.

Bread and water were shoved through a grid in the bottom of the door once a day. In the corner was an old dirty tin, without lid, for a lavatory. After the three days, one was hauled out to join in with the physical punishment. At some unearthly hour in the morning, an electric bell would ring bringing the inmates on to their feet to stand by for cell doors to open. One would stay fully dressed all the time except for boots which were left outside the door. Then it was boots on, grab some cleaning utensils, scrub out the cell, and corridor, clean the utensils and put them tidily away. Parade in the corridor with towel and soap etc., which were kept on a shelf outside the cell in the corridor and double away to the wash stands outside to get cleaned up.

For breakfast a mug of horrible black ersatz coffee. Pack drill with a 90lb pack twice a day where one had to 'double' shuffle somehow around a running track, with several sadistic Feldwebels pushing and kicking. Every so far around, one had to lay flat on the ground then get up again and continue the torturous shuffle. Much later in the day, one would get a piece of bread and another mug of horrible coffee.

This treatment went on until the last minute of the last day of the sentence, until a guard turned up at the gate where one was unceremoniously booted out, and both prisoner and guard would high tail it down the road as quickly as they could. On arrival back at the POW Lager, friends would soon have some food ready, the offender's Red Cross parcel having been saved for him.

We nevertheless carried on with our training, using the springboard which, although costly, was ideal for the job. We also got others interested and took P.T. classes, eventually finding three more for our gymnastics team.

Some thought we were stark raving bonkers, perhaps we were, but at least we kept ourselves reasonably fit and were able to entertain on the stage when there was a concert being held, by putting on a tumbling and balancing act. We also performed Indian club swinging, with clubs that had been dipped in white fluorescent paint. We became well known and were quite a success.

Books in the camp were a rarity. There were never enough to make a library, but keen swapping went on with the few books we did possess.

I had always liked poetry, especially Rudyard Kipling's *Barrack-Room Ballads*, and one day Len came into the room all excited brandishing a sheet of paper on which was written the following poem, written by a Jock corporal of the Black Watch in D Block, whose name I never knew.

CRETE

They have boasted of their Dunkirk, of the Navy's gallant feat,
But I hope they will remember the boys they left on Crete,
Who fought a losing battle, knowing that quite well,
Their lives were being sacrificed, for what, perhaps time will tell.
A Blitz Krieg had descended on a peaceful countryside.
And from a deadly German Airforce our Tommies tried to hide.
T' was not for lack of courage, nor bombardments loud report,
It was just that they were lacking the RAF support.
The fighting was furious with his parachutist troops,
Who landed on the Island to be dealt with in small groups,
The battle did not last for long, but Gawd, it, was not fun,
To see the dead and wounded and the Island overrun.
When the fighting was over, and prisoners they became,
There is an epic march which will go down in history's fame,
From Heraklion to Suda, a hundred miles or more,
They marched on empty stomachs and their feet were wore and sore.
They are not sorry now it's over and they are settled once again
Mit Deutschland's pleasant pastures to work in snow and rain,
And they are hoping, how they're hoping, that one day they'll be free,
And the pleasant Cliffs of Dover, just once again they'll see.

I liked it so much I learnt it off by heart and have never forgotten it. It sums up Crete in a nutshell.

There were all sorts of talents in the camp, activities starting usually after the evening meal and on a Sunday. One man, a tinsmith by trade, made teapots, complete with lid and spout, from empty tin cans. Solder and soldering irons were a problem, but not for long. A small piece of copper was 'obtained', fashioned to shape and fastened to a thick wire handle. Solder was collected from the joints of other tins, a tedious job, whilst flux was obtained through the guards or stolen from the loco sheds and workshop on the railway.

Herr Schultz arrived in the compound one day to announce that from the goodness of his black Nazi heart he had obtained some barrels of beer for us which were due to arrive any day and would be on sale to us in the camp canteen for a few pfennigs per litre. Amazingly, true to his word, the beer duly arrived, big barrels which must have held about 40 gallons each. They were quickly set up, taps driven home, bungs opened and poured out into any size of receptacle and hastily tasted.

It tasted quite good, like beer with a frothy top, but the alcoholic content must have been taken out before it got to us, there wasn't a hope in hell of getting merry on the stuff. However, this gave someone in the camp the idea of home brewing, winemaking.

Apparently all one had to do was to chop up a quantity of dried fruit from our Red Cross parcels, soak it in hot water (some of it had to be boiled to soften it), then place in a fermenting receptacle, add a quantity of sugar, a pinch of salt, some yeast and the necessary quantity of water. This was then put in a warm place until fermentation had stopped, carefully decanted to leave the sediment in the bottom, giving us potent 'hootch' (as we called it) ready for drinking. This all sounded too easy, the ingredients were to hand except for the yeast which wasn't difficult to obtain from the local bakery by begging, borrowing or stealing, or sometimes purchasing with coffee from our parcels. The ubiquitous KLIM tin became the fermenting vessel and soon many brews were in progress.

We then learnt that it was illegal in the UK to brew alcoholic beverages, that it was something to do with the Customs and Excise Laws, but then we were a long way from home and not a little worried, we didn't even care if the same law applied in Germany, we were going to have a go at making this 'hootch', come what may.

Another great snag was where to hide the brew whilst it was fermenting. There were dozens of different brews all needing a warm place and the warmest place was in the boiler house in the centre of the barrack block and that was supposed to be locked, the key being kept by the Germans, but of which I had made a duplicate. The brews were hidden in the roof lining labelled with their owner's name, some were knocked over accidentally which led to hard words and on the whole it was not a satisfactory arrangement.

These first brews were not very successful. The taste left much to be desired, bitter and tarty, but the brews were potent enough to give us 'thick heads'. The liquor wasn't left long enough to become clear; we would have to wait too long; it could take months and the war might soon be over (it was always going to be over by Christmas). We also realised the KLIM tins were not ideal for brewing, we needed something non-metallic and we learnt an 'airlock' was also required.

An empty beer barrel was purloined, put up into the rafters in the boiler house, all the ingredients were pooled from each room in the block and two 'experts' put in charge of the operation. For an airlock, the first one was made out of a Nescafé tin, a wooden bung, in which were two small holes, then fixed in place of the lid after filling the tin three parts with water; a thin piece of rubber tubing was acquired, fastened into the bung in the barrel and the other end into the water in the Nescafé tin. The gases then rose through the tube, bubbled through the water to escape through the second hole, the water ensuring no air passed back into the barrel.

This 'hootch', providing it was left long enough to ferment and clear, was highly successful and popular. It sometimes afforded one to escape into the depths of inebriation and forget for a few hours at least, the present environment enforced upon us. Little did I realise at the time that twenty-odd years later winemaking and beer brewing was to become one of my hobbies.

Study groups were set up, but in the academic line the degrees of success were very small as that type of study was very difficult to concentrate on. Most men turned to some sort of physical recreation, football and rugby or hockey and badminton, our P.T. school, the muscle factory, boxing, the band and the concert party, and such like. Of course, there were those who never took part in anything except to moan and criticise others, showing their selfishness. Others were ardent supporters, showing great sporting rivalry between the barrack block teams; they would also run a betting book using cigarettes for money. We were eventually able to visit the other two camps and they us in turn to compete against one another at the various games.

At first the Germans had the stupid idea that the spectators from each camp must not mingle with each other because they were afraid they would not get the same men back to their own camps. This situation did not last long and soon we were all intermingling, swapping news and making arrangements for other games.

There were also quite a few hobbies on the lighter vein, such as knitting, stamp collecting, carving, drawing and painting, music, tinsmiths, forging passes and documents, and all sorts of things to help make the time pass more quickly.

Some started keeping rabbits, wild ones which had been caught at the working sites by very clever, painstaking methods. Then the problem of smuggling them into camp, and where to keep them – under the floorboards of course, in holes dug out, the spoil carried out and dumped at work. The rabbit hutches were made from three ply wood, formerly Canadian packing boxes, put in the holes in the floor and kept scrupulously clean. One enterprising fellow who owned a large buck made a placard which he displayed, saying: 'Does your Doe want doing, results guaranteed, two cigarettes a time.'

All went well with the rabbits until one Sunday morning when Montag decided to carry out a lightning search. A new guard, keen on the job, searching between the bunks let upon a hollow-sounding floorboard which on further investigation was found to be loose, and low and behold to the amazement and ultimate amusement of the Germans, the cat was out of the bag (or was it the rabbit?).

That day was called, 'The day of the long knives'. The rabbits had to be killed, except any little ones, and put into the day's stew, which for once was pretty good. The little ones, after much argument, were allowed to be kept by the cookhouse in properly made hutches and attended to by someone on the camp staff.

The guard who 'let the cat out of the bag' was not forgotten. He came to grief soon afterwards. One night when he was on duty at the inner compound gate, a rumpus was started in one of the blocks a few minutes before he was due to be relieved. Being nosy he went along to the block, unlocked the door and stormed inside, rifle slung on his shoulder, demanding to know what was going on. He was greeted with lots of good humour and backslapping, not realising that a small poster inscribed: '*HITLER UND ALLER NAZI*

PARTEI, SCHEISSER' was affixed to his back, which was found by none other than Herr Feldwebel when he was reporting off duty. In other words, his feet didn't touch the ground, and he was escorted on the next morning's early train back to his battalion and God knows what else. There were ways and means of 'getting rid'.

We had a classic one on our job. This particular guard was a thoroughbred bastard and we promised one day to fix him good and proper.

It was the middle of summer on a very warm day during the 2 p.m. break, when someone had a dangerous brainwave. Why not pinch the bolt out of his rifle? At breaktimes it was usual for us to stretch out flat on the sandy embankment around the ganger, 'Mad Harry', and the guard who after eating their sandwiches would also lie back and doze. The guard, off guard, would lay his rifle by his side, which it was thought, by us. was a golden opportunity to take out the rifle bolt, and bury it in the sand.

An argumentative little Welshman actually did the deed, the guard, unsuspecting, carried on as usual after his doze by slinging his rifle on his shoulder and making himself a nuisance with us being extra awkward for the remainder of the afternoon.

We later marched back into camp singing away, where, just inside the gate, we came to a halt and turned to our front to be counted by the *Schreiber*, Office Clerk, whilst our guard with others paraded in front of their guardroom for arms inspection and dismissal by the Herr Feldwebel himself.

On hearing the command, 'For inspection, Port Arms', we gazed forward with apprehension, knowing that our guard would now be in a blue funk groping for the knob of the bolt.

Herr Montag was very keen on his men setting a good soldierly example at all times, especially in front of us. He never missed a trick, watching both us and his guards with his cold, steel-blue eyes.

Spotting the guard with the missing bolt instantly, he marched up to him, snatched the rifle off him and belted him with it, knocking him to the ground, then booted him inside the guardroom. We marched happily yet quietly to our own compound and huts, assured of still another success in our quest against those jailers whom we did not get on with so very well.

Needless to say, we had a new guard the next morning and the old one was never seen by us again, Heil Hitler!

The gangers were a different kettle of fish to deal with. They were only interested in work which they were very good at, and although most of them, including their bosses, dealt with us on the black-market, they had a close co-operation between themselves which made our efforts ineffective.

And furthermore, we had grown used to each other over the months of association and there was no longer any bullying.

Summer gave way to autumn and winter. It had been a good summer really, enabling us, with the event of our Red Cross parcels, to recuperate and get back some of our strength and former self. The nights were getting longer and we could expect further air raids. One morning, during the very early hours, it happened. An aircraft in obvious trouble, having been hit by flak, unloaded its bomb load a bit too close to us for our liking. It shook our camp and made us realise we were not as safe as we thought.

Making very strong representation to Herr Montag we were eventually given permission to construct air-raid shelters. But first we built those for the Germans which were made out of pre-stressed, prefabricated concrete slabs and for ours, we had to be content with a dog-legged trench with an entrance at the end of each hut and a timbered roof covered with about 2 feet of earth.

The drill now, on the air-raid alarm sounding, was for a guard to unlock the end door of each barrack hut and those who wanted could go into the shelter. This also allowed us to stand outside and watch the spectacle which we were now sure was building up in intensity. One night, after a very heavy air raid on the southern suburbs, we had more or less got back to bed to sleep when we were woken again by the sounds of many voices outside our huts and with guards bustling about opening doors.

Teltow Camp (404) had been badly bombed, smashing the huts and causing casualties to both Germans and British. So, they came to live with us whilst their camp was put to rights again. Overcrowding was inevitable. Lofty, Jock Craig, Tom Caselli and his pal, George Beaumont, along with others came into our room. The corridor doors at each end of the hut had now to be left open for much-needed ventilation. Many were housed on the floor of the dining room.

This was a great reunion, with tales of the bombing, over mugs of tea, cheese and biscuits. There was little sleep for the remainder of the time before morning work parade. Most of the Teltow boys thought the raid had been designed for their area, the marshalling yards at Litchefelde were not far away and it was generally accepted it had not been a case of aircraft ditching their bomb loads because they were in serious trouble.

The wishful thinkers and the knowledgeable ones had now to admit that our bombers did not know of our existence, nor were they even interested in us being there, as future events were to prove.

After about three weeks, the Teltow boys moved back to their own repaired camp. We had been delighted to have them although badly overcrowded and within the next week our camp was also badly bombed and damaged. We had had enough warning before the raid started and every man, with the exception of one, had filed into the air-raid shelter. The raid, which again appeared to be in the Teltow area and starting from further west, seemed to us to be getting heavier.

We were sure the aircraft which dropped its high-explosive bombs across our camp had been in great difficulty and had not meant to deliberately drop them on us. Nevertheless, the RAF were called all the bastards under the sun. But luckily the bombs had dropped on each side of the shelter and in between three of the huts and most fortunately we only lost one man, he being the one who was not in the air-raid shelter.

After the raid we went back to what had been our rooms. Ours had its roof standing up on end, the windows complete with frames had been removed right out of the wall and were lying with the glass unbroken on a lawn between A Block and ours. The room was a shambles with debris on the beds, the door of the room blown off and the walls leaning at rakish angles, but the electric lights worked in most cases.

Photographs still hung on the walls; other objects were still intact on the shelves. I had a photograph of my young brother in his choir outfit hanging on a brass nail I had taken from the heel of my boot, adjacent to the window, which was still hanging intact. A Block and B Block were the worst affected, some of the men salvaged their kit and bedding and spent the remainder of the night in the dining room. We actually stayed in our own beds with mostly the stars above us to gaze at. The German quarters had not been so badly affected, so they had no real reason to want to move us out that night.

Next day we packed up our belongings, setting off on trek in the direction of 404. But we never got there. Instead, we were shepherded into the Political Prisoners' camp, which to our amazement was now empty. It was a very old camp with smaller huts with verandas, laid out in a hexagon shape. The camp was very dirty with a terrible smell attached to it and many rotten floorboards and leaking roofs.

We made it quite plain to Montag that we did not like this one bit and before many days we were covered with lice and bugs again which were inevitably carried back into our own camp later. That weekend the general, Von Eckenvort himself, complete with entourage, all dressed up to the nines with low-slung ceremonial swords, paid us a visit at our temporary abode. We paraded and were brought up to 'attention' as he arrived at the gate, following him with movement of our head and eyes as is customary of the German army. He did not spend more time than was necessary for a very brief glimpse at the almost derelict buildings before he was out of the camp and speeding away to his next appointment.

Within a couple of weeks, we were back in our own camp again, which had all been put back together. The bomb craters were filled in; no tunnels had been unearthed. But we now decided to definitely get ourselves organised in the case of air-raid precautions. Each man had a food parcel carton into which went emergency rations of biscuits, margarine, tea, sugar, milk, dried fruit, chocolate and anything which would preserve for several days.

Some form of kit bag or box, haversack and pack containing essential items of clothing and necessaries was kept at the 'ready'. Now in the event of an air raid we could get dressed quickly, gather our kit and greatcoat and proceed in an orderly manner to the air-raid shelter.

The ex-Political Prisoners' camp we had just left was now holding Russian prisoners of war. We saw them arriving as they passed by our camp. Up until then I had never seen men in such a distressed, ill-treated condition. We had thought we were bad enough after our ordeal from Salonika, but these poor devils, gaunt and emaciated, tottering with hunger and fatigue, had been subjected to the worst treatment possible at the hands of the Nazis.

Now each day we could see a party of them digging in the field, previously dug over time and time again by their predecessors, a large hole towards which would march a small band of four, carrying a table top, bearing the corpse of one of their dead comrades who would be dumped without further to do into the hole.

There were many ugly rumours of diabolical ill-treatment of the Russians at the hands of their sadistic jailers. And yet, after the war when any German was asked about these sorts of goings on, everyone denied any knowledge of such acts. But they are liars, there were millions of them who knew what was going on and there is no one who can convince me otherwise.

By the end of October 1942, news of the war in the Middle East spoke of a huge battle raging at Alamein and in early November we learned of the first decisive victory on land for our side and our troops were steadily advancing westward.

Naturally, we thought it was just another 'push' to be later pushed back to Alexandria, but this time we were wrong. We were now getting news directly from England on a hidden radio, in that, matter of fact, unflappable BBC voice.

Our forces were steadily advancing in the Western Desert under the brilliant leadership of General Montgomery (a new fellow we had never heard of). Other forces had landed in Algeria in the west, to drive east to link up with Monty.

There were sad tales of woe from the Russian front of the German troops freezing to death in the intense cold of their second winter. The *Fumf Uhr Blatt* spoke of the encirclement of Leningrad and the siege of Stalingrad, of the Russian scorched-earth policy and the plight it had left the eastern masses in.

The winter bore down again relentlessly upon us, but this time we were much better clad and far stronger than we had been the year before.

Christmas and the New Year came and went with us having tried to make it as festive as possible. I think, however, we were mostly concerned and anxious as to what 1943 was going to bring.

During the winter months, we were drawn more together in the confines of our own barrack blocks and individual rooms than otherwise. One's personal life became a little more tedious as nerves frayed. Arguments were frequent, mostly over very petty things.

There was he who slept on the other side of the room in a bottom bunk, who having affixed some photos of his family and girlfriend on a piece of cardboard and hung it on the wall, would, if he received no mail when others in our room received some, take down his photos in disgust and put them under his mattress, only to bring them out with glee again at the arrival of a letter.

Arthur on the bottom bunk next to him would take funny turns during the night when all were asleep. He suffered from claustrophobia and would often wake up screaming and shouting whilst trying to hold up the bunk above him, and those of us would dash out of bed to help to pacify him.

There were those who wet the bed and it was God help the poor soul sleeping on the bottom bunk. But many had 'Gosunders' (commonly called a 'piss can') under the bunk or just outside the door in the passageway. It was too cold for some to go down the corridor to the 'loo' or else they were too lazy. Nevertheless, it was common practice to piss in someone else's tin or even in someone's boot, much to the consternation of their owners, but to the glee of others not affected.

Old Bill from Oldham way, who lived on a top bunk, was a quiet earnest soul, keeping mostly to himself until he had been given a trombone to practise on. During the summer nights he could get outside with it to do his practising and no one would be bothered by it, but now he insisted on one hour per night on the top bunk and what a bloody row he made, which often finished up with us all throwing our boots at him, or fleeing from the room until he had done enough. We tried to pinch his mouthpiece and bung his tubes up with paper, to no avail.

We made dartboards and sets of darts and had a great league competition in full swing. The Germans were very interested, until someone decided darts could be dangerous weapons in the hands of such skilled players, so the game became banned and forbidden.

We had brought lice and bugs back into camp from our short stay in the Political Prisoners' camp. The lice were dealt with by simply taking all our belongings through the delousing process again, but the bugs were a different problem. They came out at night-time, dropping off the ceilings on to the top bunks and then through to the bottom bunks. I slept with a towel over my face mostly, which although most uncomfortable and restricted my breathing somewhat, was still better than having the bugs drop on to my face or into an ear. The German quarters were bug free and Herr Montag turned a deaf ear to our insisting that our huts should be fumigated. So drastic action had to be taken.

Several small boxes of bugs were captured and handed over to Jack Bacon, a 43-year-old sergeant who had been a POW in the 1914–18 war and being on the camp staff, part of his duty was to help to clean out the Germans' quarters. This day he did so by putting the bugs in their beds, not forgetting the most important ones of Montag and Schultz. This did the trick; within a matter of days a team arrived one Sunday morning and spent the whole day fumigating. They made a good job of it and we were able to actually sweep up the bugs.

Another obstacle had yet again been overcome and our main concern now was definitely air raids. This was something we had not bargained for, neither could we stop them. Herr Feldwebel Montag could not understand why we were always fully dressed and quietly waiting for the block doors to be opened when the local air-raid alarm sounded. Little did he know we were forewarned by our hidden radio tuned to the Berlin station and as soon as the word came round, *'Feindliche Flugzeng Uber Hanover und Braunschweig'*, 'Enemy aircraft over Hanover and Brunswick', a mere 120 miles away, we knew it was time for us to prepare to make a move towards the shelter, and when the warning said Magdeburg and Brandenburg, we were definitely ready.

It was obvious these fellows up above meant business and did not care what or who was down below. The searchlight and flak defences were steadily being reinforced, flak trains were running backwards and forwards along the rail tracks and air-raid shelters were being hastily constructed all over the place. The war had already reached Hitler's midden.

In May, we were delighted to hear that the North African campaign had been won. The Germans had been well and truly pushed out and the Italians had been very little help to them. The Eighth Army had fought from Alamein to Tunis in six months, We now knew the tide was changing.

On another Saturday in May, we were returning from work about lunchtime or just afterwards, when after being counted in and we were walking along to our own compound, a twin-engined aircraft with RAF roundels on the underside of each wing came power diving over us in a great sweep and on to Berlin. Within seconds another identical aircraft appeared, doing exactly the same.

They had appeared and disappeared so quickly the flak had little chance to fire. We naturally were overjoyed but could never understand how such aircraft could get that far.

It would also be around this time when a new addition arrived in camp, a private soldier, too well dressed, looking too well fed and his kit looked too new. His English was far more perfect and superior to ours; we were very suspicious from the start. He was housed in A Block where most of the camp staff lived and where he was under close observation the whole time. An obvious plant by the Germans to learn the secrets of our camp, but he never got any further than A Block and only stayed a few days after realising the game was up. He was soon caught off guard when one of our members entered the room he was in and suddenly shouted in an authoritative voice, 'Heil Hitler'. The newcomer was the only one in the room who sprang to attention in acknowledgement. He must have felt very stupid to have been caught by such a simple trick and it was fortunate the Germans whipped him out quickly because his execution had already been decided. The Germans must have thought we were a lot of simple clots if we were going to be taken in with a ruse like that.

Rumour had it we were going to move camp again. We were too well in the line of the bombers. First Teltow was hit, then we were hit and now Genslagen had had a close shave. So one weekend the three camps moved lock, stock and barrel to one large camp for us all at Wulheide in the eastern suburbs of Berlin near Karlshorst.

There were great reunions between the three camps which now made a grand total of something like 1,200 or 1,300 or more men. It was also amazing how we quickly settled down as one camp instead of three separate communities. Tom and his pal George moved in with Len and myself, we worked on the same Kommando, three days per week.

We now went to work along a new length of railway running east through Hoppegarten. To get there we boarded goods vans on a line just outside our camp which took us into the centre of the city, where we marched to Anhalte Bahnhof to catch a civilian train which dropped the various commandos off at stations along the line to Hoppegarten where they worked.

Since we were now travelling and mixing amongst more and more German civilians and service personnel, we spruced ourselves up as well as we could and would march from A to B in a correct soldierly like manner with one of our own giving the orders. It looked good to see a party marching smartly along a railway platform, whilst the Germans moved out of their way, and watch them come to a cracking halt, then be dismissed to stand to one side to wait for a train.

When the train arrived, we would politely stand aside to let the civilians, mostly old men, females and children on first, then we boarded, completely ignoring any German service personnel. Our discipline, pride and bearing was such that it could not go by unnoticed. Nor did it, because, as we returned to camp one evening the whole camp was assembled into a hollow square to be addressed by the camp commandant, a lieutenant whose name I never knew.

He told us through an interpreter (although we well understood his German) that a high-ranking SS officer had complained bitterly that the British POWs were marching about Berlin like occupation troops, and it had to stop. The worst thing he did was to have told us, because we tried all the more by achieving more uniformity in our dress and to be on the lookout to salute officers (but we had always flatly refused to salute their NCOs as was customary to do so in the German army).

In July, we learned that Sicily had been invaded with very little opposition; it was completely taken over by 17 August. August also saw the start of the 1,000-bomber raids. Not only by night but now by day as well. Our shelter in this camp was only dog-legged trenches, there being no overhead protection whatsoever.

We had a grandstand view. The barrack-block doors and windows were left open all the time now and we held a nightly ritual to the trenches taking with us our food and small kit and putting our kitbags, with all our other gear in, at the end of each block in an orderly pile.

But the bombing so far had not really affected us at our new location. Directly to the west of us was a large sports stadium and next to that, was a racecourse, plenty of open ground for bombs to drop on.

The insistence of the bombers keeping formation and on course, and the ferociousness of their attacks against the many hundreds of brilliantly lit searchlights and the seemingly impregnable wall of steel being fired into their midst by flak was astonishing and credit to their airmanship.

Many aircraft were hit and set on fire; we could see their crews bailing out. Then the aircraft would dive down towards earth making a frightening noise in its death throes, until it exploded on contact with the ground and a bright flash of light and black smoke billowing high into the air. Our area was a collecting ground for bailed-out crews.

One night soon after these heavy air raids had started, the Germans employed new tactics by directing every searchlight straight up into the air. The scene was awe-inspiring; the many hundreds of white, brilliant pillars piercing as far as they could into the sky, illuminating the whole area like daylight.

The flak stayed silent, but at the ready. Everything and everyone was silent except for the loud noise from the aircraft engines. Then suddenly all hell let loose, but not from the flak; the bombs started whistling down and exploding, heavy machine guns were blazing away from right, left and centre, and the huge bombers started falling out of the sky making their horrible noise. The Germans had put up their night fighters, they simply could not miss. It was a heavy toll for our boys that night.

I still have a piece of fabric, 3 x 4 inches, on which I wrote at the time, 'BRITISH BOMBER BROUGHT DOWN OVER BERLIN, 23.8.43. PARTS LANDED AT HOPPERGARTEN. 3 OF THE CREW ALSO FOUND, DEAD!' It brought home to us once again the horrors of war.

In early September we learned of the unconditional surrender of Italy, but the Germans were there in great force and prepared to fight every inch of the way back to Germany.

The tide had also turned somewhat in the Russian campaign with the Russians steadily advancing on all fronts.

In the camp we still tried to carry on as normally as we could, but this was very difficult due to the constant interruptions caused by the visits of the allied air forces both night and day.

The daylight raids were causing great disruption of the railway system. Some days we actually got parted from our guards because we could not all get on the same train when it eventually arrived. We sometimes had to march from station to station and around stranded trains which could not travel very far in any direction. No one bothered us, we just marched along in an orderly manner, turning up late in camp under our own steam, and more often than not we would start singing as we entered the camp.

It was obvious things were getting a bit chaotic for the Germans and we were becoming an embarrassment to them. So, one night we were all assembled in the large dining room to be told by the Camp Commandant we were going to be moved yet again. But we had the option of volunteering to go to work on the Brenner Tunnel at Innsbruck. We flatly refused to volunteer for anything, anywhere, and therefore within the next few days he told us to pack our kit (already packed) as we were going to be moved into Saxony, and threatened with the coal mines.

Chapter 7

Mühlburg-Saxony 1943

We were leaving Berlin behind on this sunny day in September as we viewed the surrounding flat, featureless landscape through the open doors of the goods wagons.

The Germans had been quite amiable on our entrainment; not overcrowding the wagons; they had even apologised for the train being goods wagons and not normal passenger coaches. Hence the sliding doors were left open.

We were not sorry to be leaving, the bombing was increasing every day and it was not funny being on the receiving end delivered by our own side. All our worldly goods went with us; there was no such thing as a baggage party, we carried everything with us, which was now a considerable amount. We had also been given two Red Cross food parcels each to carry. The train chugged on all through the day and on into the night, eventually coming to a full stop in some sidings we knew not where. Our guards then quickly moved along the whole length of the train closing all doors and bolting them. No wonder we had been put in cattle trucks; some crafty German had known we would have to be locked up for the night. We were here for the night which had now turned into a miserable drizzling rain, there being nothing else to do but to get our heads down and get some sleep.

Next morning, we assembled, hoisted up our kit and the two parcels and set off on the march, where after a while we reached the main camp of Stalag 4B at Mühlberg.

We did not like the look of this place from the start. The camp covered an area as far as the eye could see. This seemed much larger than Luckenwalde, there being camps within the camp and numerous fully manned machine-gun towers standing high and ugly with a commanding view of the whole area.

We were herded into a large compound which had only one small hut, a few ablution benches, a stand pipe and an evil, vile-smelling deep trench latrine. The hut was filthy with no means of cleaning it up so no one bothered with it. This was supposed to be a holding and searching centre.

The distance between us and the next compound was about 30 feet, filled with a mass of tangled barbed wire, and we soon found out that there were British men next to us. These men had been brought in from Italy after the surrender, subjected to the usual hazardous conditions en route, with no food. They were now in a similar state as we had been when we had arrived at Luckenwalde.

Never thinking about our immediate future, we began to throw items from our food parcels over the wire to them. It was quite a sight to see more than 1,200 men hurling a barrage of tins across the wire. The German sentries did not like this one bit and made efforts to stop us, but seeing they were getting nowhere, called up the watchtowers and retreated out of range. Things went from bad to worse as the machine guns opened up, spluttering their bullets all along the wire fence. There was a terrific scatter on both sides to get out of the way, but luckily no one got hurt.

I am sure the thick-headed sentries had misunderstood what was happening in the first place. They must have thought we were bombarding our next-door neighbours in anger and they had made things worse by calling up the machine gunners.

Soon the camp commandant, with others of his staff, came along to see us, demanding to know what all the 'rioting' was about. Within no time at all, the story got well out of proportion, the sentries having to justify their action.

So that day and the next day we had no rations issued to us at all, but we did not care, nor were we unduly worried because we had enough food of our own to last a few days anyhow.

Sleeping out at night was a bit of an embarrassment and uncomfortable, but we had done it before and we could do it again. We naturally went in search of wood to light fires to enable us to cook something warm, and gradually the wooden ablution stands were taken apart, broken up and burnt.

On about the third day of this, the camp 'comedian' with his staff and a large bodyguard with two of them carrying a table, entered the compound. The table was put in position, the 'comedian' who I think was a major, stood on top of it and we all gathered round to hear what he had to say.

He was a typical arrogant bastard, who, when he spoke, cocked his head on one side and screamed out like Hitler. His interpreter translated what was, in other words, 'a severe reprimand all round', but he did not have it all his own way.

Questions were fired at him as to why we had been treated like this and why had we not been put in proper huts when we had first arrived.

They were still wanting us to volunteer for Innsbruck – to which we smelt a rat. There was something phoney and not quite right in their insistence that we volunteer and that they did not just send us there. We were unanimous; we were not volunteering for anything. Being much wiser in the ways of the Germans after two years as their guests, we were adamant we would stand fast.

The 'comedian' completely lost his temper, raving and shouting and stamping his feet; then with a clicking of the heels and throwing up his right arm in the Nazi salute screamed, 'Heil Hitler' to which we replied lustily, 'Heil Churchill'. This only made him worse. He hastily got off the table and stormed out of the compound followed by his entourage, all holding on to their pistols whilst the guards backed out and locked the gates behind them.

Next morning, a whole regiment of German infantry, in full battle order, turned up. The gates were opened, the troops marched in with rifles cocked and held at the ready, then, splitting into two lines, filed round the inside periphery of the barbed wire fence and faced inwards towards us.

We were ordered to make ready and form up to march out. When all was ready, we set off, turning to our right out of the gates leaving the camp behind us, the infantry guards accompanying us along each side of the road.

All went well for the first few hundred yards, then as soon as the first man stopped to re-adjust his kit a guard dashed in and belted him with his rifle. Soon this was happening all along the column; we were carrying everything we possessed and this made our progress heavy and awkward.

I had a haversack and water bottle across my shoulder and two kit bags tied together, slung around my neck, and some string tied round each kitbag as handles. The string cut into my hands as I tried to take the weight off my aching shoulders. After the first mile it was sheer agony.

Tom, George and Len had similar loads and so had everyone else. We were determined to stick together in the column though everyone was trying to keep to the centre to keep out of arm's length of the ever-attentive bullying guards wielding their rifles and prodding with their bayonets.

An open staff car drove past us in a cloud of dust – with the 'comedian' and another in the back seat – which then positioned itself at the next road junction. The 'comedian' then stood up in the car with his right arm bent, and fingers tucked inside his tunic, Napoleonic style, urging his guards to press us on more quickly along the road. The guards did exactly as they were told and the whole column began to surge forward as they brutally attacked us on both flanks with rifle and bayonet.

How far we were destined to go we knew not, but we were well out into the countryside now. Men began to ease their burden by offloading articles, throwing them off to the side of the road. Some staggered to a full stop and dropped exhausted and fainting; other men fell over them pressed on by those behind.

The column was now really feeling the strain and becoming a shambles. This was a mass punishment forced march, just to let us see who was really in charge. But we still jeered at that blasted 'comedian' as we struggled by, hoping that one day one of us would meet up with him after the war and repay him for his kindness.

Those who fell out behind were soon revived by one means or another, then chased along the road as quickly as possible to try and catch up with the main column. The roadside, littered with an assortment of kit, looked like another retreat from Dunkirk.

Eventually, utterly exhausted, weary and aching in every limb, we came in sight of a camp ahead and what a camp. In fact, the whole area gave one a feeling of foreboding.

A large camp with extra special thick and high barbed wire fence entanglement around it. It had railway lines running into it and through a large brick-built building, then past that was another brick building with a high factory chimney attached to it. This area was wired off separately from the remainder of the camp.

We were put through a search before being let into and counted through the gate to the compound where we were going to be housed. The buildings were built of brick, large and spacious with high windows and large double doors at each end. Outside each building was a large square mound of earth covered with well-kept grass. Inside, the floor was of hard padded earth, the sleeping bunks were five tier shelves on both sides; they were more like vegetable racks. There was a stove at each end of the building made from bricks and concrete, about 8 feet long by 4 feet square and the stove pipe going straight up out of the roof could hardly be seen because of the darkness; there was no lighting of any description.

Our water supply was from a number of wells on the old bucket winding system. A warning went round for all water to be boiled before drinking, but what the hell were we going to boil it on? The latrines outside were crude if not comical and of a definite special design. They were constructed of rough sawn timber, triangular shaped (like a ridged roof), with holes to sit on cut in the side and a flap lid over the holes. In fact, there was no seat to sit on at all, you simply had to do a squatting lean against it and hope for the best.

There was absolutely nowhere in the camp where we could sit except on the ground. We could not sit up in the bunks because there was not enough space between and it was a bit of a devil; we could not even find a comfortable seat to have our daily constitutional!

The camp smelt of recent disinfection and fumigation, but there still lingered a queer smell, a smell of death. There were the ominous-looking square mounds to consider; whatever they were they were not air-raid shelters as first was thought.

The Germans had locked up, put a very strong guard around the wire fence, and left us to it. But just to show them that our morale was still somewhat high on the chart, the Jocks got out their bagpipes (sent through the Red Cross) and gave a good display of their national tunes. This bucked everyone up no end.

For the next several days there were no rations forthcoming. We four now took stock of what we could muster between us, rationing ourselves to two small meals a day. Gradually our meagre stocks of tinned food solids, beverages and biscuits dwindled away, leaving us with only a bit of dried fruit, chocolate and several tins of oatmeal and Bemax. We existed three days alone on porridge made only with water, which was most unappetising and tasteless, but kept us going.

We also learned during this period that this camp was called Jacobstall – a Jewish extermination camp – hence the tall chimney for the crematorium, and no wonder of the smell of death. The great grass-covered mounds were supposed to be mass graves; we could well believe it.

Then our treatment changed. It was a typical method of the Nazis to suddenly become friendly. The gates were opened to bring in the much-needed rations, although we certainly had not shown any visible signs that we were on the point of starving. We also got a Red Cross parcel issue and letter cards to write home.

If the Germans thought we were going to write favourably of them, they were wrong. We put down exactly what our treatment had been since leaving Berlin and after the war I learned none of my letters had been received. They were never allowed past the German censor.

There was another camp next door to us which housed Russian prisoners of war. They, like at Berlin, were in an acute state of starvation and ill health. The same ritual of digging a large hole and the slow walk with a body on a table top was a daily occurrence.

After a total of twelve days in Jacobstall we returned to Mühlberg where our reception was much better and we were housed in proper barrack huts. The march was carried out without incident, there being plenty of time, enabling us to make frequent stops for short rests.

We were, however, still very suspicious of what the outcome of all this was going to be. The next few days were spent in documentation and having some form of vaccination against smallpox and cholera. Lists of numbers and names were posted up in each block showing the carving up of our Stalag; we were being split up into many small working parties to be distributed throughout Saxony and Stalag 4F.

Some of our naval and Marine personnel, of which we had quite a few, were given the option of going to a Marlag; in other words, a Mariners' camp. Len and one or two others decided to have a change, for better or for worse. It did not matter where they went – Stalag or Marlag – they were all the same. We would all end up in working camps somewhere. I still kept in touch with Len, however, by letter, through his wife, and in a letter from her dated 28 March 1944, learned he was in Stalag 4D and as she put it, 'His letters are very cheerful, and it seems a decent camp he is in.'

The working parties began to move out, marching to the nearest railhead to be transported to their new 'homes'. Mühlberg was about 80 miles due south of Berlin as the crow flies and about 38 miles north-east of Leipzig. I bid farewell to Len wishing him luck at his Marlag and joined Tom and George destined for Zwickau about 43 miles south of Leipzig and 20 miles south-west of Chemnitz.

There would be about eighty of us on the working party bound for Zwickau. It was rather remarkable how we banded ourselves together to form this party, because it was not as though we were all from the same barrack block in Dabendorf, Grossbeeren or Wulheide. We were a complete mixture; we even had half a dozen Cypriots with us who, with their sergeant, Ali Riza Tewfik, were good pals of mine from our days in Egypt together.

The afternoon was very dull and sky overcast when we arrived at Zwickau station in the reserved working-class carriages specially hitched on to the train for us. We assembled on the platform to move off with our kit like well-trained troops and were soon marching down the hill into Zwickau. Straight on through the town we went, busy with people who stopped to stare at us and ask the guards who we were. Being well turned out, with polished boots and buttons and swinging along in step they could not help but notice us; it was done specially for their benefit. It was good propaganda for the British troops, which we meant to keep at a very high standard.

Out through Zwickau and on towards Crossen Mulde a couple of kilometres to the north towards Mosel, where we stopped opposite a huge paper factory. On the large wrought iron gates were the words, 'Leonard and Sohn, Papier Fabrik'. So this was it, a bloody paper factory of all places; still this was better than the coal mines. We were shown to a large brick building on the side of the road across from the factory. It was now becoming dark and we had yet to see the outlines of a barbed wire fence surrounding a camp; there was none. About half of us were led through a door in the side of the building while the others went through a door in the front. As soon as we had entered, we were locked in, and finding ourselves in a not-so-well-lit basement room could only stare flabbergasted at the scene before us.

Surely, we were in the wrong place; perhaps a mistake had been made. There before us sitting at dirty tables were about twenty-odd ill-clad, dirty, unshaven men whom at first glance we took to be Ukrainians or some such like Ausländers. They hardly looked up or gave us a second glance as they continued to devour their bowls of soup and black bread. We were amazed to find they were British, from Italy, and had been here only a few weeks. There was such a big contrast between us; it was incredible we were from the one and the same army.

It wasn't long before we were talking and mixing with them, swapping yarns and finding out all we could about the paper factory set-up. Asking them where we were to sleep, they pointed up a loft and in the corner of the room was a set of steep wooden stairs leading to a huge dormitory with the usual double-tier banks far too close together, with three blankets on each.

Next morning, we paraded outside the building, to be seen by the camp commandant, a Feldwebel whose name I have forgotten, but will always remember as 'Scarface'. His face was terribly scarred, but whether it was due to the war or some other accident we never knew; all we did know was that he hated the British with such venom he showed it every time he saw us.

The boys from Italy had established their camp leader but that is all they did have for camp staff. They had no interpreter and none of them could speak any German. But we soon changed all that. After much arguing with Scarface, we demanded and got a proper camp staff going. He had really brow beaten these chaps and had it all his own way.

We were all soon put to work in the paper factory doing all manner of jobs where it was an asset to speak any German at all. Once in the confines of the factory, the gangers took over and the guards more or less disappeared, mainly keeping to the outer perimeter of the works.

It was not long before we found out there was another part of the works, but quite separate, called 'C. and F. Leonards', also manned by British prisoners and from our own Stalag IIID, and these lived in a hutted camp on the other side of Crossen village. We established ways and means of contacting each other on the works.

Our so-called camp was only temporary and I soon found myself amongst a small party selected to work on the building of a new camp a short distance away across the fields.

It was a disused engineering works and foundry and several cottages (which were in use), forming part of the camp perimeter. The army put the barbed wire fence up and we, working under the supervision of a contractor, set to work to make the old but solid buildings into a place to live.

There were obviously certain things we had to put to rights in our latest surroundings, and the quicker the better, namely, the boys from Italy had to be made to get themselves cleaned up, their rooms and belongings cleaned up and above all, restore some of the pride and self-confidence they had lost.

We did not see eye to eye for a long time; it was a struggle, like being in two camps: those from Italy and those from Berlin. We were always referred to as Berliners.

Living under a totally different environment in Italy in very large camps, which had mostly been organised by themselves with very little or no assistance from the Italians, was a huge contrast to what they had experienced so far in Germany. They had, quite naturally, thought that when Italy had thrown in the towel, they would be liberated by our own forces and it must have been a tremendous shock when the Germans moved in so quickly to snatch them out of Italy.

Although they, like anyone else, had had a rough time in transit, they must have realised by now that the Germans were definitely much more businesslike in their methods of handling prisoners and getting them into working camps.

The old story of prisoners not contributing directly to their captors' war effort needs very careful consideration. Any work, no matter what, must have been an aid to that country's economy and therefore linked with the overall war effort. There were millions of foreign workers in Germany, all well organised through the *Arbeits Amt* – Employment Exchange.

So, when in Rome, do as the Romans do, and when in Germany, well, it was a matter of them having to get used to it – liking it or lumping it.

We had learned the hard way, so that now we were well dressed, our self-discipline and comradeship was first class, we set a reasonably high standard of soldierly conduct and an emphasised example when dealing or mixing directly with the Germans.

In selecting the camp staff, we had agreed to keep the Camp Leader, Arthur Retford, who was a good man for the job, backed up by Frankie Hope as interpreter, and Blondie Horsefall as man of confidence; the latter two being 'Berliners'. The tailor, shoemaker and barber and the cooks were 'Italians'. This seemed to be a good arrangement and worked quite well. Contact for Red Cross food parcels was made quickly which made everyone in the camp much happier.

The only bad apple in the bunch now was Scarface; we thought of all manner of ways to get rid of him, to no avail. He was a pig of a man, he even tried to do a bit of Gestapo interrogation on us one Sunday morning, by having us parade and enter his office in alphabetical order to answer his questions on our personal history.

Besides stating our regimental number, rank and name, he wanted particulars as far back as our grandparents and also what regiment, corps and divisions we were from. It did not last long when he realised he was being taken for a ride, because the first few answers on family history were given fictitious names made out to be of German origin and the names of the regiments were fantastic, such as The Bagshot Fusiliers, Ali Barber's Camel Corps, and so on. He was furious with us and lashed out at Tommy Cone who bolted out of the office holding his ear, but with a big smile on his face. We reckoned Scarface must have been looking for Jews, but he was out of luck. It was now agreed that the best way to get rid of Scarface would be to cause industrial strife in the works in any form whatsoever.

Some of this included continual grumbling to the gangers about the inadequate facilities in our existing camp, the overcrowding, no showers, poor food and not even a compound to walk around in on a Sunday when we were off work; Scarface kept us locked inside. We would soon get to the ears of the Herr Direktor, the works manager.

Results were not very long in starting. Work was pushed on quicker with the new camp, the works manager took a personal interest in it, often directing operations, much to the dislike of Scarface. The food was looked into and bettered; the problem of us getting some air and exercise on a Sunday was solved by stopping the weekend leave of the guards, who took a very dim view not being able to get home.

We had numerous visits from Stalag officers; all this reflecting unfavourably on Scarface. He had left us before Christmas without even bothering to any goodbye. We could only hope that maybe we could perhaps meet up with him again after the war.

His relief was Feldwebel Yainisch, another one of the older end, who arrived just in time to move to the new camp with us. A man of about 45, a good disciplinarian but scrupulously fair, who knew exactly what he wanted from us, his guards and the works.

He toured the works often and got us a five-day week; he mixed with us prisoners in the evenings finding out for himself those things which could be made better. He honoured his word and he expected us to honour our word; life as a prisoner was not easy at the best of times and he fully realised this.

Red Cross parcels abounded. We had a large bulk store out in the compound that had been an old garage and bordered the farm road running past the camp; it could hold thousands of parcels. We also learned of another camp in Zwickau, our boys from Berlin working at a coal mine better known as Bergeschact, a dismal, dirty place – but at least they had a jolly good air-raid shelter.

One night before Christmas, we again heard the dreaded droning of hundreds of aircraft engines flying high but miles away from us on their mission of destruction at perhaps Chemnitz or Dresden. It was the first time we had heard them since leaving Berlin – not that we were very happy about it.

We again insisted on digging some air-raid trenches in the compound; it was not going to be easy with the winter upon us and the ground frozen hard.

We feared that one day the factory would be bombed. After our experiences in Berlin, there was no wishful thinking now that we would not be bombed; we expected it to happen.

The new camp was well off the main road and was approached by a rough hardcore farm track which ran past the buildings and a farm and then joined the main road again, forming the shape of a horseshoe. The railway lines to Zwickau ran along the other side of the camp.

Our exercise grounds were not very big; they were only on two sides of the building, with a narrow alleyway on the third side. The ends of the heavily barbed wire fence terminated against the fourth side of the building. One could thus walk along two sides of the camp, through part of the old foundry and then back down the alleyway to the spot from which one had started.

The two-storey red brick and stone building with its barbed wired windows housed the Germans on the ground floor, their office-cum-guardroom, living quarters and ablutions. Also on the ground floor were our ablutions, large dining room and the communal kitchen. Our sleeping quarters were on the first floor, where one large room directly above the dining room contained about 100 men and another room above the kitchen and German quarters contained about fifty men. There were three more small rooms upstairs, one of which was the camp Lazarett. In another, three of the British camp staff slept and the other was a small room at the top of the stairs which was our Red Cross parcel store. In this room the weekly issue of parcels was kept, from which a daily issue of tins was made to us.

All things considered, it was not such a bad camp, with the exception that the sleeping quarters (in which we spent most of our leisure time) were very much overcrowded and the compound outside was too small.

I was now back in the paper works doing a multitude of jobs. The yard work on the rail sidings where the wagons of timber came in was heavy and hazardous. The timber was offloaded and stacked, no matter what the weather, to facilitate the turn round of wagons. Another gang transported the timber into a large shed where it was stripped of its bark, cut into handleable lengths and then into a huge mechanical chopper, coming out at the other side in small chips on to a conveyor belt.

The conveyor belt took the chips into and through another long room, where standing along each side of the belt were about sixty Ukrainian girls picking out the knots of wood into baskets.

A door at each of the room was kept bolted on the inside (presumably to keep us out) by their overseer. But we kept good relations with them by sending soap and chocolate and such things along the conveyor when we could afford it.

The wood chips were now elevated to the upper floors of the building for storage and then into the steam pulping cupolas. After this, the pulp was drawn off into open spill tanks on the ground floor for draining and cooling, a vile-smelling place, then into a huge machine which made it into rolls of rough paper.

A better-class paper was also made in another part of the works, but a different process was used. Our pal, George Beaumont, worked on this, having a most monotonous job in the *Schleiferei*, grinding room, feeding the ever-hungry grindstone pulping devices with metre long logs via a couple of hoppers in the floor above. The hoppers were never empty unless one turned away for more than a few seconds.

One day on my way through the works I came across a weedy-looking little German struggling to manoeuvre a large steam valve into position. I automatically went to his assistance – for which he was very grateful. The next morning, he was waiting with his foreman at the main works gates and pointed me out as we passed through.

Thus, I started work in the fitting shop as mate to the little German, Fritz Becker. Fritz and I got on well together from the beginning for I was not strange to this kind of work. He had worked for this firm for many years and knowing its complex system inside out, knew just how and when he could make the work easy for himself. Later I was asked if I knew of anyone suitable to work in the joiners' shop, so I put Tom's name in and he subsequently got the job.

Christmas once again was upon us, although the weeks and months seemed to drag out for a terribly long time. Our third Christmas as guests of Nazi Germany and we wondered if it would be our last. We tried our best to make it as good a time as possible by putting on a concert show and arranging football matches with the boys at C. and F.s and Bergeschacht.

It seemed that 1943 had been a much better year for the Allies. We could safely say the tide was turning in our favour. Was not the proof of it in the air with the formations of hundreds of heavy bombers penetrating ever deeper into the Fatherland both day and night?

Chapter 8

Zwickau-Saxony, 1944

We were in the grip of a hard, cold winter although the snow was late and we learned, much to our dismay, we were about to lose our Feldwebel Yainisch who was apparently wanted elsewhere. We were sorry to lose him, which is perhaps strange to say of any German, but he was definitely a regular guy and the best commandant we had yet come across. It was quite plain to us he was not a Nazi but, nevertheless, quite understandably was proud of his country as a genuine loyal German.

His relief, Feldwebel Martin, was a different kettle of fish. About 5 feet 9 inches tall, slim, thin-faced, sallow complexion, sharp piercing eyes, firm-jawed but with a small mouth and thin lips, and he had only one ear. One had been shot off on the Russian Front. Consequently, we nicknamed him 'One Ear'.

He was an arrogant, cocksure Nazi from top to toe and was obsessed with the idea that he was one of a superior race. He was always smartly turned out and sported the Eastern Front Campaign Ribbon and displayed an Iron Cross and a Wounded Medal on the left breast pocket of his tunic.

He was inclined to be excitable, speaking with a hard high-pitched voice; the missing ear gave his face a strange lack of symmetry when he spoke, which made his appearance more sinister than was actually the case. I never knew his real age but at a guess I would have put him at about 28 or 30.

He did not like us Britishers and liked the Russians even less. According to him, we had little culture and the Russians had none, they were simply barbarians. Germany must 'Vin der Var' to get rid of the Capitalists and Communists to make the world a better place to live in. He spoke no English to us, although we suspected he often understood us.

Another new arrival was Unteroffizier Sandy, a corporal and second in command to One Ear. He was of medium height, inclined to be a bit tubby and a rather quiet, retiring type. He never said much about anything and obviously did not like soldiering. I do not believe he had seen any active service and the nearest he had come to the enemy was 'us'. He did his job as he was told and although he had no time for One Ear, he had to be his 'Yes Man'.

Also, about this time two more men were wanted on the camp staff, and myself and Nag Bevan were selected, not that we wanted the job, but such was our method of selection by majority vote, that we were expected to take it. Any job on the camp staff could be irksome, having to run a diplomatic middle line between our boys and the Germans. Fritz Becker and the fitting shop foremen tried hard to keep me but to no avail.

The method of distribution of Red Cross food parcels was much the same here as anywhere else. Every Thursday (when parcels were available) we would draw enough parcels, one for each man, from the bulk store and take them upstairs to the distribution store to be prepared for handing out on Friday night.

The doors to both the outside bulk store and the inside distribution store had two sets of keys and two locks on each door. Our 'Man of Confidence' held one set of keys whilst the Germans held the other set, the duplicate set of keys were kept in the Feldwebel's safe in the office. So, providing the Feldwebel did not let anyone have access to the duplicate set of keys from the safe, no one could open the stores without both sides being present.

One cold, snowy Thursday, early in 1944, we went into the Red Cross parcel store to carry out the usual weekly detail of preparing parcels for issue. The store was bulging with parcels at the time and the cigarette cartons had been stacked nearest the window with food parcels in front of them.

Feeling an icy cold draught from the window, we found it had been broken; the wire mesh was cut, leaving a hole large enough for two arms to reach through. There was no telling when this had happened. We had not been near the place for a week and none of our men passed this way when going to work or anywhere else outside the camp.

It was a sad blow to us. We informed One Ear who in turn brought in the Zwickau Criminal Police, whose eyes goggled as if they were looking into an Aladdin's cave when they saw all our food parcels. By the time they had arrived, we had made a thorough count of all the food parcels and none of those were missing.

The police were not very interested and deduced that some of our own men must have done it, and left it at that. We were certain that none of our men were involved, because a 150 or so men living as close together as we did could not keep many secrets from each other, especially thousands of cigarettes.

We had never had a parcel store broken into before in any of the POW camps we had been in. Certainly, the security of this one had to be tightened up, so the first thing we did was to brick up the window. Nag Bevan and I carried out the job that very day, losing no time, whilst the others carried on with the parcel detail.

There were plenty of bricks in the old foundry part of the building and One Ear produced some tools and cement. We worked like merry devils to get the job completed in the same day.

Meanwhile, Arthur Redford, our camp leader, and Blondie Horsefall, our man of confidence, had been arguing with One Ear that his security on the camp at night was not good enough; if his guards had been alert and doing their rounds properly, this robbery would not have happened.

One Ear was furious at the accusations; he played hell and fingered the pistol strap holding his Luger. He threatened to shoot those who spoke against the efficiency of the Deutsche Wehrmacht. It was very comical to see his antics; he would be furiously ranting and raving on and on, screwing up his face and his voice getting higher, whilst his corporal, Sandy, would stand rigidly to attention with fingers pointed stiffly to the ground, wishing to God he wasn't there, and when asked a question (which was, in fact, invariably a statement needing no reply), would answer in a loud voice, '*Yawohl Herr Feldwebel.*' As usual, the Germans always made a big blustering show of shouting, demanding, bullying, giving orders, getting red in the face and stamping on hats, while we Britishers played it cool – which I think made the Germans worse.

But sometimes we changed our tactics; we would imitate them and rant and rave in quite good German, also often producing the results we wanted.

However, the bitter and twisted One Ear had a queer sense of humour. When all had quietened down, he called for the British camp staff again and said that he could understand our being upset at losing our valuable cigarettes but could not understand the prisoners demanding better security in their own camp. He had not enough men to put extra guards on at night; he had not any accommodation for any more men and the Wehrmacht would not give him any more men, but he was prepared to make us an offer.

There were two guards on duty at night, one on duty in the *schreib stube* where the arms, ammunition and telephone were, and the other on patrol outside. The guards changed over with each other every two hours; we of course were thoroughly acquainted with these arrangements.

One Ear offered us the job of going on guard duty with his men so that there could be two outside and two inside. We could then watch our precious parcel store. Being freezing cold and in the middle of winter, I am sure One Ear honestly did not think we would accept, but we did. The only condition, however, being typical British, we wanted two hours on and four hours off, in pairs (as we would have done in our own army) from six in the evening until six in the morning. This was accepted and meant, however, having six men on guard.

So that evening, six of us, Arthur Redford, Blondie Horsefall, Frankie Hope, Nag Bevan, Bill Cummings and myself, got dressed in the warmest clothing we could muster and went 'on duty'. This alone must have been unique in the annals of prisoner of war camps.

One Ear did not ask us to promise not to escape. It was a foregone conclusion and obvious that anyone escaping at that time of the year would have been out of his mind.

The German guards thought we were crazy to be out in the freezing cold when we could have been in our warm beds, but anyway we did it, spending a most miserable night. The night was pitch black, it snowed like hell all the time and our clothing and boots were no match for the cold.

The German guards wore large overboots packed with straw and extra-large, long well-padded overcoats over their normal greatcoats, and big ear muffs over their ears. They were also burdened with steel helmets, rifles, respirator canisters, ammunition pouches and side haversacks.

One night of this was enough, nothing happened; we thought it better to let the Germans enjoy their own weather! The store was now well bricked up, the roof was good, the door was big and stout and we had examined the locks and keys with One Ear. There was no doubt the security was as good as it would ever be.

There were also Ausländer camps in the area and we thought they were worth investigating in case they might lead to some clue to the robbery. Ausländer camps were those holding foreign workers who had been brought into Germany by force or trickery and made to work to aid the German economy. There were several camps, men and women from Poland and the Ukraine and men from France and Belgium. All these were civilian camps and not POW camps, whose inmates lived a miserable existence, being ill-fed, badly clothed and ill-treated at every opportunity.

But the investigations, both by ourselves and the Germans, came to nothing. The winter continued with its customary harshness and the incident was gradually forgotten.

Life in camp went on as usual; new guards came and went, and the Allied Air Forces were spreading their activities throughout Germany. By many indications, it was time for us to complete the digging of the air-raid trenches inside our perimeter wire and be ready to get our heads down.

The next incident we were concerned with was over a Leica cine camera. One of the men in C. and F. Leonards had somehow or other obtained this excellent cine camera from a German guard, but another guard had later seen photographs or films showing the camp, various individuals and part of the factory. This guard had instantly blabbed to the camp commandant who in turn started a full-scale search for the camera, but not before the boys had been tipped off by the first guard who had done the deal.

The camera found its way through C. and F.s to our part of the factory and then into our camp where it was given over to the camp staff to hide as C. and F.s camp was being torn apart board for board in an attempt to find it. This was serious for the Germans as there was no telling what had been filmed. They even searched the works – again a hopeless job. The camp commandant reported the matter to Stalag HQ and they in turn turned the matter over to the Gestapo dogs. Their investigations also come to naught. We had been informed of all the proceedings almost hour by hour. The next move the Gestapo made was to pay our camp a visit one Sunday morning when we were all in. It was a complete surprise; we had no idea they were coming. Every man was chased indoors and the camp locked up. Then, after we had been individually searched, we had to file out of the main door into the compound.

There were three Gestapo men, dressed in long, dark, shiny mackintoshes, dark trilby hats and polished black shoes. After we were all in the compound, they started to search the camp, insisting on doing the job themselves, they wanted no help from One Ear or his guards. All this took several hours, until at last the three emerged via the front door and went off to the office to One Ear. The camera was quite safe.

We all dashed into our rooms; every bed had been torn apart and every man's kit was strewn about having been thoroughly gone through.

Suddenly, one man came storming through to the camp leader and insisted he had lost two bars of Lux soap. Arthur, Blondie and Frankie Hope went quickly to One Ear and reported it whilst the Gestapo men were still there. Were they being accused? Yes, they were!

The three were very annoyed and as usual there was much loud talk and threats. One Ear never spoke a word until he butted in to dismiss our men.

Later after the Gestapo men had gone, One Ear sent for our camp leader and gave him the two missing bars of soap, with the explanation that he had told his visitors the only way to prove their innocence was to turn out their pockets, which they surely would not mind doing to vindicate themselves. Hence the two bars of soap, a feather in the cap for One Ear, a boot up the arse for the Gestapo men, and a camera safely hidden in the German quarters without them knowing. The camera was soon recovered, re-hidden several more times and after considerable time handed back to its owner in the other camp. The Germans had at last come to the conclusion that there had never been a camera in the prisoners' possession, but the photos must have been taken by one of the guards; consequently, more stringent discipline was applied to them.

One Ear was going on leave for a week or so and his relief, another Feldwebel, turned up to stand in for him. I forget his name, but he had been on recuperation leave after spending some time in hospital from wounds received on the Russian Front. He was expecting to be sent back there and dreaded it. He was a young, active man, more like ourselves, and was so enthusiastic about soccer that he insisted on playing with us. When we went to the football field at Crossen, we would go already dressed in our football kit with a battledress blouse over our shirts and carrying our boots. The Feldwebel did the same, borrowing a battledress blouse and joining our ranks whilst four of his guards accompanied us to the field. He did this so that no one else would recognise him and he passed off as one of us. It was a pity he did not have a longer stay with us. One Ear was back all too soon and he soon put the camp back on its old footing again with his petty restrictions. He had now well and truly fallen out with our 'Vertrauance' (trusted) man, Blondie. They disagreed violently every time they met.

Blondie Horsefall, a bombardier and regular soldier of the Field Artillery, was a man of his word. Always clean and smart and well turned out, speaking German now quite fluently, he hammered away at One Ear on every possible occasion for better facilities and conditions for us.

I had known him from our early days. He was a good sportsman who loved playing any kind of games and had taken part in our gymnastic sessions with great enthusiasm. In the end One Ear got rid of him, posting him to another camp miles away, somewhere in Poland. The next and last time I saw him was after the war when we were both hurriedly changing trains somewhere en route to our new units. The next man to take over Blondie's job was Bill Cummings, a shrewd, likeable Northern Irishman from Belfast.

We soon lost another one of our camp staff who had got on the wrong side of One Ear: Nag Bevan, a true Welshman in every sense. He was posted to Bergeschacht in Zwickau (as all Welshmen were miners). Harry Hammerton took his place. He was a 6-footer, corporal of the Military Police and a good steady, dependable type.

The next new development was the calling in of our camp money which the Germans were going to exchange for Deutschmarks (DM) at the rate of two for one. We had never at any time ever considered our camp money as a purchasing power between ourselves, as did the French or other prisoners. To us it was pretty worthless, except to pay exorbitant prices for almost worthless goods when the Germans stocked the so-called 'canteen' each month.

The greatest use we had found for our money in Berlin was to donate as much as we possibly could to the International Red Cross through our *Vertrauance* man via the Germans to Switzerland, if it ever got there; at least we were trying to do some good with it.

Changing over to DM threw a new light and purchasing prospects on the whole subject of money, although the country was well sewn up with strict controls, rationing and issues of various types of dockets required for any mortal thing one could think of. But loopholes were found and although we still contributed to the Red Cross, we found good use for what was left.

We managed to get permission to go to the Zwickau swimming baths, in two sessions, on a Sunday morning, paid for in DM. This was also a very useful propaganda march through the town for us.

Through our weekly visiting French medical officer, we learned that he could give us a medical certificate to enable us to buy, through German civilian sources, spectacles, false teeth and chiropodist treatment, all to be paid for quite legally in DM.

I badly needed a part upper denture for four teeth and I had no trouble in obtaining the necessary *Schein*, certificate. Having had several visits to a dentist in town, accompanied each time by a guard, the day had now come when I was to get my teeth and of course pay for them.

So a guard and I sallied off forth one bright sunny afternoon to town, chatting about this and that and the war. Like most Germans, he was utterly fed up now the tide had turned against them and made a rude grimace as a train went down the line with its locomotive bearing the following slogan, written in large white letters on its side, '*Alle müssen arbeiten für den Sieg*', 'Everyone must work for the victory'.

Our afternoon darkened as we entered the town; we were both walking on the pavement, I walking nearest to the road and my companion gazing in the shop windows, when from nowhere up loomed a German officer.

I slung him a smart salute up quick, to which he repaid the compliment, looking me straight in the eye, and adding, '*Guten Tag*', 'Good Day'.

The guard had completely ignored him; he had not even seen him as he had gazed in the shop windows, and we were only about three paces further on when the officer bellowed for him to stop. And stop he did, to receive the biggest reprimand he had ever had, and made to march forward three times to salute the officer, in full view of everyone passing by.

I honestly did not know where to put myself, I could only stand in the lee of a shop hoping to be as inconspicuous as possible, but an old German civilian, deciding to take a hand in the matter, bellowed at me to get into the gutter. I bellowed back in equally as good German that it had nothing to do with him and I was staying where I was. Then the officer spun round and told him to get on his way and mind his own business.

The officer next glared at me, looking me up and down, from my shiny boots to the top of my sparkling RE cap badge and barked, '*Englander?*' '*Yawolhe Herr Offizier*,' I replied, (I did not know his rank), whereupon he told us both to go upon our way. With another salute, and moving off smartly, we both could not get away quick enough.

Neither of us spoke again until we got into the dentist's, and there he told his tale of woe while I was getting my final fitting. The old dentist, heavy bespectacled, commiserated with him and when he could get a word in, related similar stories of the First World War, seemingly soothing the guard.

I was very happy with my teeth, paying for them in full, plus a bonus of a bar of chocolate which I slipped to him around the counter, laying it on a shelf. Then with '*Guten Tags*' and '*Auf wiedersehen*' the guard and I stepped out into the warm sunlit afternoon, and more trouble.

From here we had to proceed to the *Deutsche Kaserne*, German Barracks, where the guard had business to conduct for One Ear, and we had not gone far when the air-raid alarm wailed out. 'Oh!' we said, 'It must be a false alarm,' the bombers had always gone around us, surely 'they' would not bomb Zwickau.

We carried on our way whilst most other people, mainly old men, women and children, hurried on their way to the various shelters, for what they were worth (because Germany had been very late in constructing air-raid shelters).

The sound of aircraft, hundreds of them, could now be heard, and looking up into the clear blue sky we saw a huge smoke ring forming above us and one solitary aircraft leaving the area, The flak started its rumpus pushing shell after shell into the sky, and looking further afield we saw a mass of bombers in perfect formation heading straight for us, and the Pathfinder's smoke ring.

A policeman shouted to us from the other side of the road to get to a shelter just around the corner of the next street. Running forward at the same time as the bombs began to whistle down, we had just got inside the doorway of the shelter when the first ones began to explode. With thumping hearts and the draught of exploding bombs to help us on our way we tumbled more or less down the stone stairs to the shelter below, which had been converted from a cellar. There were several electric bulkhead lights fitted to the walls, the ceiling had been strengthened with cross timbers and shored up with heavy uprights. A rough bench seat ran round the room. We were the only occupants.

We planted ourselves on the bench just around the first corner of room, whilst outside the noise was deafening and increasing in its density. I was silently praying that my number would not be on one of the bombs, at the same time gritting my teeth, new ones forgotten and cursing the RAF

Then the cellar shook, bits of debris fell on us and the lights went out. My God, I thought, they are after us good and proper this time. The guard was now moaning. I thought he had been hurt, but he was on his knees praying aloud, '*Mein Gott in Himmel, Warum hast du mich verlassen?*' 'My God in Heaven, why have you forsaken me?' saying it over and over again until he was almost hysterical.

The raid increased its intensity and viciousness for what seemed an interminable length of time. I could now see a weak shaft of light at the bottom of the stairs as my eyes got used to the darkness. The bombing suddenly decreased and stopped altogether, leaving only the flak shooting at the departing raiders, then all was quiet. I spoke to the guard, saying we must get moving. He was still shaking like a leaf and followed me up the steps to the street above. What a sight met our eyes; half the street had collapsed.

We made our way back the way we had come, all thoughts of going to the barracks forgotten. Our best place now was out of town and fast, heading for camp. There were palls of smoke and dust over the town which completely obliterated the sunlight. This indeed had turned out to be a dark day.

The 'all clear' had not gone, but we still made our way hastily over piles of rubble and on to the edge of town to the long straight road leading to Crossen. About halfway back to camp we heard the dreaded noise of more aircraft coming towards us. The flak opened up and the second raid started.

We both slid into the field which was below the road level but really offered no protection at all. The guard was moaning again that we should have stayed in the *Keller*. But we could at least see what was going on, and from here it did not seem to be as intense as the last one. Once again, the bombs went en masse for the town.

After the raid, we continued back to camp, the guard asking me over and over again not to tell anyone what had happened in the air-raid shelter. I gave him my assurance and this is the first time I have ever mentioned it. He had done nothing to be ashamed of, it happened to many in those days of great danger.

Not far from the camp, as the 'all clear' sounded, we met Arthur and Bill with another guard coming to meet us. They had decided to come into town to see what had happened to us and six others of our men who worked in town at a milk factory. Luckily, they eventually found our men in town safe and sound, if not badly shaken. The whole camp buzzed with excitement at this raid and there was much speculation as to whether the paper factory would become a target or not for another day.

Various grades of paper were manufactured and quite a lot of the better-class paper was loaded into refrigerator-type railway wagons and sent to Turkey. We were told that from Turkey the paper found its way in one form or another to England, but we never knew whether this was true or not. However, one thing is certain, throughout the war these two factories were never bombed!

Of the few Cypriots we had with us, two of them decided to make an attempt to get to Turkey by stowing away in one of the refrigerator wagons. The idea was all right, except for one or two snags they had not thought about: the wagons were not ventilated as ordinary goods vans, and no one knew how long it took for them to get to Turkey; these were the two main factors for survival. The two stout hearts stowed away late one afternoon, the wagons were closed and sealed, and the remainder of the men came into camp after the day's work.

The Germans soon discovered that there were two men missing and the usual search began by locking up the camp, counting and recounting and informing the local barracks and police. Meanwhile, our camp leader, having been told where the two men were hiding, sent for Ali Riza Tewfik, their leader, explaining to him the danger they were in inside the refrigerator wagon with its limited amount of air space, and if something was not done about it, the two would not last out till morning.

Ali, realising what danger they were in, agreed they must be got out, or else they would land up in Turkey as dead turkeys. It was a hard thing to do, but the Germans had to be told as the two men had now been in the wagon for several hours. So, the wagons on that consignment were duly opened, eventually coming to the one where our two men were; they crawled out utterly exhausted from the effects of the bad air. It was a good try for a spontaneous effort and given a bit more thought could well have been developed into a good escape route. But it was too late now, the Germans really tightened up their vigilance on that particular loading ramp and the security of the men working there.

The business of escaping cropped up frequently. There were lengthy discussions both for and against – which usually ended up in a heated argument. Deep down in everyone's heart was the burning question: how to get home and do it safely. It was not just a question of getting out of the camp, the main problem was getting out of Germany. We all wished at one time or another to be able to fly over the wire like the birds and away into infinity.

It was not difficult to escape from a working party, the only snag about this was it only gave one a head start and nine out of ten attempts were quickly recaptured. Escaping from the camp at night after returning from work was not much of a problem. The best time to go was after the 9.30 p.m. check parade which would at least give one a few hours grace until the next morning's check parade and even more time if one could carry out a cover-up operation for another few hours.

There were the usual risks involved when negotiating the heavily barbed wire fences. One had only three choices: under, through, or over the top, and one could be unlucky enough to be making the bid when the guard dogs were being exercised or when a trigger-happy guard was on duty.

Preparation was absolutely essential. There was always much argument as to whether to go off dressed as a civilian worker or stay in our own uniforms. The majority favoured staying in our own uniforms as this was definitely the safest if one was recaptured to establish one's true identity. Being caught as a civilian worker could lead to untold unnecessary trouble with the Gestapo who showed no favours to anyone.

The preparation and hoarding of suitable food were all important. Food mainly came from our Red Cross parcels in the form of chocolate, dried fruit (such as raisins, currants, dates, apricots etc.), biscuits, home-made oatcakes and cakes made from Bemax and the odd tin of bully beef and the like.

This of course had to be hidden in safe places for we never knew when the Gerry would pounce on a hut to do a thorough search, usually when were all out at work.

We had no such thing as an escape committee because from our very first days of captivity we had had no trust or confidence in our senior NCOs. Therefore, all would-be escapists kept their plans to themselves and quietly disappeared when the appropriate time arrived, with only their own room-mates knowing of their departure and the reminder of the camp knowing when the Germans realised someone was missing.

Maps and compasses were almost non-existent. There were many rumours and much speculation of these being hidden in Red Cross sports and games requisites and although every item was thoroughly searched, I never knew of one instance when anything was found. The only possible method of getting anything like this was to bribe and blackmail the German guards.

The biggest and most important problem of all was how to get out of Germany and then occupied Europe. Which way to go and where to make for was not an easy decision to make. Germany itself was under such strict security control by the Gestapo, the Criminal Police and the Wehrmacht that even the Germans found great difficulty in movement from town to town without the necessary correct documentation. There was no doubt about it, the Germans had the whole country pretty well sewn up.

There are always two sides to everything, and as it was with our thoughts and arguments on the subject of escaping. Why should we escape? Why should we risk our lives again and again, and for what? A grateful country eager to have us back so that we could be used as gun fodder again?

Does anyone think the politicians and generals thought twice about us after we were made prisoners? Not on your life they didn't. We had served our usefulness; we had gone through hell for them; we had seen so many men of both sides killed and wounded, maimed for life, shell shocked (or is not the modern term, battle fatigue?), and now we were, to use a good old army term, written off. The only people to do anything for us now were our own next of kin, relatives and friends and those wonderful voluntary workers throughout the British Isles. And we were not altogether out of the war yet, though some people might think we were safe behind our barbed wire camps. Did the politicians and generals think about us when they ordered Germany and other countries of Europe to be bombed and blasted and annihilated, and to be shelled and shot at right up to the last minutes of our liberation? Not on your life they didn't. They have no idea what it was like under the mass bombing because they were not there as we were.

So the greatest percentage of POWs of all grades stayed put to sweat it out until one day the liberation armies moved in.

We were now well into 1944 and we kept wondering how much longer the war was going to last. We had been keeping a very strict count of Red Cross parcels since the robbery earlier in the year and up to now all was well. There had been a shortage of parcels at times and the weekly issue had been one between two men or even one between three, but we had survived the winter very well and the store was beginning to fill up again.

One Thursday, after counting out the correct number of parcels for the weekly issue, we found that there was one missing. We checked and double checked and we had to recheck without arousing the guard's suspicions; we were absolutely certain, though we couldn't believe our eyes!

We decided to play for time, so knocked over one of the stacks of parcels to give us time for another count. They were so well packed that none of the contents could come to harm. The stack came down; the guard played hell and fetched One Ear, who ordered us to carry on with the parcel *ausgabe* (output) and restack later. This was just what we wanted, so the next day we started restacking and recounting until there was no mistake, there was definitely one parcel missing. Someone was getting into the store, but when and how we had still to find out.

After the next Thursday's count, we found that there was another parcel missing and during the following week when two of us we walking round the old foundry we found a parcel still tied up with string, evidently ready for collection by somebody later on.

The others on the British camp staff were told, and we all debated whether or not to leave it there and keep a watch to see who came to collect it. We decided against this action, for although we had ways and means of getting out of the camp at any time we liked, we realised that whoever was watching would soon be missed by the guards and also that the spot would have to be covered day and night.

So, we took the parcel up to the camp leader's room without being seen by anyone, and then invited One Ear up to show him what had happened. One Ear refused to believe that the culprit could possibly be one of his men and we equally refused to believe that it could be one of ours. Something had to be done and we needed his co-operation. First, we had to find out just when the parcels were being taken and to do this, we would have to count the parcels every morning. But this would arouse the suspicions of the Unteroffizier and the *schreib stube* clerk who were normally in the camp all day and also any of our own men who happened to be off sick from work in the factory.

To overcome the difficulty, we persuaded some of our men in the factory to cause a little industrial unrest, which meant that One Ear could send the two Germans into the factory to smooth out the trouble, leaving us free to count the parcels.

We did not tell our men the real reason why we asked them to cause a disturbance and the plan came off, because One Ear took the usual reprisals by sending all the sick men to work, leaving the other four of us free to go with One Ear to the store to count.

For a week or two we kept our ears and eyes open amongst our own men and One Ear kept a sharp eye on his guards. Soon something emerged from our efforts. We found, to our delight and to One Ear's amazement, that when a parcel disappeared, it was when two particular Germans were on night guard. This was at least once a week, though not always on the same night of each week and there was a separate weekend roster.

One Ear wanted to wheel the two guards in there and then on the spot, charge them both with theft and get the whole thing cleared up. He was beside himself with rage and raved on and on, saying that both would be shot for letting down the honour of Germany. We pointed out that in all probability one of the two guards was innocent and that it would be quite wrong to accuse them both, also that if they were charged it might be impossible to prove that one was guilty, for lack of evidence.

I said, rather rashly, that the only way to prove anything was to catch the thief in the act, then I wished I hadn't spoken because One Ear immediately took me up on it, and, in effect, said 'OK, get on with it, you said it, you do it!'

We five talked about the situation on and off all day, I couldn't back out, and the more I thought about it the more determined I became that I had a plan which would work. The plan was that I should be locked in the store on a night when these particular guards were on duty, on condition that someone else came in with me, but no one had volunteered.

I worked out that One Ear would have to sneak us out of the main building and lock us in the store, using his own key and ours. We would have to go out through the back door of the cookhouse and One Ear would have to leave the padlock off that door to get us out, then re-lock it again when we were safely inside the parcels store.

I was also thinking about what would happen when we caught the culprit. He would be armed with rifle and bayonet, in fact he would be in battle order, complete with tin hat. We could not afford to slip up and let him get trigger happy; he would have to be disarmed and overpowered quickly.

I was still thinking in terms of 'we' and what 'we' would have to do, when one of the British camp staff came up to me and said he would come with me. This was Harry Hammerton, a big fellow, a policeman in civilian life and a corporal in the Military Police. So we went to see One Ear to put the plan to him. He was all in favour, but would not have anything to do with it personally. I realised that, as a Feldwebel, he could not allow himself openly to aid and abet his prisoners; it was obvious that it would cost him his job if anything went wrong. Nevertheless, I reminded him that it was his duty to help us and that he was already deeply involved.

One Ear presented all sorts of theories about getting us out of the building at the required time without any of the guards finding out. He then decided to give the task to his Unteroffizier, but immediately changed his mind as he did not trust the fellow. We also had to do everything without our men knowing, for some misguided soul might have given the game away and somehow put the guards on the alert. The fewer who knew about the plan, the better.

One Ear wanted to know whether we could get out by ourselves with one of the British camp staff locking the door after us and then getting back to his own bed. We would not even hear of this. How could we get out, we asked, when he had the place so well locked up?

With a smirk on his face, One Ear said that he knew we could get in and out and that some men had done so in the past. One of us then quietly and smilingly replied that, that statement had yet to be proved as a fact. However, it was true that we could get in and out of the buildings; it was a bit tricky and dangerous, but we weren't going to tell him how. So, it was decided that one of the Germans whom we could trust would have to be approached. We chose the Obergefreiter, One Ear's interpreter, Seifert, who was an intelligent type and anything but a soldier. He was tall, lanky and skinny, with a bit of a Jewish look about him and his English was quite good.

That evening, Seifert was detailed for parcel *ausgabe* duty and so were Harry and I. We first began talking about all sorts of things and then we broached the subject of our plan to be locked in the outside parcel store.

Seifert was completely flabbergasted. We thought he was going to faint, then he sat down on a stool and put his head in his hands. He did not know what to say and if he had known he would have been speechless with fear. I offered him a cigarette and told him to take his time, just to talk quietly, when he could. In the meantime, we were dishing out tins of this, that and the other to the men queuing up on the other side of the counter.

Eventually Seifert was able to talk and I told him that I would fix everything with One Ear if he would give his word to help us in the presence of One Ear. We would then finalise the details of how he would get us out of the building, into the store and then get himself back inside his own room, without anyone being any the wiser. I explained that if he wouldn't agree to help, we would have to tell One Ear of his bartering and black-marketing with us, because we couldn't afford to have him around any longer. This would mean that he would be posted immediately, perhaps to the Russian front! As we expected, Seifert agreed.

After the parcel *ausgabe* was over we locked up, said goodnight to Seifert and went along to see the camp leader to tell him that we were ready for the final phase. He hadn't liked this idea of mine from the start and wanted a further discussion on it, so we found the other two members of our camp staff and called them in. We five were still the only ones in the camp who knew anything about the missing parcels.

After a lot of discussion, it was decided that we would go through with the plan, but the responsibility would be entirely Harry's and mine. The other three obviously didn't really want to be responsible because they were not able to take an active part, and if anything went wrong, they would have to explain things to the other men. But Harry and I were quite happy with this, provided they gave their word to keep it all secret and just carry on as if nothing was going to happen. Anyway, Harry and I could not back out now that we had brought Seifert into our confidence.

I had even kept this business secret from my own bosom pal, Tom, something I hated doing, because normally we had no secrets from each other and we shared everything we had. But so had some of the others on the camp staff, and we had agreed from the beginning to keep it all to ourselves.

I had to get through the rest of that evening as normally as I could. On going to bed, I found it very difficult to get to sleep as I had all sorts of ideas running through my mind. I was thinking of how I would use pepper to blow into the guard's face as he came near to us in the store, and then, gripping my round cigarette lighter, make my hand into a club to belt him sharply behind the ear. I had made this lighter in the fitting shop in the paper factory with the aid of Fritz Becker, using a heavy copper tube about 1 inch in diameter and about 3 inches long; just the right size to make one's hand form a good weapon for knocking out guards.

We saw One Ear the next day and told him that Seifert had agreed to help us. Seifert was called in to One Ear's office to confirm this and so the game was on; we now had to make the final plans as to how we could be 'sneaked' out of the main building and across into the store, also for Seifert to be able to get back into the German quarters without arousing anyone's suspicions.

The route would have to be from where we slept on the first floor of the building down the main stairs with the locked gate top and bottom, across the hallway and through another locked door into the kitchen. Then across the kitchen, through another locked door into a corridor, down some steps and through the outside door which was not only locked but had a metal bar across it on the outside, secured by a stout padlock. Once there, a quick dash for about 12 or 15 yards across to the parcel store and then Seifert would have to lock us in.

Seifert had the worst job, for not only would he have to contend with the two men on guard duty but also with the other guards who slept in the same room as he did. He must also not forget Unteroffizier Sandy who slept in a separate little room opposite the office-cum-guardroom.

Seifert would have to get the padlock and bar off the outside kitchen door beforehand, then take the padlock off the inner kitchen door, hoping that while it was off and he was coming upstairs for us the guard on duty would not discover it.

Seifert would also have to make sure that the door from the Germans' quarters into the kitchen was locked behind him so that we would not be disturbed when crossing the kitchen. He would have to put the key to this door into his pocket and replace it on the Germans' side of the door when he had locked us in the parcels store, before getting back into his own sleeping quarters, and the number of keys involved meant that he would have to make himself familiar with each key by touch. Valuable time couldn't be wasted by fumbling and searching for keys; they would have to be kept in separate pockets – for silence and speed were essential.

When the Germans went on sentry duty each night, they helped the Feldwebel or the Unteroffizier to carry out the check parade on the British prisoners at about 9 p.m., after the parcel *ausgabe*. Then the main doors were locked, barred and bolted from the outside as well as the back kitchen door. The official 'Lights Out' was 10 p.m. when we, the prisoners, had to retire to our sleeping quarters on the first floor. The guards then locked the gates at the top and bottom of the stairs and went back to their own quarters by way of the kitchen, locking the kitchen door behind them and also the door leading to their own quarters. They then went through to the office-cum-guardroom, hung up the keys on the key-board and one of them would then go on sentry duty. They would do two hours on and two hours off.

The tour of sentry duty took the guard first to the main gate where he would stand for a while, then patrol around the perimeter of the camp (they did this patrol in two halves and it didn't matter which half was done first), from the main gate along the hardcore track as far as the wall of our outside buildings extended. While doing this part, the guard could not see into the camp confines. Then he would go back to the main gate for another little rest, after which he would patrol in the opposite direction, turning right at the corner and going towards the railway, turning right again to walk to the far extent of our buildings and returning by the same route. On this part of the guard's patrol his view into the camp yard was limited, which was ideal for our plan. The guards seldom walked round the inner confines of the camp at night once the doors had been locked and barred, so if Seifert was careful and didn't get into a panic, we would succeed.

We discussed all this detail with Seifert and the more we went into it, the more enthusiastic he became. It showed us that truly there is a spark of adventure in every man, whatever his nationality. At this stage we had reached the point where we had to decide on the date. Which night should we choose?

We consulted One Ear and he decided for us; it was to be on Saturday, 17 June, 1944, eleven days after D-Day. It appeared that he was going home for the weekend from Saturday morning until early Monday morning; there would also be a number of guards away for the weekend and Unteroffizier Sandy would be in charge of about ten men only.

One Ear gave Seifert a telephone number to ring in case we were successful with our plan; otherwise, if nothing happened at all or if something went wrong, it was obvious that he would deny all previous knowledge of our activities. Seifert also realised this, it was the only time he seemed to waver and want to back out of everything.

The day, 17 June, finally arrived. One Ear went off smartly for the weekend and then it was a long, long day for the five of us on the British camp staff waiting for night to come.

At last, everyone started to get ready for the check parade, then the two guards, with Sandy in attendance, locked up as usual and left us alone. I took particular notice that the two guards we suspected were on duty. It seemed ages before everyone went to bed and settled down for the night. Even after the lights were out, by the dim glow of the pilot lights, some horseplay would be going on between the bunks, and guitars and other instruments would be played. Home-made candles would be lit, groups of men would gather to talk about every topic under the sun and arguments would be started which would often continue the next day. A hundred or so men in one room was no joke and there had to be some outlet for our feelings.

Eventually things quietened down, candles were extinguished and most of the men went to the urinal before settling down for the night. There were two toilets at the head of the stairs to which one could just see the way with the aid of the pilot lights. Some men did not bother to go to the urinal during the night but kept a tin can (usually a German 7lb jam tin!) under the bunk and emptied it out the following morning.

It must have been in the very early hours that I heard a noise from the stairs. I was already dressed and I slipped quietly out of bed and went over to the place where Harry slept.

He was awake and he too was already dressed. We heard footsteps coming towards our room as if someone was trying desperately to be quiet and we thought of Seifert. Surely, he wouldn't be such a fool as to wear boots, he would either take them off or wear plimsoles or something like that.

We were amazed to see the figure, not of Seifert, but of one of the two guards on duty coming into the room. He didn't see us, but shone his torch across to the other side of the room and then walked up the alleyway between the bunks next to where I slept; he actually passed my bed and didn't notice that I was not in it. He walked very steadily, seeming to know exactly where he was going and he went straight to one of the bunks and did a bit of silent bartering for his black-market activities – coffee and cigarettes.

Then he tiptoed out of the room and locked the door again behind him. This was one of our worst moments. This guard was one of the two whom we suspected; he did a lot of black-marketing and always made out that he was very friendly towards us. Seifert, I thought, was probably foxed, he must have seen the fellow go upstairs and would have to wait for him to get down again before he could start to come up. Harry and I both hoped to goodness Seifert would come as promised. As a precaution, while waiting, we fixed up our beds to make them look as if we were still in them.

We didn't have long to wait after all. Seifert appeared and I couldn't help chuckling, for he looked so comical with his long, lanky figure bent almost double, tiptoeing along in stockinged feet. He looked like the villain bent on mischief, in an old cloak-and-dagger film.

Harry and I each grabbed a blanket and were just starting to follow Seifert towards the stairs when someone started to pee in his tin, which seemed to make a terrific row; then someone sleepily came from between the alleyway of bunks to go to the toilet at the head of the stairs. He didn't see us and we followed him as far as the stairs where he went on and we slipped downstairs, locking the gates behind us.

The hallway was in complete darkness and so was the rest of our route, but we knew exactly where to go. We got safely through the kitchen holding on to each other, through the door into the corridor, down the steps and to the outside door which we carefully opened, taking care to lock all the doors behind us as we went.

It was pitch dark outside and we stood still for a while to try to detect where the sentry was. At last, we spotted him through the barbed wire fence making his way towards the railway line. This was fortunate for us; in fact, it couldn't have been better.

We helped Seifert to put the bar across the door, by which time we had left the main building and locked it. We walked over to the parcel store, unlocked the padlocks and went in. Seifert lost no time in wishing us good luck, locked us in and silently went on his way. Harry and I had no reason to doubt that he would not be successful in getting back undetected, for the man acted like a natural burglar.

We settled down in our pre-arranged corners on our folded blankets on the concrete floor. It was pitch dark and got colder and colder. It became difficult to keep our eyes open in such utter darkness; we whispered a few words of encouragement to each other and then there was silence. I must have started to doze because the next thing I knew was that Harry was giving me a shake and whispering that there was a noise at the door as if someone were outside and trying to get in. I woke up instantly and with a horrible cold chill running up and down my spine, stood up and gripped my cigarette lighter in my right hand. Harry was already on his feet. The locks were being removed from the doors; one half of the door began to open and a chink of light shone in, getting bigger as the door opened wider. I could see Harry opposite me and we both stood motionless as the intruder came nearer. It was only then that I realized in a flash that I was on the wrong side of the door to be able to use my right hand properly to 'belt' the fellow and my heart was beating so loudly that it seemed it could have been heard a mile away.

Suddenly Harry and I moved out together. It was all over before one could say 'Jack Robinson'. I could see the man's outline quite distinctly and it certainly was a German guard. We forgot the pepper and Harry hit him right in the midriff, but in striking the blow hit the guard's lamp which was hooked on to the centre of his belt.

The lamp flew off in bits to the floor and the guard grunted. While this was happening, I reached out for his steel helmet and after pulling it forward, grabbed him by the front of his tunic and belted him on the side of the face. He went down like a pole-axed pig, bounced off a stack of parcels and slumped to the floor.

Harry and I got hold of the guard, got him to his feet and it didn't take long for him to come round. I felt for his bayonet and withdrew it from its scabbard. I was now quite cool and calculating; from then on, I spoke in German, quickly and crisply.

I told the man not to cry out or do anything to raise the alarm and prodded him with the bayonet just to let him know I had it and would use it if necessary. I then asked him where his rifle was, but he was reluctant to answer until again he felt the gentle persuasion with the bayonet. Harry had got the man firmly held in a typical policeman's grip and so we marched him off to the guardroom, his own guardroom! We left his rifle, which was leaning against the wall at the side of the kitchen door, until we could get back for it later.

The guardroom door was locked. I asked our prisoner for the key and told him to open the door. When he said he hadn't got it, I clouted him across the head with my hand and told him not to try to be funny, but to produce the key immediately, for surely by this time he knew we meant business. At that, he produced the key from his pocket and opened the door.

We pushed him through into the passageway and opened the first door on our left which led into the office-cum-guardroom. I switched on the light and we saw the other guard asleep on a 6-foot table under the window. There was a small counter with a hinged flap on it just inside the door and Harry pushed our prisoner through this into the centre of the room and sat him down in a chair. I told him, or reminded him again, to keep quiet. Harry then went over to the rifle rack and stood with his back to it, well in control of the room, while I woke up the sleeping sentry who sat bolt upright when he saw me.

We must have given him a terrific fright. I told him to sit quietly on the table, that all would be explained to him very soon and that I was going to get Seifert, Sandy and our own British interpreter as well. I knew exactly where Seifert slept but there was no need to put the light on in the German quarters as he was out in a flash. He went to get Sandy while I went back to the office.

Seifert and Sandy soon came in, Sandy brandishing a pistol. I told him not to be such a b— fool, but to put the pistol away or else we would take it from him. By this time, Harry was standing holding a loaded rifle ready for use.

Everybody started to talk at once, but after a few minutes of babble Seifert began to unfold the whole story to Sandy, while the culprit sat with his head in his hands.

Sandy was most upset at being kept out of the picture, knowing nothing at all about this beforehand. Seifert, however, as a junior rank, was really enjoying himself relating his and One Ear's part in the plot.

Once the explanations were over, Seifert phoned One Ear and we went out with Sandy to lock up the store and collect the guard's rifle which was still leaning up against the wall by the kitchen door.

The culprit's name was Fischer, the man who had come upstairs to do his black-marketing and the man who claimed to be the prisoners' friend. His friendship had cost us dearly, for he had had a great many parcels out of our store for some weeks past, but he claimed to have no knowledge at all of the cigarettes which were originally stolen and which started the whole affair. While we were all in the guardroom, I asked Fischer what keys he had used to open our store. He said that it was easy to get the key from the key-board and had tried several other padlock keys from the board to open our padlock; one, the key to the indoor padlock on the kitchen door, had nearly opened it and he had been able to fix this key to fit the store padlock.

Dawn was breaking when Harry and I returned to bed. We called in at the camp leader's room to tell him that all had gone well and that we had caught the thief. News soon spread through the camp and we did not get much sleep on the Sunday morning as we had to tell the story over and over again. My own special friend was amazed and wished he could only have been in on the night's activities.

One Ear came back that morning instead of Monday and sent for us. We told him exactly what had happened. He had already sent Fischer to the Military Barracks in Zwickau under escort to detention. After he had heard all the facts, he told me to write out a report stating briefly what had happened.

Within a day or two, a German major arrived and sent for Harry and myself. His English was quite good and he congratulated us on the job we had done but also said that it was a most unusual affair which could have had disastrous consequences for all concerned. One Ear had obviously had a good 'telling-off', he was wearing a new hat and standing rigidly to attention by the major's side. The major then dismissed us and that was the last we saw of him.

Later, the other guard who had been on duty told me that when I awoke him that night he thought the war was over and that we were taking over the camp. It was easy to see that he could have added, 'What a pity it was not so!'

One day, after the excitement of catching the culprit had died down, I asked One Ear what would have happened to Fischer. He explained that, although the penalty for stealing food in wartime was death, being a soldier he would most likely have been posted to a 'Straf' Battalion on the Russian Front, in which there was very little chance of survival. I remember that at the time I felt neither hate nor remorse for Fischer. The only thing that mattered to me was that this had put an end to the stealing of our parcels.

As is always the case in events like this, there were repercussions. One Ear had been presented with another problem, it was obvious that his security of the British prisoners of war had been sadly undermined and he realised that if we could get one of his guards to help us in such an escapade, we could also get them to help us in other activities.

Eventually, the incident was forgotten; I expect the copy of my report which I duly handed over to One Ear was filed away in an office at the barracks and, like files in all the armies in the world, stayed in a cabinet until it was time to be disposed of after the requisite number of years, but I still have a copy of that report to this day. A report of what might have been the only occasion when two British prisoners captured a German guard and handed him over to his own guardroom.

The long-awaited day, D-Day, had arrived with the Allied landings in Normandy on 6 June 1944; they were steadily gaining a foothold and consolidating their positions.

We were most jubilant now, expecting the war to be over by Christmas. The German attitude towards us changed overnight showing more goodwill than they had ever shown. Even One Ear was far more amiable and suggested that maybe a few of us would like to go to a 'holiday' camp which had been set up for some time at Genshagen, Berlin. We had read about this camp in the POW German edited news sheet, *CAMP*, issued monthly to us, and we had learned through individuals from other camps who had been to Genshagen that it was nothing more but a breeding ground for the 'British Free Corps'.

Der Freiwillinge Corps were set up by the Nazis and comprised volunteers from all different nationalities to fight against the Russian communists. There was certainly a British Free Corps because members had been seen wearing the German-type field grey uniforms and the shoulder titles – British Free Corps. Whether they ever went into action or not, or what induced them to join forces with the Nazis, I would not know. Anyhow, we were not having anything to do with it or Genshagen and told One Ear so; he never mentioned the subject again.

Autumn came with still more good news from the fronts of the Allies and the Russians who were closing in tighter on Germany. But September's news of the loss of Arnhem after a terrific battle was terrible.

The German guards were being thoroughly sifted out for duty on the fighting fronts and were being replaced by *Deutsche Volksturm*, a Home Guard of men whose ages ranged from 60 upwards, who were not in the best of health and had no interest whatsoever in their duties.

One Ear told us of the new secret weapons such as rockets being fired on London; a self-propelled tank with high explosives directed at the enemy lines by radio; Der Panzerfaust, a new infantry anti-tank weapon; a new jet aircraft which we had indeed seen for ourselves, flying over Zwickau; all of this information he got out of the daily newspapers. We continued to impress upon him that no matter what new weapons they brought out, only something short of a miracle could now alter the course of the war. It was now only a matter of time and they were paying dearly day by day, just as we hoped they would.

Zwickau, however, had not had many air raids since the one the guard and I had been caught in and these had been night-time visits and more pinpointing of targets than mass attacks on the town. By the approach of Christmas, Red Cross parcels were getting scarcer and we had to introduce strict rationing on ourselves. The two cats belonging to the civilian cottages at the camp disappeared one weekend. They had been well fed and fattened by us for months and made a tasty meal in the Sunday stew cooked by Tanky, our cook, who said we would not know the difference between cat and rabbit, and he was right.

We were surprised one day by the arrival of Feldwebel Yainisch and two British prisoners who had been captured at Arnhem. A new camp had been established in Zwickau itself of men from Arnhem, and Yainisch was trying his best to get it organised but was having a lot of trouble.

The two Britishers, Lance Sergeant Ord and Corporal Simpson, told us of their troubles: no Red Cross parcels; nothing to keep themselves clean with; dirty camp; poor rations from the Germans; and having to go out to work. There were about 230 in the camp, many of whom were sick; there were many malingerers which made matters worse; morale was rock bottom and discipline very poor.

Yainisch was trying to do his best for them, but his resources were now more limited than ever. It was he who suggested bringing them to our camp to have a talk. We could only tell them that their troubles were the natural troubles of all beginners in this life and they would just have to get used to it. They had one consolation: that it could not possibly last much longer.

Materially we gave them what soap we could spare and anything in the way of warm clothing. We also gave them an issue of Red Cross parcels, of about one between four, that we could ill afford to give. They went back to their camp more enlightened and less embittered. Our camp now became the central holding centre for Red Cross parcels for the four camps in the area. This ensured an equal distribution weekly, if supplies were available. To this end, Bill Cummings worked ceaselessly to get supplies and saw that each camp got its fair share.

The 'Para boys' and Yainisch now made another request that two men from our camp should go to their camp to help to get it on its feet. Apparently, the bad apple in the bunch was Unteroffizier Fritsch whom Yainisch could not get rid of because he was also the interpreter and Yainisch could not understand English and the Britisher trying to be interpreter was not up to the job, his German being very poor. Fritsch, therefore, his English very near perfect, had things all his own way.

We talked it over at some length and in the end decided I would change camps, providing my pal, Tom, could go with me as interpreter, and also providing we could come back at any time if we wished.

Tom and I thought about it, the war could not last much longer, a change of faces and scenery may do us good, though it meant leaving George behind who did not really mind. So, we agreed to go, first week in the New Year after spending Christmas (yet another one) with our own camp, for there was no point in missing the various forms of entertainment we had been helping to prepare.

We did, however, arrange for the Para boys to attend the concert party we staged and afterwards everybody mucked in to share a mug of tea and biscuits with them. They were most impressed by our hospitality towards them and we hoped their few hours' stay with us had shown them that being prisoners of war did not mean all was lost. We had all been through what they were now going through, but at least they knew they could depend and benefit by our experience and we were not so very far away from them.

One Ear, with his warped mind and queer sense of Nazi humour, nearly put the kibosh on the whole of the Christmas by suddenly deciding to carry out a search of the camp on Christmas Eve. Luckily, we got the tip-off through the cookhouse staff via the guards, which gave us a few precious minutes to hide forbidden items.

Some of our boys had been working at the nearby *Schlachthaus*, slaughterhouse, and had managed to get some lumps of pork fat and pigs' trotters and various types of sausage meat. Others, like myself, had managed to get cakes made outside the camp by Germans, at the factory. In my case I had supplied the dried fruit and some sugar, sent them to Fritz whose wife had made the fruit cake, with enough fruit for herself. They had not had such luxury for years.

So, on the warning that One Ear was on his way, everything was hung on the barbed wire on the outside of the windows and the blackouts put in place. He had a good look round but went away empty handed, muttering to himself, knowing there must be something hidden somewhere, but he never thought of looking outside the windows.

Some wood alcohol had found its way into camp; this was a by-product, made in the factory under special security, and the three men who drank it nearly came to a sorry end, having to be sent to hospital, violently sick, for emergency treatment, their Christmas somewhat spoiled.

Visits were made to Bergeschacht camp and our other Crossen camp to see their concerts and to have a good natter with old friends. There was much optimism all round that this was definitely our last Christmas in Germany, and although we knew everything was going to get much worse in the way of acute food shortage, a very cold, severe winter as usual and the bombing, we did not care or mind any more. We could only hope and pray that God, whom we had often decried, would in the end bring us through safely in one piece, if not a little hungry.

Chapter 9

The Days of Reckoning

Tom and I, accompanied by Feldwebel Yainisch and pulling all our worldly possessions on a borrowed German handcart, arrived at the Para boys' camp next door to number 135 Adolf Hitler Ring, Zwickau, one dark, freezing cold late afternoon in early January 1945.

Approaching the camp by way of the Ring which followed the River Mulde in a wide arc along the eastern side of the town, we passed the main road bridge to Chemnitz and Dresden and came in view of a dark, stone-built four-storey building standing a few yards off the main road, a stone's throw from the bridge, and opposite equally dark-looking stone-built flats on the other side of the road. A high, heavily barbed wire fence with a double gate in it, stretched the length of the frontage of the building along the pavement, and owing to the building standing oblique to the road, the far end of the fence was only about 10 feet from the corner of the building whilst the other end finished near the side of the house, number 135, on the roadside, leaving enough space for a 5-foot wide single barbed wire gate with a pathway down the side of the house leading to the German quarters and office. This pathway was also bordered by a high barbed wire fence and at the far end was another gate leading into the very small camp compound. An armed guard patrolled back and forth along the length of the pavement and another guard was on duty down the pathway. Both guards stood to attention and clicked their heels in salute to Yainisch as we approached.

The single-storey dwelling on our left as we walked down the pathway was entered through double doors at about its centre into a dimly lit hallway with stairs leading to the floor above, a door to the left and a door to the right. We went through the door on our right which led into the office. Seated at a table in the centre of the room, writing, was the man we had been looking forward to meeting with some anticipation, Herr Unteroffizier Fritsch. He immediately stood up, clicking his heels and giving the Nazi salute to Yainisch, saying 'Heil Hitler', and then, moving from the chair, stood with his hands behind his back, back to the fire, glaring at us through his rimless glasses.

Grunting at our introduction by Yainisch, he then asked us in perfect English, did we not salute German non-commissioned officers. We answered in equally as good English that we did not salute non-commissioned officers in our own army and we would only salute commissioned officers in the German army. So he did not take kindly to us from the start.

This was the bad apple in the bunch: Fritsch was an old man of about 60 years or more, small and thick set, heavy-jowled face and bald head. He had been given the rank of corporal, *Dolmetscher* (interpreter), purely and simply for his usefulness on account of his excellent knowledge and speaking command of English.

Still scowling at us, Fritsch spoke in rapid guttural German to Yainisch, saying the two bunks had been allotted to us in a small room on the first floor close to the Camp Revier (sick bay) and that after we had gone through the customary search, he would take us to our quarters as it was getting late and the *Arbeits Kommandos* would soon be returning to be checked in through the gate, which was one of his duties.

Yainisch in reply said the searching would not be necessary in our case, whereby Fritsch opening a drawer in the table took out a large key and switching instantly to English growled at us to follow him. We said *Guten Tag* to Yainisch and that we would see him later – all in German – and followed Fritsch. We simply had to let Fritsch understand right from the beginning that we had understood all that had been said between them and that we could reply equally as well in German, no matter how fast or guttural a dialect he spoke. In fact, we had to 'out German' him on every possible occasion.

It was now quite dark outside. Fritsch pressed a light switch in the entrance hall which put on a light above the door and another light above the door of the camp building. The guard on duty outside slid the bolts off the barbed wire gate leading to the compound as we turned left out of the office and walked towards him. A few yards across the compound, Fritsch unlocked the huge main door to the camp building with his large key and after ushering us inside, locked the door behind him, leading the way up a dimly lit, stone spiral staircase, ascending anti-clockwise to the first floor, the Revier, and the small room we were to be housed in. Here we were greeted by Frank Polley, Dave Simpson and Bill Ord whom we had met previously when they had visited our camp at Crossen.

Fritsch then departed, leaving Tom and I talking to our new friends, sorting out our belongings and bunks and generally getting settled in.

We then made a quick tour of the building, starting with the Revier, a good-enough room with single bunks, but not very clean and with dingy lighting.

The second floor, which held most of the camp's accommodation, was, as usual, overcrowded, dingy, dirty and contained many very untidy bunks. Large piles of ashes surmounted the base of the huge slow combustion stove. The third floor, which included the kitchen and dining room, was very much the same. We met the three cooks, Petch, Lane and Fitzpatrick, who were busily engaged preparing the evening vegetable stew (for what it was worth). Lastly up to the top floor where the washroom, showers and toilets were situated. Tom and I looked at each other, we were not at all impressed by what we had seen. The whole place was filthy and needed a good cleaning up.

As we trooped behind each other down the stairs again, the working parties were returning to camp, cold, hungry and somewhat looking dejected. They paid not the slightest attention to us as they passed us on the stairs.

Yes! this was our Dabendorf days all over again; we knew perfectly well how they were feeling. It was the normal natural process of all 'beginners'.

After the evening meal of unappetising, mucky-looking vegetable stew and the issue of dry rations, we assembled in the upper room for our first check parade. Tom and I stood out in front whilst Ord and Simpson arranged the parade, in fives, for counting. There was much talking going on, no doubt about us.

Yainisch, Fritsch and a guard appeared; a hush fell on the room and the count began, a laborious process for any German. All three carried out the count, agreed the number, then Yainisch totted up those on parade, those in the Revier downstairs, plus those away in hospital, and including Tom and myself came to a grand total of 231, correct.

Speaking to the assembly and translated by Fritsch, Yainisch said a few words about our coming to the camp, of co-operation with us and hoped that life would now settle down a bit and run more smoothly for everyone. He was doing his best and it was up to them to make it better for themselves. With that he left, saying to Tom and myself that he would see us in the morning, when we would go through the working parties and the general set-up of the camp.

We then asked the parade to stand fast so that I could have a few words. I had just begun to speak and at the same time looking each and every man from one end of the parade to the other straight in the face, when I heard one man in the centre, quite near to me, say 'collaborators'. I dashed quickly into the ranks and grabbing the man by the scruff of the neck dragged him out in front, shaking him like a rat.

I was livid with rage and slung him roughly against the front rank with the parting words that if anyone else said anything like that again, I would make him eat every word of it. I also told them that we were not afraid of any of them and that the best two amongst them might as well stand forward now because if it was a fight they wanted, we might as well get it over with now.

There was a deadly silence throughout the room, no one stood forward. I broke the ice again by telling them they were not the only ones who had gone through a rough time, we had all had the same. We had come here to help them and if they were not going to give us a chance to try, then we might as well go back to our own camp the next morning, letting them get on with it in their own way. With that, we went off to our own room whilst the parade broke up into groups and a hubbub of talk.

Later that evening, when we were talking it over with the other members of the staff, a delegation arrived with the man who had caused the upset, saying it was the wish of everyone that we stay and there would be no more trouble.

Next morning, we were up as early as anyone else. Taking special note of the departing working parties, it was difficult to tell who had been washed or not owing to everyone being so muffled up with coat collars and scarves and red berets pulled down right over the ears to keep out the biting cold; we suspected very few had.

Going quickly through the huge rooms, it was plain to see that no effort had been made to leave the bunks tidy or to sweep the floor or to clean anything at all. This would not do; we could not go on like this. So, I sent the word around that all the camp staff and all those having reported sick, lame and lazy, would assemble in the Revier downstairs, in half an hour.

At the assembly, I put the sick at one end of the room whilst I told the camp staff that whatever else they thought they were going to do that day, they were first going to clean up the camp from top to bottom; we would all get mucked into it, including some of those who had reported sick but were able to work.

Every bed in the camp would be made down like Tom's and mine. The washhouse and latrines would be scrubbed from end to end, and there would be hot water for when the men returned back from work that night. The rooms would be swept, the stoves would be cleaned and there would be no skiving.

Next I turned to the cooks and the one who looked after the dining room. I told them to get their fingers out and to get the kitchen and dining room absolutely spotless, and that also from now on there would be no more of their special friends or all and sundry milling about in the kitchen when the evening meal was being dished up. There would be some 'sick' for spud bashing and we would have some cleaner stew in future. The cooks did not like this, and I soon fell out with them.

Then, sending them all off on their way to get cracking on the tasks ahead, I lastly pounced on the sanitation, medical orderly, better known as 'Sani', who got a rocket straight away for allowing the Revier to become such a dump. A good camp had a spotlessly clean Revier with clean beds and nobody in them. It was up to him to make sure this was so.

Accompanied by Sani, we next sorted out the sick parade which was a most difficult job and a thankless one. We had the same system as all the other camps in the area, whereby we were visited once per week, in our case each Monday, by the travelling French medical officer.

He was a very busy man with dozens of camps to visit throughout the week, covering a wide area; quick and efficient, he did not waste much time.

He was doing a good job of work, hampered by petty German restrictions and the increasing Allied bombing.

The obvious dodge was to report sick on the Monday night, hoping to make it last out the remainder of the week and go back to work the following Monday. There were, of course, the legitimate sick and this is where Sani came into his own with his very limited resources.

Number 91474, Fitzgerald by name, I soon realised he was a first-class medical orderly. A medium-built young man, a very pleasant manner and a most likeable disposition, he soon dealt with the various ailments such as boils, sore feet, stomach disorders, odd bruises and the common cold, and of course extra special treatment for those on the skive with 'idleitis' by way of a number 9 and two days off work to get over it.

Later in the morning, while the camp was being well and truly dug out, Tom and I went to the office where Yainisch and Fritsch showed us the neatly arranged camp distribution board on the wall with every man's POW number, a name and trade on a little tag, all hanging in straight rows opposite whichever *Arbeits Kommando* he worked on. There was a separate line for the camp staff, for the sick in camp and for those away in hospital.

I wrote down in a notebook every man's particulars according to the board (which I have in front of me now as I write). The following is the composition of the camp on that particular day in January 1945:

Arbeits Kommando	
Werdau	28
Zwickau I	74
Zwickau II	42
Neumark	60
Mosel	12
Staff	14
Away in hospital (91896 McDowell)	1
Total	231

As I was writing this, Unteroffizier Fritsch went into the camp to see Sani and the sick and Tom talked to Feldwebel Yainisch. Fritsch had, up to now, with his excellent knowledge of English, taken it upon himself to deal with the daily sick parade and he alone would decide what had to be prescribed in each case. He made matters worse by taunting and belittling each man, saying they were all lazy good-for-nothings, which in return only caused a lot of insolence and bad feeling.

This morning he found that the job had already been done for him and he came storming back into the office demanding to know who the hell we were and on what authority we had attended to the sick. What he did not know was that we had briefed Yainisch about the sick parade while he, Fritsch, was out of the office and Yainisch had agreed we had done the right thing and he would like to see the sick himself later.

He soon quietened Fritsch down giving him other duties to perform concerning the guards. I could see we were getting on the wrong side of him, which did not bother us one bit. What we had to do was to keep on the right side of Yainisch.

During the next few days, I arranged to visit each of the working parties to look into the conditions out there. I had no illusions what it would be like for I was too old a hand at the game to expect anything but graft from the Germans. But many things could be bettered.

The camp was getting a 'face lift'. More fuel must be found for the stoves and the hot water boiler, and an endeavour must be made to get the rooms some better lighting, as we had noticed not all the lamp sockets had bulbs in them. So, Fritsch was sent off to the German barracks to use his 'charm' to produce the extra light bulbs, and I decided to ask the men working on the coal sidings to bring back a little coal in their pockets each day and to get Yainisch to stop having them searched when coming through the gates.

We could now see much more of our surroundings in daylight. Looking out of the windows at the front of the camp, we overlooked the main road with the four-storey flats opposite. To our left was a street crossing with more flats and houses and it was here the local children had made themselves an excellent ice-skating rink; there being very little or no self-propelled vehicles on the roads made it a safe place for skating. We often watched them, and enjoyed their antics.

To the rear of the camp, we overlooked the river Mulde with its black, icy waters flowing swiftly below. It was quite wide here, the water lapping up to the base of our building. Along the bank at the base was a mass of entangled barbed wire extending the length of the building and then out into the river for some yards at each extremity.

The building had been a furniture-making factory before being made into a prisoner of war camp. On the ground floor was housed all the woodworking machinery, work benches and other stores, all preserved and sheeted until the day they would be brought out again after the war.

When Yainisch came round on his inspection of the camp during the afternoon, he was amazed and delighted to see what a difference the camp staff and those sick but able to help had made in cleaning up the camp.

Tom and I had taken special interest in the kitchen. It was now spotlessly clean with a much better vegetable stew in the making than they had had previously. The dining room orderly had also been very busy scrubbing the tables and benches and floor. So all was set for the men coming in from work.

Watching for the men returning from work from one of the upper windows, I could see Fritsch waiting, torch in hand, and muffled up against the biting cold ready to make his count as they came through the gate. The first ones in were usually Zwickau I and II, the Neumark, Mosel and Werdau parties having much further to travel. They were long days, Reveille being 4.15 a.m. to be at work for 6 a.m. and arriving back in camp again at about 6 p.m.

Seeing the men returning in such a downtrodden, demoralised state brought home to me what we must have been like when we had first arrived at Luckenwalde. No wonder the Germans had insisted on giving us drill parades, though they were not a success, and the misery of our first working camp at Dabendorf through a very severe winter which had been sheer hell.

I simply shuddered at the thought. Maybe Tom and I were now acclimatised to the German ways and daily routine. Sometimes it seemed we had known nothing else, and we had been here for ever such a long time and God only knew how much longer.

When one pauses to think that these Paratroopers and airborne troops had been trained for a long, long time to achieve a peak of efficiency, besides many of them having sampled action before Arnhem and to have been boosted up in the public eye and keyed up for the greatest and most dangerous mission of their lives, was there any wonder after the chaotic events they had been tossed into, that they should find themselves, within days, prisoners of war, in a completely different environment, so downhearted and miserable?

From the stories they told me about Arnhem, it would appear that the planning, intelligence reports and execution of the campaign was a brilliant piece of mis-management. The brunt of the battle had been borne by those courageous officers, NCOs and men, whose efforts were so outstanding to the bitter end.

These were now very disappointed men: alas, had we not said the same of Crete. Their only consolation was they would not have to endure this life much longer; they would not have to go on year after year as we had done.

The men were genuinely surprised to see the transformation we had made, in one day, of the camp. The stoves were lit, producing a reasonable heat and upstairs there was hot water to wash in.

There were a few grumbles about the evening meal not being dished up before all the working parties were in, as previously, when the last ones in had to take pot luck. The camp staff could not have their meal first either, they had to queue up with everyone else and Tom and I were there to see that all got a fair share.

That night on parade, I told them that in future they would be expected to make up their own beds and sweep the rooms up. On Sunday there would be a blanket-shaking session in the compound and further cleaning up. Anybody with lice had better let me know immediately so that I could make arrangements for them to be deloused.

I also told them I did not care how much trouble they made whilst at work, but here in camp I wanted them to consider it a piece of Britain and to make it a place worthwhile to live in, if only temporarily.

My message went home alright, because from that day on they made steady progress which never dropped back. There were the occasional few who had to be 'chased' and a particular one who had to be taken upstairs and scrubbed.

Within the first week I realised there were three sergeants in the camp. Only one had tried to do anything for the camp, the other two just strung along with everyone else. I asked them point blank why they had not come to the fore to do their 'bit' as was expected of them; they had no excusable answer. So, I told them I would stand no nonsense; if they stood on the fringe arranging the ammunition for others to fire, I was going to have their co-operation or else they would have to go. I got co-operation.

Keeping well in touch with Bill Cummings at Crossen with regard to Red Cross parcels, Tom or I would take a party from the camp staff, hot-footed with a couple of handcarts for collection – hail, rain or fire.

Feldwebel Yainisch borrowed two bicycles and he and I pedalled to the various jobs to see the conditions and to try and make things better. I enjoyed the cycling; it was good exercise. Zwickau I and II were about 5km away, the working parties having to march it. Neumark was 12km, Werdau 10km, and Mosel about 7km away. The work was much the same on each party, unloading or loading wagons on the railway sidings with coal, farm produce, pit props, even manure. I suggested to Yainisch that since he and his men depended on the same kitchen as us for food on continually shortened rations, he should stop Herr Fritsch from carrying out his petty searches when our men returned to camp and I would get them to bring in such things as coal, carrots, turnips, potatoes and the like, which would supplement the rations, and his guards could turn a blind eye. He made no promise but wagged his finger at me for a naughty suggestion. But the searching stopped, our vegetable stew got thicker and we managed to make a reserve of vegetables.

As the weeks went by, even Fritsch came round to our way of thinking, becoming much friendlier and more amiable. He poured out his life history to us one day, telling us that he had belonged to a textile firm and had learned his English at their London office where he had spent some time before the First World War and many years up to 1938 before the present war. There is no doubt that his knowledge of English and the British Isles was first class. His only trouble was, he was a German. But like many other

Germans who, realising the end was nigh, his attitude towards us had made a remarkable change.

Most of our Wehrmacht guards were now being posted to the fighting fronts where there was an increased shortage of men daily. They had been a poor lot of downgraded men to start with, there being only about four of them left who were excused just about everything but breathing, the remainder being old Volksturm men. They were scraping the bottom of the barrel; the writing was now on the wall.

One early morning, as the working parties had left the camp and there was sufficient light to see across the road, I was gazing out of one of the upper windows at the cold, desolate scene, when a young lady, probably about my own age, walked by and, glancing up, gave me what I thought was a wisp of a smile, but I was not sure. The next morning the same happened again, so I told Tom; I had no idea where she came from, but it was a very pleasant change. But one night after check parade when Tom and I went to the office to do our usual arranging of men and sick for the next day, who should be sitting warming her knees against the fire (from coal which our boys had brought in) with another girl friend, but our 'lady of the road'.

Yainisch and Fritsch were present, Yainisch making the introductions. Both girls stood up and shook hands with us, I trying to show no sign of recognition to Maria, the one who had passed by our window; I think the other girl's name was Anna.

A few months ago, this scene would have been absolutely unheard of for to even be caught speaking to a German female, the penalty was at least ten years' hard labour. A notice to this effect was posted up on the wall by the kitchen hatchway at Crossen camp, which I remember so well because years had been spelt 'jears' and we made fun of it.

We carried out our business plus a lot of small talk, including the girls, and I wished Maria would not look so intently at me all the time, for both Tom and I were a bit embarrassed. Nevertheless, from then on we looked forward to seeing them. We saw them night after night, but sometimes there would only be Maria and thus we found out that she lived in a flat above the office with her mother and father. Originally, the whole house had been theirs until the furniture factory had been made into a prisoner of war camp and the ground floor had been made into quarters for the guards and the office.

Maria's mother and father were getting on in years, her father being the caretaker of the factory, going on his rounds every day through the ground floor to see that all was well with the machinery and stores, but we had never yet seen him.

January, cold and biting, gave way to an equally cold February and alas the restarting of more air-raid alarms which would wail out both day and night. On the first few occasions of the alarm sounding at night, we heard the noise of the hordes of aircraft by-passing Zwickau, bound for other targets, but we were alert, dressed and ready for moving out of the camp. The same applied during the daytime until we realised we had not got an air-raid shelter and our compound was quite inadequate to hold one.

I soon took this matter up with Yainisch who also realised what a plight we would all be in should Zwickau become a target once more, which I was sure it would. He soon got busy with the local authority who, to say the least, were not so very bothered about us. But I pointed out that should there be any casualties, the Burgermeister would be held responsible and would answer to the liberation forces when they arrived, and probably with his life.

The safest air-raid shelter was situated over the nearby bridge and in a hillside on the left of the road; it would hold thousands of people, but it was not for us. Instead, we were given a shelter made of precast concrete slabs, half sunk into the ground in a bastion design and covered with packed earth.

It was situated not very far away: we turned left out of the camp, a few hundred yards to the next crossroads where we turned left again, passing houses on each side of the street, until we came to a small park, again on our left, which stretched from the street down to the river. Inside the shelter was a row of wooden seats along each side, but there were no lights. This was better than nothing; my next problem was to get the men use to it.

The problem solved itself one night when, without any warning, about midnight, the sound of crashing bombs nearly blew us out of bed. There was a mad scramble to get dressed and down the spiral staircase to the door, which the first there hammered on to get the guard to unlock it. But they were too late, the air raid was over.

It had been a quick one, by not more than three or four aircraft, who had seemingly appeared as if from nowhere, to light up, pinpoint and bomb with such precision some oil storage tanks at a small refinery about ½ mile along the river from our camp.

Several of us dashed up the stairs to the top floor where we could look out of the windows high up in the building. There before our very eyes was a mass of flames and palls of black smoke billowing up into the sky. There were more explosions as the fires spread, sending flames shooting high into the night sky lighting up the whole area. It was a great sight to see and it certainly boosted our morale that night. But one thing was certain, when the next air-raid alarm sounded the men would not take much getting out. It was not all going to be such precision bombing.

The Battle of the Ardennes during December and January had been a near setback for the Allies, but now that was over and won, the German defence lines were getting smaller every day; the Allies were advancing, the Russians were advancing and we in the middle, so to speak, wondered who was going to get here first.

Naturally, we wanted our own troops to get here first, and so did the Germans. They definitely did not want to be overrun by the Russians or the Americans. We could understand their feelings about the Russians, because both sides had been carrying out such vicious warfare, with a total disregard for the Usages of War and Geneva Conventions, and was on a par with the Japanese.

When I asked why they did not want the Americans to take over, they said they did not trust them, but they could trust the British to give them a square deal.

A widespread theory by the Germans at this time was that the Western Allies should now come in on the side of Germany and strike forward with everything possible against Russia. The Hitler regime was collapsing anyhow, so why not salvage what little remained before it was too late and strike an everlasting blow at Communism. I must admit that looking at the events over the years after the war, they had a point.

Day after day, we now saw hundreds of marching lost souls coming through Zwickau from the east. God knows who these miserable half-starved people were. There would be long columns of women, aged from 16 to 60, ill-clothed, with sacking tied around their feet and legs, old shawls and blankets over their heads and shoulders, urged on by armed civilian guards with yellow armbands. They slept where they stopped and fed when they could, which was very seldom. They were being driven from A to B to no purpose, like a lot of cattle. There seemed, in those last three months, to be a mass exodus from the east; where were they all going to? What was the meaning of it all? Europe had gone mad; it was terrifying to see these shambling columns of human wreckage.

Our rations were cut to rock bottom, the basics being bread, potatoes, sausage meat, ersatz cheese, ersatz coffee, jam, sugar and salt. There were very few Red Cross parcel issues now.

Bill, at Crossen, was doing his level best to get supplies. He managed sometimes to give us some bulk supplies which, if carefully used, would strengthen our evening stew for a few days. I had more arguments with the cooks, and one day Petch attacked me but I was too quick for him and sent him hurtling over my back through the kitchen door to crash on to the floor of the passageway outside. Tom, as usual, was at my side, steady as a rock, watching the others should they make a move. I could always depend on him. But nothing more happened, I had won the day and Petch and I became firm friends after that, which was just as well; he was a damned good cook and worked very hard with the other two, getting very little or no thanks for it, as usual.

The air-raid alarm was sounding nearly every night now and I got the men organised with their kits as we had done in Berlin. There was never any panic. We would make an orderly exit of the camp, having the door locked behind us, form up in the yard with the guards and march off to our air-raid shelter around the corner, after we had let streams of civilians pass by our main gate on their way over the bridge to the deep shelter in the hillside.

Many a time the flak would be blasting away at the thousands of bombers above as we got near to our shelter. The noise was terrific from the bursting shells, drone of the engines and crashing of bombs. Very often the bombers would fly straight over us without even so much as spitting on us. But their very presence was enough to drive fear into the hearts of everyone in the town.

March arrived and with it sad news of Feldwebel Yainisch having to leave us once again. He sent for me and told me a Stalag Staff Feldwebel and a Staff Interpreter had paid us a visit. It seemed that his services were again wanted elsewhere and his relief would be arriving in the next day or so.

His relief was Feldwebel Zahn, a man who had seen much active service. He had been a regular soldier before the war and after having completed so much service had then worked at the Zwickau post office, from where he had been recalled to service when the war started. He had been wounded several times, the last one being so serious as to make him definitely unfit for further active service. A man of medium height, pleasant face and direct manner, he made no bones about his feelings over the war and the Nazis. He had Fritsch screwed down from the first moment he took over. We shook hands and said goodbye to Yainisch and that was the last we saw or heard of him.

My next blow arrived when Tom fell ill. At first, he thought he had a bit of a cold, but he gradually got worse. We had missed the weekly Monday visit of the French medical officer so I persuaded Tom to go to hospital. Sani agreed with me and I arranged with Feldwebel Zahn to take a guard with me the next morning to put Tom on the train at Zwickau station. This train came along every day at about 8 a.m. and on it was a German guard and medical orderlies who would pick up any sick cases and care for them en route to hospital, either at Lichtentanne, Hohenstein or Reichenbach.

So the next morning, the three of us set off to the railway station, a considerable walk to the other side of the town. Tom, dressed in his greatcoat with polished buttons, polished boots and a French beret with his Middle East Commando cap badge in it (shaped like a knife), trudged wearily along the road with a pack on his back, while I carried his kit bag. How he ever managed to get to the station, I do not know. The last few hundred yards were all uphill, but he did it by sheer guts. I wanted to take his pack as well, but he would have none of it; even the old guard would have carried his pack.

We did not have long to wait at the station, the train was in, loaded and away again in minutes. I shook hands and said Godspeed and a quick recovery and stood sadly on the platform watching the train until it disappeared down the track. I had lost a very good pal. I did not see Tom again until after the war when I had been home a couple of weeks. I was on the main street in town when a voice hailed me from the upper deck of a trolley bus, and who should it be but Tom, safe and sound and looking well, having been well cared for in hospital, and now on his way home a few miles out of town. I was overjoyed, we had a lot to catch up on. But on the day I left him at the railway station in Zwickau, I felt anything but joyful. I felt very lonely, now on my own and although I had no more trouble in the camp and had made some good friends amongst them, it was not going to be the same without Tom.

On our way back to camp, the old Volksturm guard and I walked smack into an air raid. The warning siren sounded, the people nowadays were well trained to get to the shelters quickly and orderly. The guard and I followed the crowd and joined them in an air-raid shelter.

Then came the usual sounds of flak, aero engines and the eerie whistling and crashing of bombs, near enough but not directly over the top of us. The people in the shelter looked thoroughly fed up with it all and stunned that it could be happening to them so far inside Germany.

There were lots of them staring at me and much mumbling, which I could not pick up on account of the noise outside. But when it quietened down and I heard people asking the guard, 'Is he an Englander?' 'What is he doing in here?' 'Why is he not outside with the bombs?' 'They are murderers, bombing defenceless people,' and so on, I thought the best thing I could do was to either retreat gracefully or else speak to them.

One or two of the women appeared to be getting a bit hostile; they were chattering about losing their husbands and sons, so I quietly stood up and speaking to them in a loud, clear voice, in German, told them, 'Yes! I was an Englander, in the same boat as they were. Was I not being bombed the same as them? Did they think it would make any difference if I stood outside? Did I not want to live, as they wanted to live?'

I told them not to blame me for the war, it was not my doing, but to blame Hitler and his friends. I said a lot more, no doubt mixing up my words and repeating myself, but many eyes were now downcast or they were looking away as if they were ashamed. But they had got the message; I had driven my words home alright.

Then suddenly I said to the old guard, 'Come, let's get out,' and as the old boy stood up the people around beseeched us to stay because the 'all clear' had not sounded. We left nevertheless, walking quickly back to camp, the 'all clear' sounding as we came in sight of it.

Our worst air raid was on Monday, 19 March. I still have a notebook starting from that date and an everyday record until I left Germany after our liberation. I quote the following entry I made about the raid, Monday, 19 March, 1945:

'Zwickau, bombed, air-raid shelter withstood the nearby bombs. Nearest 10–15 metres away. Lager (camp) had two near misses in yard, one through the roof which finished up in the workshop in the basement, weighed 300lbs. Our district heavily damaged. No water in main.'

On that day the raid started about 10 a.m. and went on until about 12 noon. The composition of the camp was as follows:

Werdau	20
Zwickau I	53
Zwickau II	34
Neumark	45
Mosel	13
Work	165
Sick	36
Staff	13
Total	*214*
In Revier Lichtentanne	7
In Revier Reichenbach	6
In Lazerett Hohenstein	4
Full Total	*231*

So, with thirty-six sick and thirteen staff, that made forty-nine of us in camp. When the air-raid alarm sounded we trooped in an orderly fashion out of camp, taking all the bed-ridden sick with us as well. The only two guards left in camp went with us. Feldwebel Zahn and Unteroffizier Fritsch stayed behind, but finished up (so they told me) running like hell for the hillside shelter across the bridge when the bombing started.

It has often been said that you cannot hear the bomb which is going to hit you. No one has ever come back to verify this statement, but it is certainly true that you can hear the very near misses. We had hurricane lamps lit in our cold damp shelter, giving a very pale-yellow light, enough to be able to see each other sitting shivering, along each side of our leg of the shelter.

When we heard the angry hissing of the bombs, we were certain they were coming straight for us; we all, including our two guards, automatically 'hit the deck'. The explosions were absolutely terrific and ear splitting; the force of air being driven into our shelter by the blast actually blew out the hurricane lamps out and knocked over men who had not already 'hit the deck.' Men were crying out, I thought we had had a direct hit. Then somebody shouted for the 'bloody hurricane lamps to be lit'. I heard one of the old Volksturm grumbling and fumbling for his ancient flint lighter and the lamps were eventually relit.

During the next lull, I went along the line to see that everyone was alright; we had not been hit, but it could not have been far off. The men were swearing and cursing in true soldierly fashion at the so and so's above who were bombing us; I know I did my share of swearing. After the raid, we climbed up the stairs out of the shelter into the open air. The rim of a huge bomb crater was right at the entrance with several more lapping each other. The whole area was pitted with craters; it was devastated. All that was left of the houses was a straight line of rubble along the street. As we climbed in and out and over the rubble on our way back to camp, I noticed that in one house, with only the stairs and the chimney breast standing, there was a woman dressed in black, standing at the top of the stairs on the landing with her arm outstretched holding on to the knob of a door. A guard and I climbed over the rubble and gingerly climbed the stairs, and as we spoke and reached out our hands to the woman, she toppled over falling into the rubble below. She was stone dead.

We retraced our steps and caught up with the remainder of the party before they reached the camp. I, as usual, carried out my silent counting of the men before they disappeared into the building. This time there were only forty-eight including myself and, drawing Ord, Trim, Simpson and Polley on one side, told them we were one down.

They could not believe it, we must be wrong, so while Simpson paraded everyone in the yard and re-counted, the other four of us took a landing each and bounded up the spiral staircase to search the rooms. The camp had been hit, but we did not know then that we had a couple of unexploded bombs in our midst.

The room I went to was approached by a short landing, one side of which was covered with hardboard panels. One of these panels had been completely blown out and as I looked through the hole I saw my missing man, standing over the large cast iron stove. I shouted out to him, 'What the bloody hell do you think you're doing?' and turning very calmly towards me, replied, 'I'm making a brew of tea.' I was so pleased to see him, but I gave him a real good 'rocket'. He had been in bed the whole time the raid was on, not daring to move.

When the others from below came in we soon found out about the unexploded bombs. There was a gap through the roof and a neat hole through each floor which a bomb had made, and it was lying on its side in the workshop. Another bomb was sticking up out of the yard below and next to it a big crater. Most of the windows were shattered, with glass and plaster debris lying on the bunks. The water main was broken and was never repaired again.

Chaos was not the word for it; everywhere was bedlam, both inside and outside the camp. Getting hold of the camp staff, I told them to get those men who were able to work (which was most of them) organised, and get the rooms sorted out again and the holes in the floors covered over. The cooks had to be given some help. I was going to see Zahn and Fritsch about the bombs and water, and also to get some information, if possible, on our outside working parties.

Zahn and Fritsch were sorting out the office which had been knocked about a bit. They knew about the unexploded bombs and had phoned for the Bomb Disposal Squad at the barracks.

They did not know about the water being off, so we quickly decided that Fritsch would take some men and the handcart, get some containers from the local dairy and produce some water from somewhere. This he did with all urgency; it was the best and most efficient job he had ever done for the camp. As Zahn and I were walking over to look at the unexploded bombs, David Simpson arrived with Dipaola, our camp barber. They were both sappers like myself and David told me Dipaola had done a bomb disposal course, and would have a look at the bombs.

Dipaola, a British South American, whose name none of us could pronounce correctly, was normally called Pancho. Long and lanky, with jet black hair and swarthy features, a very pleasant fellow and a jolly good hairdresser, he now changed into a serious sapper and inspected the bombs.

He soon pronounced them 'duds' and asked for a moveable spanner to take out the fuses, which was soon produced by Zahn. Pancho, the hero of the day, had them out before the Bomb Disposal Squad arrived who, when they saw what had happened, wanted him to go with them to see more duds. But we were not having any of that, 'charity began at home' for our own safety and it was their business to deal with all the other duds.

We could not get through on the phone to the working parties at Zwickau I and II, but Mosel, Werdau and Neumark rang in to say they were all alright. So, after a cup of coffee and a bite to eat, Zahn and I got out the two bicycles, setting off to the other side of Zwickau to see for ourselves how they had faired. But firstly, I asked him if we could call where Maria worked (which was on our way) to see if she was alright. He raised his eyebrows at this, and nodding his head in the affirmative, said, 'Alfreds – Williamstrasse, isn't it?' 'Yes,' I replied. Off we went, having to make several detours and sometimes carrying our bicycles over bomb debris before we arrived at Williamstrasse. The street was untouched, we parked the bicycles against the kerb and walked into Alfreds, the jewellers. Maria beamed all over her face when she saw me. Zahn asked if everything was alright and seeing that it was, we departed as quickly as we had entered before anyone else in the shop saw us. We had learned all we wanted to know, there was no use lingering. I was to learn why later.

On our way to Zwickau I, we met Zwickau II marching back to camp as their sidings had been attacked, leaving considerable damage, but luckily we had no casualties. We were given hurried and garbled accounts of what had occurred and I told them quickly about the camp.

We could not get to Zwickau I quickly enough, but on arrival were relieved to find that although they had had some near misses, again fortunately there were no casualties. There was no thought of any more work that day by the civilian gangers, who, quite naturally, wanted to get home to see if their beloved ones were alright. Zahn told them to march back to camp. That evening we held great council in the camp, apart from hearing many tales of what had happened, with the usual soldier's emphasis and not without a little exaggeration.

These Para boys knew their 'aircraft recognition' off by heart and told me (I was hopelessly out of date and could only remember the Blenheims, Gladiators and Hurricanes) that besides being attacked by Flying Fortresses flown by the Yanks, there had also been some rocket-firing Typhoons and single-engined fighters. By all accounts the Allied Front was getting closer. We decided we must keep urging the men to go to work as long as possible, the main reason being that as long as they were outside the camp, the more possibility there was of being able to get food. The leaders of the working parties agreed; it did not go down well with some of the men but they were in the minority.

The sick parade had now got so large that we were having to keep a roster for whose turn it was going to be next. Sani was having a difficult time trying to prescribe for such ailments as swollen legs and ankles, strains and back troubles.

When I went down to the office that night, there was only Zahn there. He made the excuse for the absence of Fritsch by saying he was getting worried about the guards. Most of them being old Volksturm, he thought it best that Fritsch should from now on stay with them as much as possible, which would deter them from deserting. If he suspected this, it was good news to me, it showed that German confidence was waning somewhat.

Maria came in, and the three of us sat around the table and talked about the day's raid. Much damage had been done, mostly to the residential and shopping areas. The railway had been damaged, telephone communications had been affected, our area especially had been cut off from the water main, leaking gas mains had caused many fires, but remarkably enough we still had electricity supply. Worst of all, there had been many casualties amongst the civilians. When I got up to leave and said 'Goodnight,' Maria also arose, said, 'Goodnight' to Zahn and went out into the hallway with me. Zahn just replied the same and stayed at the table, not bothering to come with us. In the hallway, Maria put her hand over mine as I reached out to put the light switch on. She left me for only a moment, then was back thrusting a loaf of bread into my hands which she must have previously planted on the stairs. Putting the loaf inside my battledress blouse, I held her for a moment to whisper my thanks and to say I would see her the next night.

We could hear the guards talking in the room opposite and Fritsch's rasping voice. It was not policy to hang around too long, so she went off silently up the stairs and I opened the outside door and stepped out into the dark passageway to find the guard to let me into the camp building. But this time I had to find him, for he was on duty alone, and from then on, I realised there was only one guard on patrol at night instead of two.

I noted in my diary:

Wednesday. 21 March 1945
07.15 hours.   Veg – Joe, Nick, MoGaugie, Atherton.
Bread – Joe, Dave, Frank.
07.30 hours.   Water, Blackouts, Latrines, Bomb crater.

These were some of the entries which meant that a week's supply of vegetables and bread had to be collected from the town. Also, water had to be collected for drinking, and water from the river for washing and to keep the latrines functioning. The bomb crater also had to be filled in. I scribbled some more hieroglyphics, working out our bread issue for that day and the following interesting note:

'INSTONE, STRUCK BY CIVI.'
'(WHY) MATTICE USING BAYONET. Z.1.'

This news came through on the telephone during the early afternoon. Zahn sent immediately for me and we both pedalled off to Zwickau I as fast as we could to see what the trouble was. When we arrived at the railway sidings, we found Mattice, the Wehrmacht guard, with fixed bayonet trying to get the other three Volksturm guards to help him get our men into some goods vans to look them up. He was shouting and gesticulating with the rifle and bayonet whilst our boys tried to keep dispersed. The Volksturm guards were not so enthusiastic about it and were trying their best to calm Mattice down.

It was an ugly scene of an overwrought guard and fifty-four men who might at any moment decide to take the rifle from him and to hell with the consequences. The civilian who had caused the trouble had fled; he was nowhere to be seen. We parked our bicycles and Zahn stepped in quickly, making Mattice sheath his bayonet, then calling the other guards together demanded an explanation. I joined our men, confronted Instone, and demanded an explanation from him. Everybody wanted to talk at once, so I took Instone on one side to get the story out of him quietly. He was a reasonable sort of man who did not cause any trouble and certainly would not go looking for it.

A few of them had been unloading a wagon when along had come the civilian who had started on to them in a mixture of German and bad English, about the bombing and the murdering airmen. He had become rather agitated and hot under the collar, whereupon the men had stopped work and told him to push off (in four-letter words). Taking great offence at this he had climbed on to the wagon, attacking Instone, who had, naturally, retaliated and some of the others had broken it up and pushed the civilian off the wagon. Mattice had then come upon the scene, got hold of the wrong end of the stick, as usual in such cases; the whole upset had become distorted and enlarged, and while Mattice was arguing, the civilian had quietly slipped away.

But someone on the sidings had quickly phoned through to Zahn, which was just as well. He had soon taken complete command of the situation, and asked me to tell the men to finish off the wagons they had started to unload and then we would all get back to camp and call it a day. These sorts of misunderstandings could easily end up with some poor unfortunate bod getting shot, similar to what happened at Teltow when a prisoner who was walking away from a guard was told to halt and wouldn't. The guard had promptly shot him in the back and killed him. In this very unfortunate case, the ganger had taken complete charge of the situation, taking the guard's rifle away from him, had the dead man fastened to a table top and had marched the whole Kommando, including the guard, back to camp. By his quick action he had probably saved the situation getting out of hand and more men being shot.

Our main objective, now the end of the war was in sight, was to keep alive. There was simply no point in sticking one's neck into trouble. And although there had been a marked change in the German attitude towards us in the past few months, there was no doubt that this terrible heavy bombing from the air was straining our relations now.

Had we been confined in a non-working camp miles away out in some remote part, we would not have given two hoots about the bombing. But being in daily contact with the civilian population and living in a built-up area as we were, threw an entirely different light on the matter; we were having to live with it daily.

My notebook goes on to say that day after day those who were left in camp were kept busy bringing in fresh water, and water from the river for washing and flushing the latrines. The latter job was by far the biggest because many gallons of water had to be carted all the way to the top of the building to fill up, I don't know how many beer barrels were carried.

I have a note of keeping 88775 G. Mackay in camp because he was a carpenter and he repaired the gaping holes in the floors which the bombs had made. I also had a 'whip round' the camp to collect 275 Reich Marks to buy some French cigarettes which were then shared out.

Two men, who shall remain nameless, came to see me about escaping. They did not want to see anyone else but me. I listened carefully to what they had to say; briefly they were fed up and wanted to try and get to the British or American lines which they thought could not be far away to the west. They proposed to break out after the first available air raid at night, after being in the air-raid shelter and on our way back into camp. OK I said, if that was what they wanted, I could arrange to cover up for them, at least until the next day. But I asked them if they had saved any provisions at all, they would certainly need some, and if they knew what route to take. Did they not think it best to hang on another few weeks – the end and our liberation couldn't be far away now. They had not thought about food or anything else, so they decided to wait a while and make some preparations. Chocolate and dried fruit were what they needed and it would pay them to stay in their own uniforms for sake of identification.

Exactly two weeks later, on 4 April, they decided to make the attempt. They skipped camp alright without being missed, but in the early hours of the morning they decided to come back and rang the electric bell push button on the gate. On hearing the bell, the old Volksturm guard was so alarmed that he could not believe his eyes. During their few hours of freedom, they had not even got out of Zwickau; I don't think they had studied their route carefully enough. Spending a most miserable night getting colder and colder, they eventually agreed the best place for them was back in camp.

Zahn sent for me. Naturally, at such an unearthly hour I knew something was radically wrong and my first thoughts were that the two men had been recaptured or, worse still, one of them had been hurt. I was not surprised to see them sitting in the office, giving me a weak smile as I entered. I was pleased that no harm had befallen them. I smiled back at them, asking them what the hell had gone wrong. They retorted without bitterness that they had not got out of the bloody town, so had decided to come back and make the best of a bad job.

Zahn sent them under escort into the camp then turning to me, remarked that it meant Straf Lager for the two of them. Yes, I admitted, that would be the normal course of events, but in this case, they had come back of their own free will; would he not take that into consideration and also, I stressed, the war was nearly over.

He was silent and thoughtful for a while, and I chipped in again by saying that he might as well send me with them to the Straf Lager because he knew perfectly well that I was consorting with Maria, which was wrong. Lifting up his arms in a gesture of submission, he looked up and said, '*Du gewannst,*' 'You win,' and that was the last I heard of it.

Saturday, 24 March 1945

We spent most of the day in the air-raid shelter. The 20 men on the Werdau Kommando walked all the way back from work. We drew 34 loaves of bread for the 170 workers and 8 loaves of bread for the 45 non-workers (the latter being 13 staff and 32 sick). We had 16 men away in hospital.

Sunday, 25 March 1945

Again, most of the day was spent in and out of the air-raid shelter. Orr and Pritchard and myself braved the air raids and went to Crossen to collect parcels. One parcel between two men, a Godsend. We did not have to open them up and put them into store to give out tins each night any more. All that nonsense had gone by the board due to the bombing and the inconsistency of parcel issues. It was good to get an English cigarette again after those damnable French ones.

Monday, 26 March 1945

The sick parade shot up to 47. There were all sorts of ailments and several cases of men fainting. The French MO did not arrive.

Tuesday, 27 March 1945

The number of sick went up to 52, and still no MO.

Wednesday, 28 March 1945

The French MO arrived in the afternoon in an army lorry with two orderlies and dumped 12 sacks of parcels (personal parcels) on to us. The normal postal channels had been so disrupted that he thought it best to leave the parcels with us and he would inform the various owners, of which he had a list, that they would have to come to us to collect.

There were 175 parcels for 140 different destinations. Of these two were for our own camp, five for Bergeschacht, three for C. & F. Leonards and two for Leonards & Sons. The remainder of the parcels were mostly for French and Serbians working out on the farms. I listed the whole lot in my notebook and there is one interesting entry: *Zwickau jail, two parcels, drawn on 29/3/45*.

Bill Cummings collected these together with the parcels for the Crossen camps. Some months ago he had got to know from a Frenchman who delivered various goods to Zwickau jail during the week, that there was a Britisher imprisoned there. Bill had made enquiries and had actually been given permission to visit the man and had given him considerable aid. I understood this man was a merchant seaman who had been imprisoned for sabotage. But now there were two parcels for two different Britishers. Who was the other one? Bill set off in great haste to find out and I did not hear any more about it until later.

April arrived bringing much better weather, if nothing else. Rations were now at their all-time lowest, not only for us but also for the Germans around us. There were columns of miserable, hungry Ausländers marching wearily in all directions, a legion of lost souls forced into a bottomless hell by the Nazis. For those who lived through it all, they were, after the end of hostilities, to become known as 'Displaced Persons'.

We had often said, with much bitterness, that one day the Germans would be made to pay for their wrong doing. Well now they were paying very dearly, but in our eyes, it was the wrong ones who were paying. The women and children and the old people were paying, by starvation, the destruction of their homes and losing their lives. We saw it all daily and it made us sick. The days of reckoning were at hand.

It was now a nightly pilgrimage to the air-raid shelters, while during the daytime there would be five or six alarms, with thousands of people scurrying over the bridge into the hillside. It reminded me of the story of The Pied Piper of Hamelin.

Saturday, 7 April 1945
Good news – Red Cross parcel issue at Crossen, those wonderful life savers. I spoke to Crossen on the telephone something previously unheard of telling them I had 216 men

in camp and I would arrange the collection tomorrow, Sunday. The issue would be one parcel to two men, but there would be 50 cigarettes each.

Sunday, 8 April 1945
In my notebook I wrote:

CROSSEN, ORD, SEED, SANI, DAGNALL, FLINT, HOWART.
Sani to write prescriptions of patients.
To go for water as soon as ready.
Kane to see doctor Monday.
Reveille 06.30.
Parade 08.00.
Rooms to be finished as soon as possible.
Parcels issue.
Beer barrel may be filled (what with I forget).

We went off to Crossen as early as possible, pulling the old handcart and wondering if the air-raid alarm was going to sound. It did, just as we were leaving the town, but we kept on going. We saw the aircraft flying over in their hundreds, well away from Zwickau. It looked like we might be left alone this Sunday. Duly arriving at Crossen, Bill took me on one side while the parcels were being loaded on our cart and he told me that this would be the last food parcels we could expect to receive. The cupboard was now well and truly bare. He gave us enough for 224 men, 112 parcels, ninety of which were Christmas parcels, and twenty-two American parcels. This was indeed bad news and meant we were going to be mighty hungry if the war did not finish quickly. All the way back to camp I wondered how I was going to tell the rest of the men. I did not have the heart for it but they would have to be told, sometime.

It is amazing how in those last few weeks we tried to carry on as normally as possible. The camp was much better now than it had ever been. There was practically no grumbling over the extra chores to be done in bringing in water and climbing to the top of the building with it. Air-raid drill we had off to a tee. Meals and ration queues were orderly. There was a much better spirit in camp and morale was high.

We now knew that the Western Allies had crossed the Rhine and strong American forces were racing towards us. The Russian steamroller was reported to be near Berlin and driving towards us from the east. The British were thrusting into the Ruhr. We wondered who was going to get here first, we certainly did not want the Russians.

The parcels were issued out as soon as we arrived back in camp. Meddlesome Fritsch wanted to poke his nose in and have them all opened up under his scrutiny, but Zahn soon put a stop to his nonsense. That night on check parade I told everyone not to expect any more parcels, we would have to tighten our belts. Those working on the sidings handling turnips, potatoes and such like would have to try and bring some back to camp each day to help the stew out.

From Monday, 9 April to Saturday, 13 April our men went out to work under great difficulties: there was no transportation of any kind; the work on the sidings got less and less; the sick mounted from forty on the Monday to sixty by the Saturday. The French MO was never able to come again, but those who were definitely ill we managed to get to hospital. Our total in camp was now 209 out of 231.

Erich Zahn and I talked over the situation on the Saturday night in the office. We were getting to the bitter end. He said he could not guarantee us getting any more rations, we had enough bread for about three days at six men to a loaf and the same for his own men. Maria came in and told us that there were no more provisions in the shops to be had; the local bakery was empty and people were trying to barter their more valuable possessions for food.

Erich decided to have a walk along Adolf Hitler Ring for some fresh air; he was fed up and the air would help to clear his head and perhaps think better. He asked us to go with him, saying he would be glad of the company. He was not very well and suffered from severe headaches. So with Maria in the middle, holding my hand tightly, we walked and talked of the problems facing us.

What would happen when the Allies arrived? He emphasised that he did not want a *Schiesserei*, shooting gallery to start. He had a fear that our men would get hold of the guards' weapons, but I tried to dispel his fears by saying that when the time came, I would hold the camp staff responsible for the good conduct of our men and the arms would be kept under lock and key and there would be no trouble. I was confident that there was no one in camp bent on revenge of any kind, and we were all too well trained and disciplined to do anything silly. We agreed to issue all the rations out on the next day and there was no point in the men going out to work anymore.

As we retraced our steps slowly back to camp, we heard a very unusual noise. We must each have heard it at the same time, because we stood still together and listened. Erich then said one word, *Panzers*, tanks, there was no doubt about it, it was the sound of very many engines a long way off. I thought, well, it must be a German Armoured Division on the move, but Erich thought otherwise. The noise came from the west, they must be British or American.

As we reached camp, Erich went into tell Fritsch and the guards. I kissed Maria a quick goodnight and hurried indoors to tell everyone in the camp. The Germans were now in the compound listening. I awoke Simpson, Trim, Ord and Polley and asked them to listen at the door. Then they heard it, there was no question of it being aircraft, it was definitely armour on the move and the news soon spread round the camp.

Reveille 05.00 hours. Parade 07.00 hours. Two men, Mackay and Jordan return from hospital, bringing our strength to 211. At about 08.00 hours I was sent for, an old Volksturmer trudged tiredly up the stairs to tell me the Herr Feldwebel would like to see me.

Down in the compound, not far from our door, stood Erich Zahn, Fritsch and another Feldwebel, who I was told was a Staff Feldwebel from Stalag IVB HQ. He, like Erich, looked tired and war weary; on his tunic he displayed two Iron Cross ribbons, the East Front Medal, and three Wounded Medals, the Black, Bronze and the Silver. He spoke quietly but curtly in a commanding voice to me, saying that in one hour's time he wanted every man in the camp to parade with their kit and two blankets each, ready to march off. He had been instructed to move us to a safer place.

'*Nein*,' I said, '*wir gehen nicht, wir bleiben hier.*' 'No,' I said, 'we are not going, we are staying here.' The Feldwebel stood spellbound, he was speechless for some moments. He had no doubt never been answered back so spontaneously before by so lowly a rank. He stood looking at me incredulously. I thought he was going to explode, but he didn't. Instead, he said, 'Come with me,' and we all trooped over to the barbed wire fence. Pointing through the wire at the bridge he told me that the German sappers were preparing it for demolition. True enough, I could see soldiers carrying the all-too-familiar boxes of explosives from their trucks to the underside of the bridge.

It was nice to know what was going on, not that we could do very much about it. There would be hell of a bang when it went up and a lot of damage would be done to the surrounding buildings, including ours. I was also wondering what would happen to the shelter in the hillside, which was, to say the least, the safest place, but on the wrong side of the river. If the bridge was blown, more than half the population would be cut off from the town.

Turning to me again, he asked what I thought about it now. I still replied the same as before, we would prefer to stay put. I noticed that Erich Zahn and Fritsch had been non-committal and had not sided with the Staff Feldwebel either. We also heard something else: distant gunfire; there was no mistake about it. Looking at each other as we walked back to the door of our building, the Staff Feldwebel said he hoped we knew what we were doing. I had made the decision, be it on my head. With that, and *Gutes Gluck*, good luck, he left and we never saw him again.

I bounded back up the stairs, two at a time, calling to Simpson and Trim to assemble everyone – except those sick in bed – into the big room. Telling them all what had happened and that if they listened carefully, they would hear the distant gunfire, they all cheered like mad. All were excited, it was a stirring moment. It was a fine day, as I remember. Zwickau seemed to be more than quiet, as though waiting in anticipation for the final blow to fall.

Erich Zahn and I went along to see what our air-raid shelter was like around the corner. We climbed over and around the bomb debris which had not been removed from the street and finally as we went down the steps into the shelter, we found it all flooded. This had been caused by the burst water mains; there being nobody to fix them, we could not possibly use the shelter any more.

There was now only one thing for it; when the time came, we would all have to move into the hillside shelter and muck in with the civilian population; they would have to move up a bit to make room.

Later in the day, four more of our men turned up from the hospital at Litchentanne, McCann, Scarfe, Kirk and Kane, making our total in Camp 215. I was able to see Maria several times during the day. There were no air raids and the night passed quietly.

Monday, 16 April 1945
Bread issued last night for 3 days – Sunday, Monday, Tuesday,
Today skilly (meal) spuds, macaroni, meat.
Get washing water and drinking water in, clean the billet up a
  bit, in case of alarm.
Cooks 05.30 hours. Reveille 07.00 hours.
We had 18 bed patients in our own Revier.

There was no need to worry about the normal Reveille, we awoke at first light to the sound of artillery gunfire. It was a good way off, there was no panic. Everyone got dressed and stood to, and Sani had enough men ready to move the sick out first, to the hillside shelter.

Petch and his cooks continued to get on with their work; there were not enough rations to make a meal for tomorrow so he was determined that today's skilly, as it was generally called by these boys, would be a good one. There was no shortage of helpers to prepare the potatoes and other vegetables. The water detail was arranged and I went with them into the compound to see that there was no delay in getting the guards to take one party for fresh water to the hydrant a few streets away and the second party to the river for the washing water.

Erich Zahn met me and told me he had only four old Volksturm guards left. He went on to say that Fritsch and the others had changed into civilian clothing during the night and had 'hopped it'. 'What!' I said, 'deserted?' It was unheard of in anybody's army, least of all the German; not that it really bothered us at all.

Erich was very sad, there was not much he could do about it now as we estimated the oncoming forces would be in Zwickau within the next couple of days, if not today. He and the four old men insisted on staying with us right to the bitter end, otherwise they would not be able to lift up their heads amongst other men afterwards.

It was not long before American fighter aircraft appeared over the town. Twin-engined, rocket-firing planes shot up the railway, barracks and road blocks; The single-engined fighters chasing down the length and breadth of the streets, looking for targets.

We dashed out of the office into the compound where many of our men were waving to attract their attention. White bed sheets were collected out of the Germans' quarters, taken into the camp, where they were laid on the floor, sewn together and with paint and brush, the words, 'BRITISH POWs' was daubed on in as big letters as possible.

Lengths of string were then tied to the corners of the sheet and the whole thing was slung outside between the highest windows of the building and made fast; it looked splendid. Meanwhile, others had found more paint, smashed a way through the attic doors to the roof, which fortunately was not a very steep one, daubing on a big white cross and the letters POWs.

It was some time before one of the fighters spotted us; he came in close several times to have a look at us, then he waggled his wings in recognition. His pals came in and did the same, flying so low they almost touched the chimney pots. To say we were excited and very much relieved is an understatement. No pen of mine could ever describe the scene adequately, with men sitting on the roof waving, hanging out of windows waving, and down in the compound doing something like an Indian war dance. We could now only hope they would be able to contact the ground forces and the 'five-mile snipers' to pinpoint our position so that we would not be a sitting duck for their shells.

We managed to get some water in after a bit of a struggle of dodging down the streets, not knowing if the shells were going to come raining down or whether any German opposition may be met. The Volksturmers were left behind in camp as it was thought they would be an encumbrance.

There were very few civilians daring to venture forth from their homes. I told Maria to be ready, with her mother and father and whatever food she could muster, to go into the hillside at a moment's notice. Erich Zahn and I made sure the rifles and ammunition left behind by the deserters were securely locked away. We tried to get through to Crossen and Bergeschacht camps on the telephone but the lines were dead. By mid-afternoon it was obvious the fighting was getting closer. It was coming from the direction of Crossen, though it could have been further away. The noise of tanks was much closer, heavy machine guns could be heard at intervals; the sky was never short of fighter aircraft with very little opposition from the Germans.

The air-raid 'fore' alarm sounded, which was the signal for the town's population to take shelter. They soon started coming in droves past our camp and over the bridge into the hillside. I saw Maria and her parents off with their little bundles of belongings and told her I would come and find her later.

Our 'skilly' was ready, the sick and their helpers were fed first, then off they went to the hillside with the Volksturmers helping. The remainder of us soon wolfed down our share, then with our bits of kit joined the others in the hillside. As Erich Zahn and I with the tail end were crossing the bridge, shells began to land in the centre of the town. It only lasted for a short time as if it was a reminder for all to take cover before the real shooting match started.

Towards evening, a lull had settled over the area as though the participants had gone back to their corners for a breather before the next round started. We talked about the impending demolition of the bridge, there were no soldiers guarding it that we could see. Erich suggested that he and I should walk along the track by the riverside to follow the electric demolition cable to see what and who was at the other end. We went very carefully for several hundred yards until we came to a point where we could see two uniformed, steel-helmeted 'beings' sitting on the edge of a newly dug slit trench. The two 'beings' were both Hitler Youths and not more than about 13 or 15 years old. They stood up and saluted Erich as we approached, then, after passing the time of day, asked who I was.

I answered for myself in a typical German voice and whilst they continued to talk to Erich, telling him how hungry they were, I noticed that in the slit trench was an exploder with the electric wires unattached (these were lying on the side of the trench) and the only weapon they seemed to have was a new Panzerfaust, the new rocket-firing anti-tank weapon which had only come into prominence after the Normandy landings. We talked for a while; they seemed uncertain why they were there. Their orders were to wait until someone came along to connect up and blow the bridge, and they had only been told how to fire the anti-tank weapon. Erich promised to come back with some bread for them, which was as much as he could do. I noticed he did not offer them a rifle apiece.

Back in the steps of the hillside shelter I told Simpson, Trim and co. what I had found out and that Zahn and I were going back to see them again. It was getting on towards dusk and there was a chance of someone going over the low wall on to the river bank to cut the electric cable and destroy any safety fuse there might be connected to the detonators and ignition sets at the bridge. Meanwhile, Erich had collected some bread from some of the civilians and we both walked back along the river bank to give it to the two Hitler Youths. I said nothing about the bridge to Erich, I thought it best not to implicate him nor to confide too much in him; after all, by rights, he was still one of the enemy.

The Hitler Youths were ravenous and very grateful for the bread which they gorged in record time. It was a pity to see such young boys fanatical Nazis, waiting to give their lives for a useless cause. They could not possibly win and they just did not know how to lose.

It was coming dark when we got back to the shelter; it had been a long, tiring, hectic day and I for one was ready to get my head down for some sleep. I was quietly given the tip-off that the bridge had been 'fixed' good and proper, which really made the day. Picking up my two blankets and other kit, I went along the shelter to a pre-arranged place to Maria and her parents. We were glad to see each other, I could see their faces light up in the dim light of hurricane lamps, the only illumination we had.

Everybody had been warned to stay in the shelter until further notice on account of the bridge having to be blown, and our men were given a portion nearest to one of the entrances. Sitting down on the rough bench seat next to Maria, we shared our blankets wrapping them around us and tried to get some sleep. It was cold, damp and uncomfortable but I slept for quite a long time until my head fell sideways, waking me up with a start, thinking that I had broken my neck. After that it was just a matter of fitful dozing.

Tuesday, 17 April 1945
Our morning started with distant rumblings and earth tremors. The hurricane lamps were lit, bodies began to slowly shift about on the uncomfortable wooden benches, stretching arms and legs; some stood up to get a better stretch and flap their arms to restore their blood circulation. I could hear children further along the shelter whimpering; the poor little devils must be cold and hungry, but who wasn't, I was starving. I had one knob of bread left, my full water bottle, some dried fruit and a bar of chocolate. I still had a few cigarettes left, but there was definitely no smoking down the shelter as the air circulation was extremely poor, having to rely solely on the natural ventilation through the entrances.

Maria stretched from her curled up position against me, saying so softly, '*Guten Morgen*,' looking up and giving me a smile. Then she leaned forward touching her mother and father opposite us, speaking to them in an equally quiet voice. The old couple answered. I don't think they had slept very much.

I went along the shelter to see Sani to find out how the sick cases were getting on and seeing they were no worse than yesterday, carried on towards the entrance, talking to the remainder of our men en route. Also meeting Erich Zahn, we went along together. At the steps were some of our men, lying at the top carefully peering over to see what was going on outside. We could hear the shelling and machine-gun fire, heavy mortars and fighter aircraft, yet, when we took a turn to peep over the top, we could not see much except columns of smoke going up and the aeroplanes buzzing over. There was no one to be seen, and definitely no one guarding the bridge; the day was fine though cloudy. The action seemed to be coming from our right, from the direction of Crossen. Erich said he thought this would be the last day; I wholeheartedly agreed, silently hoping and praying it would be.

We sat in the steps and had a smoke, talking of what we would do when the advancing forces arrived. Erich agreed to hand over the rifles and ammunition and his pistol to me when I gave him the word. We made white flags ready to wave from the top of the steps, and instructions were passed to all our men to stay where they were until they were given specific orders to move. I did not want a bottleneck in the entrance should they suddenly start a shooting match due to our men dashing out of the shelter in the excitement of the moment. I wanted to see 215 live men at the end and I could then say that my job was done.

Going back to Maria, I gave her what news I had, which was not much. Her mother and father dug in to what rations they had which was a dashed sight more than I had; passing some to Maria and including me. I told them I had a knob of bread but they waved me aside telling me to eat. I was very grateful for their kindness to me and could not help thinking that these were the sort of people who were having to suffer. It was all wrong. I looked along the line of faces of mostly young and old women, children and old men, feeling very sorry for them.

The battle outside raged all day, each hour bringing it closer and closer, but no liberation. By evening time, there were a few lulls as though both sides were getting ready to jockey for fresh positions.

I decided to give the children nearest to me a special treat to end the day. Bringing out my bar of chocolate I distributed it as far as it would go amongst them, finishing off the remainder by giving them pieces of dried apricot from a 1lb slab. They had never seen anything like it before, while I had never known such joy as I got from the happy look on their faces.

The only note I made in my notebook on 17 April was the names of those who were away in hospital: Chandler, Flannery, Clarke, Taylor P, Martin W. Overington, Instone, De Boureier, Dixon, Glover, Vickers, Caselli (one S and two Ls), Broughton, Charlesworth, Pearce and Malloy, Total 16. Thus, we had to spend yet one more night in the shelter.

Wednesday, 18 April 1945
I wrote the following simple brief words:
Free approx. 3.30 p.m. American tanks and armoured cars entered Zwickau after shelling for three days. One G.I killed on bridge. One GI wounded on bridge. No losses in camp.

This day started like the previous one with the rumpus of war going on in and around the town, coming to its final crescendo about midday, then a lull, then odd spasmodic small-arms fire.

Peering over the top of the shelter steps towards the bridge and across the river, we suddenly saw a tank appear on the Adolf Hitler Ring. Behind it trundled another; both had great big white stars painted on their sides – American. We could now see armed soldiers walking behind the tanks and others flitting from door to door along the Ring. They halted short of the bridge; they could not possibly miss seeing our camp with its big white sheet with the huge crude letters, BRITISH POWs, tied across the upper windows.

We shouted to them like mad, as hard as we could, at the same time waving the white flags. A machine gun from somewhere splattered bullets all around us, making us duck down in the steps, and we were swearing like hell. Within a few more moments we heard an American voice shout, both in English and German, 'Come out with your hands up.' I quickly sent word to Erich Zahn below that this was the finale, then four of us stepped outside, hands raised.

Six well-armed American GIs confronted us with their automatic rifles pointing straight into our midriffs; a sight never to be forgotten; we all started to talk at once. I remember saying, 'Why has it taken so long for you to bloody well get here?' Another said, 'Why the hell are you firing at us, we are bloody British?' Someone else said, 'Have you any gum chum and I am dying for a smoke. The Yanks kept saying, 'It's the Tommies, they're OK.'

We all shook hands, we felt like kissing then. One with a walkie-talkie set was speaking into his instrument saying that they had found us and we were OK.

The rifles were passed up from the shelter and I strapped Erich's pistol on to my belt. The GI with the walkie-talkie told us our orders from his leading commander were that everyone had to stay in the shelter until told to come out; as yet the town had not been completely taken over and they did not want any street congestion. He asked the four of us to go over the bridge to see the officer who wanted some information from us.

Leaving two GIs at the shelter, the four of us started off towards the bridge in pairs, I and a GI coming up last. We could see the huge Sherman tank standing on the other side of the bridge at its junction with the Adolf Hitler Ring. Other tanks and armoured cars were spread out at intervals. GIs were kneeling, crouching or in standing positions behind the tanks or other strategic points.

Tingling with excitement we were halfway across the bridge when all hell let loose with several things happening at once.

An open-type German truck, something like our open, desert, 15cwt trucks, came careering down the hill towards the bridge. At the same time, a German machine gun opened up on the bridge from a position in some trees at the top of the hill behind us, above the shelter.

Just before going to ground, I saw the truck with several people in the back, a woman in the passenger seat and its soldier driver frantically trying to stop it and turn around. The Yank and I hit the deck as fast as we could, with bullets screaming angrily around us and ricocheting off the bridge. The others had just dashed off the bridge scurrying under cover over a low wall on to the side of the river. There did not seem to be any fire coming from the Americans. Then I heard a Yankee voice hailing us, telling us that when the tanks opened up to make a dash for it. I was absolutely petrified lying there with no protecting cover, feeling stark naked, expecting any moment to feel something tearing into my body.

The tanks' heavy machine guns began to blaze away and it seemed to take me ages to get up on one knee. I shouted to my GI pal and gave him a shake; it was then I noticed all the blood underneath him; poor fellow was dead. Feeling nauseated, I grabbed his rifle and with bullets firing in all directions, ran, doubled up, over the bridge, diving over the wall to the others. I must have been shaking with fear and desperately frightened as many willing hands dragged me under cover of the wall.

The tanks' heavy cannons came into use, making a hell of a noise, and just about blew the top off the hill where the German machine gun had been positioned. The American officer we had been asked to see was with us under the wall. He passed me a lighted cigarette, which I took with a none-too-steady hand. The truck on the other side of the river which had tried to turn around on the steep descent to the bridge had overturned and was lying on its side, having spilt out all its occupants, though we could not see any of them.

Another of the Americans with us had been wounded but had managed to get to safety. He was now being attended to by one of the others; these fellows seemed to carry everything. As the shooting ceased from the tanks and also the hilltop, a GI with another walkie-talkie set could be heard calling forward the medics. I was now able to tell the officer that the GI on the bridge was dead, but we were not out of trouble yet. From the opposite direction, down the continuation of the Ring leading into town, some Germans began sniping at us from the upper windows of some buildings on both sides of the street.

The tank nearest to us manoeuvred to a new position, machine gun coming into action and then the cannon. The second tank trundled forward, turning into the street, blazing away with his guns as well, knocking hell out of the area of the windows where the Germans were shooting from. It only lasted a few minutes, then all was quiet.

The officer was now asking us about the bridge, was it safe and would a couple of us stay until their sappers came forward, who were now being called for on the walkie-talkie, and show them what had been done.

Being free to move back on to the road now, we climbed over the wall to walk over to the tanks. It was then I noticed an armoured personnel carrier a little way off with two blokes lying on the top of it calling to me. I could not believe my eyes. Who should it be but Arthur Redford and Bill Cummings from Crossen who had insisted on coming into Zwickau with the advancing Americans to show them where we were and, as Bill said, 'didn't want us to land in trouble', an understatement if I may say so, but I was very, very glad to see them. Arthur was wounded, having been shot through the fleshy part, high up on one of his legs, whilst he was on top of the carrier. He was taking it very well, saying it wasn't much, which was typical of him.

All the personnel of both Crossen camps were all right, they had been liberated two days ago and since then the Germans, though only a small fanatical force of Hitler Youths with veteran officers, had put up much fierce resistance from behind road blocks and the use of their Panzerfausts.

Bill said that our next 'port of call' was Zwickau jail to release the two known Britishers being held there, then on to Bergeschacht to release the 'miners'.

The Americans were delighted to have us with them, so with two waiting to meet their sappers to show them over the bridge, the other two of us went with the leading infantry accompanied by a tank to direct the way to the jail.

They still took no chances! The infantry moved cautiously down each side of the streets, hugging the buildings. As we passed street intersections, we could see other American tanks and infantry fanning out through the town. There was still fighter activity in the air, though they had no opposition; the flak was dead, there was practically no more shooting of any kind, the German resistance having completely collapsed.

At the stout prison doors, which we could see as we turned into a small square, the prison commandant and some of his assistants were awaiting our arrival. They stood stiffly to attention and saluted the American officer who, taking not the slightest notice of them, ordered them in excellent German to open up and parade all the inmates on one side of the prison grounds and all the German guard on the other side, also to bring forward at once all British and, if any, American prisoners.

Three Britishers were eventually brought forward. They looked shabby and ill-fed, but with smiles on their faces and tears down their cheeks they came towards us and we hugged each other. We took them back to our camp, telling them they were welcome to share in whatever we had; at least we could give them a bed and it would not be long before we got some food from the Americans. We told them to muck in and make themselves at home. Bill continued on to Bergeschacht where he found everyone safe and sound and in good spirits.

Back at our camp, we found the Americans were now releasing everyone from the hillside air-raid shelter. The town had been taken and all were told to go back to their homes and stay there, as from now there would be a strict curfew, no one being allowed on the streets for at least twenty-four hours. We were also told to get back into camp and stay there until further orders, but some of our men had already skipped into town searching for food, which they soon discovered and brought back to feed the whole camp.

On the road by the bridge, the Americans had lined up scores of German prisoners. Anyone dressed in uniform was there, even railwaymen and postmen. I went along with a Yankee sergeant to find Erich Zahn, telling him that Erich was in a poor state and needed medical care. I found him still with his old Volksturmers, true to the last. Talking briefly to him, I could only wish him well and hoped it would not be long before he was back home again. He asked me if I would go and see his wife who did not live far away, Maria knew the address, so I promised to go as soon as I could and let her know what had happened. I shook hands with him as they moved off to wherever they were going to be housed, now prisoners of war.

Retracing my steps back to camp, a little sad and sick at heart, I went upstairs to the flat to Maria and her parents. They greeted me with open arms, saying thanks to God, that I was all right, for they had heard about the episode on the bridge. I was so overwhelmed by their emotions that I could not help but sit down and with head in hands wept and sobbed for long enough, all the pent-up feelings of the past few days now being released.

After a while, Maria's mother patted my head, offering me a cup of coffee, which I very gratefully accepted. It was black, with practically no sugar (there had not been any milk for weeks), and as I drank, I realised I was terribly hungry. It had been a long hectic day and apart from being hungry, I was tired and weary. Frau Sahm, being a resourceful woman, had managed to make some sort of a meal and the four of us sat to the table to enjoy every morsel of it. Tomorrow I would have to go out hunting for food as there was now very little in the house and with the curfew on, their chances of getting any were remote,

As we ate, I could see into the compound below, through netted curtained windows, where quite a few of our men were milling about and talking to some of the American GIs on duty in the area. A wine cellar had been found (supposedly reported to be a Nazi one), so with crates of the stuff being carried up to the rooms, helped by GIs, there was soon sounds of merry making and singing, which went on well into the night.

We in the house retired early, having had enough for one day. I slept on the divan in the living room whilst Maria and her parents slept in the one and only bedroom overlooking the river. Slipping my loaded pistol and holster under the pillow, I lay down and could not help thinking of all sorts of things from the day's events: the bridge; the poor dead GI; Arthur and the other wounded; to persons of the past whom we had so often said we would like to meet when the war was over and vowed that justice would be done, meaning the Germans, of course. There were those from the Salonika days who had started the ball of hatred rolling, and those later, some whose names were remembered.

Montag had not been so bad, compared with others, but I would love to have met that swine of a major from Mühlberg who cocked his head on one side, and then there was Scarface and those brutes of gangers on the railway. With my mind in a turmoil, I thankfully went into a deep sleep. I suppose at that time there was understandably much hatred in each and every one of us. But many of those we hated we never saw again and after that night I seldom thought of them, my thoughts being taken up with the future.

For Thursday, 19 April I did not make any entry in my notebook but it was a day of activity, mainly searching for food. The Americans let us roam around the town at will during the daytime but they did not want us out at nights because our iron-shod boots made a noise when we walked, and being trigger happy, they would shoot first and ask questions afterwards. Nevertheless, they were indeed most kind to us, they gave us plenty of rations, cigarettes and the inevitable chewing gum. In fact, nothing was too much for them.

I met Lieutenant Arnold, a transport officer, who was doing his best not only to supply us with rations but to arrange us transport to take us west. He explained, however, his difficulties in keeping in touch with his transport, who were strung out in a long line throughout the Third Army. There were still many pockets of German resistance operating on the line along which the Third Army had made their fast advance

Knowing that transport for our evacuation was trying to be arranged gave our men the idea of looking for their own transport amongst the Germans. Several civilian cars were found (which had been salted away for the duration) and confiscated, serviced, filled with American petrol and made ready to move off.

I also met three American sergeants and a corporal who had come with some men to load and take away the explosives from under the bridge. We got along fine with each other and they promised to come back that night to swap yarns over a bottle of wine. I later wrote their names and unit in my notebook – Sergeants George McLain, Howard Bradford, Edward Lange and Corporal Paul De Pierro, all of 168 Engineer (C) Battalion, G.P.O. 230 G.P.M., Third US army.

They turned up for the party which we held downstairs in the ex-German quarters, bringing food, cartons of cigarettes and Coca-Cola, and, above all, goodwill. I tried to get Maria to join us, but she declined, probably for the best, to let us get on with it in our own way.

There were about eight of us; we talked of everything – America – England – the war and personal experiences. The wine flowed freely; the Coca-Cola being forgotten. We sang and drank and smoked. Some of our songs we sang together, some were sung by individuals – some funny, some sad, some not too clean soldiers' songs (it was a good job for me that Maria upstairs could not understand what we were singing about), but we had a great night. The Americans had to be back at their units for 23.00 hours and at a quarter to, a jeep rolled up for them. They piled in, still singing and joking, very merry but not drunk, and were whisked away to a chorus of goodnights.

The wine certainly went to my head, I was not used to this. I made my goodnights to the others, leaving them, like me, a little inebriated. Finding the stairs, I went up on all fours, to be helped through the door at the top by Maria who had been waiting for me, it seemed, with some hot black coffee ready. That was about the last thing I remembered before sinking on to the divan and feeling as though I was slipping into a bottomless pit.

Friday, 20 April 1945
THE CAMP RATHER UPTURNED, ABOUT HALF THE CAMP LEFT IN CIVI CARS, OTHERS BY U.S.A. TRANSPORT. I HAVE DECIDED TO STAY UNTIL THE LAST MAN HAS GONE.

Waking up early with a thick head, to be cleared by more black coffee, something to eat and the smiling, knowing looks from Maria and her mother, I could hear lots of feverish preparations to move going on in the compound with the 'borrowed' cars. Some were being towed, some pushed; bonnets were up with lots of willing hands rummaging about with the works. But by lunchtime all were mobile and being driven on test around the streets.

Later in the day, the US transport officer arrived with some trucks. Everybody eagerly clambered aboard; the convoy of trucks and civilian cars lined up with engines ticking over ready to move off.

I tried to make a last final count, going along the convoy asking how many there were in each vehicle, but it was hopeless, they were not even interested in who was there. I was certain there were some men missing so I declined to get aboard, telling Lieutenant Arnold I would stay behind to round up the stragglers and anyhow, I had done my best for this lot, they did not need me any more.

As I stood alone in the road watching the convoy move slowly off amidst the pleadings of some of the men to go with them, I felt strangely elated and free. They were soon out of sight along the Adolf Hitler Ring and as I turned to go back into camp alone, I spied a solitary figure coming towards me from the town. It was Jock Stewart. I told him he had missed the boat, but he was not in the least bothered. He said there were a few more men in the town, which was just as I had thought.

Friday, 20 April 1945
CAMP JUST ABOUT EMPTY, 9 OR 10 MEN LEFT, MAYBE WE GO MORNING.

The curfew had since been lifted on the town's population and notices were being posted telling all to go about their daily business as normally as possible and that on Monday, 23 April everybody would be expected to report back to their usual place of work.

It was a nice day, so Maria and I decided to pay Frau Zahn a visit at 10 Pohlauer Strasse, just out of town on the Chemnitz road, as I had promised Erich. There was another couple at the house when we arrived and they all looked pretty scared when I was introduced as an Englander, especially as I was wearing Erich's pistol on my belt. I shook hands with them all including Erich's little boy, and soon assured them that I was on a friendly mission. I told them of the last few days, that Erich would be all right and I hoped he would soon return home.

What else could I say? We stayed for about an hour, having coffee and home-made biscuits. I wrote down the address and that of her friends, Marianne and Reinhold Schulze, and, shaking hands, again departed.

When Maria and I arrived back at our camp I found Jock Stewart patiently waiting for me, grinning all over his face. His first words were, 'You've missed the boat chum.' While we had been away, an American truck had been sent to pick us up to take us to Gera, but Jock had waited for me, and the truck had gone on taking the rest of the men. Still, we were not in the least worried, there was no real hurry to leave, we had a good bed, a reasonable amount of food, the freedom of the city and some very good American and German friends.

Saturday, 21 April 1945
Jock Stewart with me, two boys rolled in from another area, Taffy Ninniss and Koyli.

Jock and I had been out into the town to report, as we did daily, to Major McMillan, the American town major. He was very good to us in every respect, giving us packs of K rations, cigarettes, underclothing and new boots. I met at least one of my friendly American sergeants daily, whose generosity was phenomenal, nothing was too much trouble for them. On our way back to camp we had met Taffy Ninniss and Koyli. Taffy and I had known each other from our Berlin days, he having been captured on Crete also. A member of the Welsh Regiment who had suffered very heavy losses, he was very fortunate to be alive because he and some others had been put against a wall and shot during the height of the battle for Malamie and Galatos. Only Taffy had lived to tell the tale, he having the scars on each side of his neck where the bullets from the German tommy gun had grazed him. He had fallen forward to the ground with the others and had been left, presumed dead.

Koyli was a Yorkshireman whose real name I did not know. He was a member of the King's Own Yorkshire Light Infantry, hence the nickname KOYLI. He had been taken prisoner somewhere in the desert, having spent some time in Italy, then been carted off to Germany.

We settled them in the ex-Germans' quarters downstairs, sharing our food and whatever else we had with them.

I also heard further from Sergeant George McLain that he and another were going to Gera for the weekend, leaving about midday the next day, Sunday, and that they would take us with them. This good news indeed called for a celebration, so we arranged to have one that night, our last in Zwickau, and which this time Maria attended.

In the early evening before the party started, Maria and I walked alone through all the rooms of the camp. I wanted one last look around. Entering the room I had occupied, there, still hanging on the wall, were a couple of pairs of Indian clubs I had spent hours twiddling and swinging, and two guitars I had tried to knock a tune out of.

On passing the store where our parcels used to be locked away, I noticed it was still locked and remembered that there were still some parcels left by the French doctor, which had not been collected. Rummaging through the inside pockets of my battledress blouse I found the keys and on opening up, there on the floor were five parcels.

We carried them downstairs, also collecting my Indian clubs and the two guitars, and took them into the old office, to the others. We debated what we should do with them. The owners certainly would not be coming for them now, they would not even be bothered about them anymore and we could not do anything to find them. There was no point in leaving them to rot, so we decided to open them.

The majority of the contents was food, hard and stale but still edible, and would help to supplement our rations. I still have the entry in my notebook of where the parcels were destined for, and sincerely apologise to their owners for the action we took.

Our party that night went with a swing and plenty of music; no one got tight, a good time was had by all. Maria enjoyed herself (her parents would not join us) and then off to bed looking forward to starting our journey home the next day.

Sunday, 22 April 1945
CAMP FULL OF RUSSIAN POWs. 12.00 HOURS LEFT FOR GERA, BUT SOON CAME BACK, 8,000 POWs THERE.

Our day started with Jock dashing upstairs to tell me we were being invaded by a horde of Russian prisoners of war. There down in the compound was a mass of hungry-looking individuals. They simply tore the camp apart, and while they were doing it Taffy and Koyli dashed off to tell the Americans. We had previously heard ugly rumours that these Russians had plundered and raped when they had first been set free.

A squad of Americans were not long in arriving but they seemed at a loss to be able to get them out of the building. Then a saviour in the form of Herr Sahm made his appearance and, speaking fluent Russian, told them the Americans wanted them to be orderly, and march off to the barracks where they would be properly fed and cared for. (The Americans also wanted to make sure they were under control and not able to wander in marauding packs around the countryside.)

It worked like a charm, the camp was empty within ten minutes, but what a mess they left behind. We settled down again to our preparations to move. A little later in the morning, Frau Sahm came hurrying out of the bedroom where she had been working, to say that another two Russians had been looking in at her through the bedroom window and gesticulating. They eventually came round the front, through the small gate and up the stairs to the room we were in. How my pals downstairs missed them, I don't know! I quickly told Maria and her mother to go into the bedroom. Herr Sahm was carrying out his daily routine inspection of the workshops.

Standing in the middle of the room confronting the Russians, and speaking in German, I told them who I was and asked them what they wanted. They replied that they wanted the Frauen (the women).

So taking their meaning that they were bent on rape, I whipped out my pistol and at point blank range fired two shots directly above their heads, the bullets smacking into the wall above the door, making the plaster fly in all directions and the noise sounding like a cannon going off.

They stood absolutely petrified, saying, 'Komrad, Komrad, don't shoot, we go.' I bawled at them again, telling them I would shoot them if they didn't go quickly. Then bolting down the stairs, almost falling over each other, with me after them brandishing the pistol, they ran smack into the arms of two of the American sergeants who soon bundled them on to a jeep and sped off to hand them into the barracks with the others.

At 12.00 hours we left for Gera, after saying our goodbyes and not without tears. Frau Sahm who had so often called me her son, and had certainly treated me like one, was sorry to see me go and wished us Godspeed and a safe journey.

Gera was about 30 miles away to the north-west, along past the paper factory and on through Mosel to the Autobahn, then westward to the turn off for Gera. The journey took us an hour and on arrival we were most disappointed to find the town absolutely congested with ex-prisoners of war of all nations, but mostly British. There they all were, the two Crossen camps, Bergeschacht and ours, and many others housed in German flats (the occupants having had to move out to wherever they could find to live), trying to feed themselves on American rations.

They had no idea when they were going to be moved again and they were all grumbling about it. The American lines of communication were so stretched and overworked that it was taking them all their time to look after themselves without also trying to cope with thousands of ex-prisoners of war.

Everyone would have been better off to have stayed in their own camps, where at least there was some form of organisation; all we would have needed was food.

The four of us soon made up our minds to go back to Zwickau the next morning when the two Americans returned. The war was not over yet, we could wait a little longer, there was no hurry. Gera was chaotic, and a headache for someone to sort out.

By midday the next day we were ready and driving out of Gera back to Zwickau. The American sergeants turned up with their jeep and a civilian car, so off we went in great style, singing most of the way.

On arrival we reported to Major McMillan, who said he did not mind us coming back. We were the least of his worries; we caused him no trouble and even volunteered to work for him in any way we could; if we just let him know when we were ready to go west, he would fix it.

Back at the camp, Frau and Herr Sahm were delighted at our return, everything being just as we had left it. Of course, Maria had reported for work that day as requested by the posters, so I did not see her until the evening. As soon as I saw her, I could tell by her red-rimmed eyes that she had been crying, and on asking her, as I held her, what the trouble was, she burst out again most upset. I thought perhaps she had been molested on her way through the town and it was not until later that night when we were alone that she blurted out her troubles.

On returning to work at Alfreds, the jewellers, it had been decided to make a complete stocktake of everything in the shop. When it came to the more expensive jewellery, these were marked off against a master list (both the jewellery and the lists having been kept in a wall safe during the hostilities and now being checked for the first time again). A diamond ring was said to be missing, so Alfreds, his wife and either her mother or his mother, who lived with them, all turned their accusing eyes towards Maria.

Maria, naturally, protested her innocence on being openly accused and had broken down greatly distressed. She now told me that Alfreds was a well-known Nazi party man and she had been afraid of him. Now, another incident came back to me of the time when Erich Zahn and myself had called at the shop after the air raid because I wanted to see if Mária had been safe. No wonder Erich had made it such a brief visit, for if Alfreds had seen us and recognised me as a prisoner of war, he might have put two and two together concerning Maria and myself, and could have had the three of us smartly put out of the way, perhaps never to have been heard of again.

Maria settled down and I persuaded her to go back to work the next day. I stressed the fact that the Nazis were now out of business and would be for a long time and that I would also take her to work and bring her back again daily for as long as I was there.

In my notebook I wrote: ALFREDS – WILLIAMSTRASSE (and the Nazi sign) and drew circles around each name and the sign.

That night before going to bed, I cleaned my pistol, placing it as usual under my pillow. Whatever made me want to keep it I do not know, but I certainly felt safer with it. Turning things over in my mind before I went to sleep, I decided I would pay a visit to Herr Alfreds the very next day and see what it would be like to put the 'Fear of Christ' up a Nazi.

True to my word, I took Maria to work the next morning and about three hours later drove up in a jeep driven by one of the sergeants and with Jock. I had it all planned out what I was going to do, but neither the sergeant nor Jock knew anything about it.

Asking the sergeant to stop right outside the shop and wait for me, I got down from the jeep and went inside. Maria was behind the counter doing something or other and was completely taken by surprise when she saw me, and I asked for Alfreds.

She pointed upstairs, so up I went into a beautifully furnished room and confronted Alfreds, his wife and the other woman. Alfreds, obviously seeing I was an Ausländer, strode towards me demanding to know who I was, what I wanted, and to get to hell outside.

I calmly withdrew my pistol, jabbed it into his belly, telling him to sit down and be quiet or else I would shoot him. As he sat down on the plush upholstered sofa, I motioned to his wife and the other woman to sit next to him. I could now see that the wind was out of his sails, but little did he know that the full magazine of bullets for my pistol was in my trouser pocket and not in the gun.

He also got a shock when I asked him why Maria had been accused of taking the missing ring, whereupon he blustered, trying to bluff his way out of it. He got a much bigger shock when I told him I knew he was a prominent member of the Nazi party and I had only to give the word to the sergeant waiting down below and the whole lot of them would be taken away.

The two women broke down moaning and crying; Alfreds, a tall, smart-looking man, now sat looking very dejected, squirming on his seat, moving from cheek to cheek.

I, standing with legs apart, typical German fashion, was enjoying this. I told him to take another stock check that day, and had he searched inside his safe? I would be back for the answer later in the afternoon when I came to call for Maria.

With that I left them to it, marching off downstairs, having a few quick words with Maria to assure her that everything was going to be alright, and moving quickly off in the jeep.

Much later in the afternoon, I went back to the shop alone; I had nothing to fear from Alfreds. As I entered, it actually looked as if they were waiting for me. They were all standing behind the counter beaming all over their faces.

Herr Alfreds blurted out everything was now alright, the missing ring had been found (in the bottom of the safe); would I like to come upstairs, coffee and cakes perhaps?

We all went upstairs and sat down; it was certainly a very luxurious room. They were babbling on, how they had found the missing ring and were so overjoyed. I calmly asked if they had apologised to Maria; they hadn't, but they did so there and then.

They asked me if I would accept a present, to name anything and I could have it. Pondering for a while as a cup of coffee was handed to me, I told them I did not want anything out of the shop, but there was one small thing I would like: his Nazi party swastika buttonhole badge.

There was dead silence in the room, even the older Frau stopped stirring her coffee. Alfreds gave a negative reply, shaking his head, denying he had ever had one. 'That's right,' I said 'everyone will deny they were ever Nazis.'

Finishing the coffee, I motioned to Maria that it was time for us to be going, and turning to Alfreds, told him there had better not be any recriminations against Maria on account of my intervention and that I would be calling for her as long as ever I was here.

As we got up to go, Frau Alfreds thanked me, and taking my hand, slipped a small round metal object into it. It was the Nazi party swastika buttonhole badge. I had won the day.

The remainder of our days in Zwickau were nothing very exciting. We developed a daily routine of reporting to the town major, of doing our Gunga Din act of water carrying, obtaining food and cooking. We were able to move around quite freely, visiting the local American unit and enjoying the pleasure of their mobile bath outfit. I do not know about the others, but I was becoming more and more settled in my own mind. It was difficult to realise that we could move about freely without having armed guards with us.

One day, Jock and I calmly walked into a barber's shop for a haircut, which we were badly in need of. There were two in the barber's chairs and about four waiting when we entered, who made room for us to sit down. It was the first time we had ever been in a German barber's shop; it was not unlike a British one.

The barber, looking suspiciously at us, asked what we were wanting. I told him we were Englanders and wanted a haircut. His whole attitude instantly changed to one of friendliness, saying he would not keep us long, we could be next in the chair. I replied that we were not in any particular hurry and we would take our turn with the others.

Soon we were all talking about the war (which of course was still going on). The Tommies and the Americans were the 'Goodies' and the Russians the 'Baddies'. Nevertheless, we got our haircut, shampoo and dressed, it was a great treat which only cost us a few pfennigs and was well worth it.

Maria and I spent a lot of time together in the evenings and weekends visiting her friends and Frau Zahn again.

On Saturday, 5 May, we heard officially from the Americans that the ceasefire orders had been given. The shooting was to all intents and purposes, finished. What a price had been paid for peace and freedom.

We also heard that Hitler and others had perished in their command bunker in Berlin, but most Germans would not believe it. The Russians had steamrollered their way into Berlin almost knocking it down stone by stone. It was Germany's final collapse.

Our American friends told us that our area was due to be handed over to the Russians according to pre-arranged Occupational Zones; it was time for us to be going home. They were due to pull out to Gera on Monday, so we decided to have one last party together to celebrate the end of the war and our departure. I also gave much thought to taking Maria home with me; her parents agreed that it would be for the best, but she would not leave them, they were getting on in years and had lost one son and not heard of another one for many months. Looking back, I am sure she did what was best.

So, we left Zwickau for good, with two of the American sergeants, on Monday, 7 May 1945. This time it was much harder to leave. I can remember quite clearly the camp, the bridge, and the cobbled set stones of the Adolf Hitler Ring receding from view as we gathered speed on our departure.

There were still thousands of ex-prisoners at Gera but we stayed with the Americans, departing for Erfurt about 50 miles to the west, on 9 May.

At Erfurt, one of the sergeants contacted a pal of his in the Air Force who promised to take us to Brussels on his next trip. Erfurt had also thousands of ex-prisoners waiting patiently to go home.

On Friday, 11 May the Air Force pal told us to be ready to move off the next day; they could only take us as far as Brussels and then we would be on our own (British-controlled) territory.

George McLain and Howard Bradford took us to the airfield where we were handed over to the crew of a Dakota aircraft. After saying their goodbyes, we boarded the plane and, sitting on the wooden bench seats along each side of the fuselage, peeped out of the portholes waving to them as we taxied out to the runway.

At 10.30 a.m. we were airborne, the only passengers on the aircraft. Occasionally, as we flew almost due west we could look out and see the many war-torn devastated towns and cities below us.

We arrived over Brussels at 12.30 p.m. where we had to join the flying circus. Flying round and round the city at varying heights were hundreds of different types of aircraft, all waiting their turn to be called in to land, and as fast as they were landing, others were taking off.

Our turn came after flying around for nearly half an hour, when we landed safely, about 460 miles further west than we had been a few hours previously. We climbed out on to the tarmac and with a brief cheerio to our benefactors, watched them taxi away to make way for others to land.

Standing in the middle of this vast airfield we looked about us to take stock of our position. Over in one direction we saw what appeared to be a khaki-clad infantry battalion on the move by some airport buildings; they were all wearing Balmoral type caps so we naturally thought they were a Jock Regiment (we did not know until much later that they were ex-POWs going home, after progressing slowly for weeks along the normal channels of evacuation). We thought it best to keep out of their way, we would be back in the army soon enough.

In another direction we spied a Salvation Army hut situated on a green patch between two taxiing thoroughfares. We picked up our bits of kit, making a bee line for it.

At the hut were two gracious ladies serving free tea and eats and cigarettes, the first English ones we had met for months. It was a grand day and after being served we went outside to sit on the grass to eat and decide what our next move was going to be.

There outside, on an upturned box, sat our Angel Gabriel, drinking his tea and eating his wad, a Royal Air Force sergeant in full flying kit. We got talking to him straight away, asking him if he was going back to England and if he had one of these 'big' aircraft 'over there'.

He told us he was one of the crew of a Lancaster bomber due to set off about 3.30 p.m. and that he could not promise us a lift, but the aircraft was not 'bombed up', though they were on patrol duties and there was no harm in us asking his skipper.

And see his skipper we did. A tall, young flying officer, whose rank and name I never knew, looked us up and down with his sparkling eyes with some amusement. He spoke very softly and kindly to us asking us wherever had we come from, whilst his crew members stood behind him watching on.

Once he had heard our story it did not take him long to make up his mind. Yes! he would take us home, we could have hugged him there and then, but first, he said, we would have to help to push the huge aircraft on to the tarmac. Then allotting us to various positions, one behind the rear gunner, myself by the mid upper gunner, and the other two by the navigator, we taxied off to the start of the runway.

At 3.30 p.m. the great Lancaster gathered speed along the runway, taking off like a huge bird and with its four excited and very grateful passengers. We were told over the intercom that we were travelling due west, about 325 miles, to land in the south of England at approximately 4.55 p.m. Someone made a crack to please fly over the White Cliffs of Dover, which was instantly relayed to the skipper.

About an hour later we were given word to position ourselves where we could see out, and there below us, plain to see, were the White Cliffs of Dover; I couldn't help thinking of Jock's poem:

> *And they're hoping, how they're hoping, that*
> *some day they'll be free,*
> *And the pleasant Cliffs of Dover just once*
> *again they'll see.*

Landing at Horsham in Sussex we deplaned and waited for the skipper and his crew to convey our sincere thanks to them for bringing us back. To the skipper, as a small token of gratitude, I gave a German Ost Front

Medal (Russian Front), one of a handful of German medals the American sergeants had given me at one of our parties.

We were soon surrounded by Royal Air Force Service girls, one of whom picked up my bit of kit and, linking her arm in mine and talking all the way, walked me over to one of the huge hangars bearing big 'WELCOME HOME' signs, where we were further met and welcomed by ladies of the Voluntary Services and ushered down to a meal.

This indeed was IT, we were finally HOME.